Alma Guillermoprieto's

SAMBA

"An unforgettable personal experience...told in sharp, vivid prose. You must continually wipe the sweat from your brow as you find yourself deep in Rio, and in the samba."

> —*Cosmopolitan*

"[A] brilliant social chronicle...informative and always entertaining."

> —*Newsday*

"Here is the samba world without the bullshit, without the TV hype for tourists, and without prejudice. These people come alive, with their joys and (yes) their horrors, living in a Rio favela. Beautiful."

> —David Byrne

SAMBA

Alma

Guillermoprieto

SAMBA

Vintage Books   A Division of Random House, Inc.   New York

VINTAGE DEPARTURES

FIRST VINTAGE DEPARTURES EDITION, AUGUST 1991

Owing to limitations of space, permission to reprint previously
published material may be found on page 245.

Library of Congress Cataloging-in-Publication Data
Guillermoprieto, Alma.
Samba / Alma Guillermoprieto. — 1st Vintage departures ed.
p.   cm. — (Vintage departures)
ISBN 0-679-73256-X (pbk.)
1. Carnival — Brazil — Rio de Janeiro. 2. Samba (Dance) 3. Rio de
Janeiro (Brazil) — Social conditions. 4. Rio de Janeiro — Social life and
customs.   I. Title.
GT4233.R5G85   1991
294.2'5'098153 — dc20   90-55687
CIP

Manufactured in the United States of America
10 9 8 7 6 5 4 3 2 1

Obrigada Mangueira

Contents

SAMBA

Prologue

When I first arrived in Rio de Janeiro several years ago, I rented an apartment in Ipanema, an elegant oceanfront neighborhood, and along with the refrigerator and the bed and a couple of chests of drawers I inherited a maid: a stocky, very black woman in her fifties whom my landlady insisted she loved as one of the family. Nieta was nice, the landlady then warned me, but she had a tendency to steal little things, and it was important that as a foreigner I start off by imposing my authority, otherwise Nieta would, as maids do, start to get "uppity" on me. My secretary issued the same warning, and so did almost everyone else I met at the time. "Don't let her take advantage of you or you're in for trouble," they said urgently, as if the entire Brazilian social order were at stake. I liked Nieta enormously, but I was on the lookout for insubordination.

"*Ciao!*" she would say in the mornings, sending me off to work with a smile, one hand on hip, the other waving gracefully in a pose learned from television. In my own country, Mexico, maids were not supposed to be so casual or say sophisticated things like "*Ciao.*" Was this a sign of uppitiness? She had been trained to stand whenever she was in her employer's presence, but I had not been trained to provide a television for the tiny room off the kitchen where she lived.

Consequently, when I came in late and found her watching television in the study she would stand up and I would sit down and we would watch television together. I encouraged her to sit, but I worried. Was I asking for trouble?

Despite the awkwardness of the situation, I enjoyed watching television with her: she was hip, in the way Cariocas—the people of Rio de Janeiro—are, and she had excellent information on the singers who appeared on the screen: which ones were fakes, which ones had spoiled their talent by going commercial, which were involved with the underworld. She filled me in on the background of the prime-time soap operas. One then playing was set in nineteenth-century Brazil, and Nieta didn't think much of the lead actress. "That woman has no originality, her body isn't expressive," she commented. And another night, as we watched the heroine being waited on by her favorite house slave: "Whites adore soap operas set in the old times. They really love to look at the slaves."

The first time we went to the market together I asked her why she was calling the elevator at the back of the hall. She rode down with me in the front elevator. We did this a second time, and then the third time she refused, saying a neighbor had seen us and complained to the doorman. "We're not supposed to ride the front elevator," she said then, for the first time, and I was too confused to ask her if the "we" referred to blacks or maids. In theory, Rio de Janeiro city codes prohibit servants, delivery people and tenants in bathing suits from using the front elevators. In practice, the regulation ends up discriminating mostly against blacks.

Nieta went home on weekends and invariably came back edgy. Sometimes her problems had to do with the complicated lives of her two adult daughters, but more often it was a question of money. Refrigerator door off the hinge. Rains caving in one of the two rooms in her house. She lived about two hours away by bus, and when I suggested that she (that is, I) might prefer day work only, it was clear she had no appetite for the daily commute or the unrelieved contact with her own misery. Instead she said that some weekend she would like to invite me out to her neighborhood for a meal at home. But before I could make the trip—only a few weeks after she had begun working for me—I became convinced that she *was* stealing things like sugar and helping herself liberally to my makeup and perfume, and the loose change. I agonized over the unfairness of her situation:

perhaps the level of stealing she indulged in was normal and expected from underpaid servants in Brazil. Perhaps the sugar bowl and the small-change drawer were producing evidence of nothing but my own paranoia, fueled by a landlady's slander. Perhaps I had taken at face value a warning that she had intended not against Nieta but against the entire black race, meaning, "You've got to watch these people; they're unreliable." Perhaps it wasn't Nieta's fault that I couldn't trust her. But I couldn't, and I fired her.

I missed her very much after she wished me "everything good" at the kitchen door and waved *"Ciao!"* for the last time. For one thing, she was the only person who had—or could invent—answers for the growing pool of questions in my mind. The odd situation of blacks in Rio provoked my curiosity much more forcefully than the freewheeling culture of beer and chatter common to white Cariocas of my income level, but I realized only after Nieta left that she was my single contact with the culture of a race that constitutes nearly half the Brazilian population. The new maid, a shy white woman from the Minas Gerais countryside who had converted to evangelism, certainly could not provide the answers Nieta could have come up with. Why aren't there any black waiters? Where can I find black music? Who is the black woman with blue eyes and a metal gag whose plaster image appears in all the religious-supplies stores? Just what, exactly, is a samba school? Why is it that at sunset, when the beaches in Ipanema are emptying, black women will sometimes approach the waves and toss white flowers into the foam?

The heat bloomed in December as the carnival season kicked into gear. Nearly helpless with sun and glare, I avoided Rio's brilliant sidewalks and glittering beaches, panting in dark corners and waiting out the inverted southern summer. Nevertheless, certain rhythms, an unmistakable urgency in the air got through to me. Although there were still three months left to the carnival celebrations that would close down Rio for nearly a week in March, the momentum was already building. The groups of men who normally gathered for coffee or beer in front of the tiny grocery stores that dot Rio were now adding a percussion backup to their usual excited conversation. They beat a drum, clapped their hands in counterpoint and toyed with a stray verse of song before letting the rhythm die out again.

There was a faster, more imposing beat to the sambas on the radio. I made tentative inquiries: Carnival? Boring. Vulgar. Noisy, some people said, and recommended that I leave town for that horrible weekend. Samba schools? Tacky, some said. Highly original, said others, and volunteered that the "schools" were in reality organizations that compete on carnival weekend with floats and songs and extravagant costumes, each group dressed entirely in its official colors. But was it true that carnival was something that happened principally in the slums? Why? There were shrugs, raised eyebrows. Who knows. Opium of the people. Blacks are like that. We Brazilians are like that. You know: On the day of the coup, back in 1964, people were happy because it meant they had the day off and could go to the beach. I recalled the way Nieta's gestures became expansive when she mentioned carnival. Opium, yes, probably. But surely it was fun? In March, I ended up on carnival weekend with a ticket for the first of two all-night samba school parades.

In the official parade grounds—the Sambadrome—I thought the silence eerie until I realized it was in fact a solid wall of sound, a percussive din that did not sound like music and advanced gradually toward the spectators on an elaborate loudspeaker system set up on either side of the central "avenue," or parade space. At the head of the noise was a gigantic waggling lion's head that floated down the avenue and overtook us, giving way to dazzling hordes in red and gold. A marmalade-thick river of people swept past; outlandish dancers in feathers and capes, ball gowns and G-strings, hundreds of drummers, thousands of leaping princes singing at the top of their lungs. Drowning in red and gold, I struggled to focus. In the ocean of feathers and banners faces emerged: brown, white, pink, tan, olive. Young black men bopping in sweat-drenched suits; old women in cascades of flounces whirling ecstatically; middle-aged men and women with paunches and eyeglasses bouncing happily in their headdresses and bikinis. What kinds of jobs did they have in everyday life? How much had their costumes cost? Why, in Brazil's pervasively segregated society, had all the colors decided to mix? Four Styrofoam elephants trundled past on golden platforms, followed by gigantic Balinese dancers in red and gold. There were acrobatic dancers with tambourines; more spinning old women; a flag-bearing couple, who should have been paralyzed by the weight of their glittering costumes, twirling and curtsying instead through a dance that looked like a samba-minuet. Nothing was familiar or logical, and I was reduced to the simplest questions. How could that large woman over there in the sequined bikini be so unconcerned about her cellulite? Why was everyone singing a song about the Mexican chicle tree, and who had come up with this idea? Why were a spectacularly beautiful woman dressed only in a few feathers and a little boy in a formal suit pretending to have sex with each other for the audience's benefit, and why was everyone involved so cheerful? Were all these people from the slums? And if they were, how could they look so happy when their lives were so awful?

It was well after dawn when I left the crowd of ever more enthusiastic spectators, as the seventh samba school was about to begin its slow progress. Beyond the Sambadrome were the squalid last alleyways of a moribund red-light district, and beyond that the favelas—the slums, perched on their outcrops of rock. Back home, the Ipanema universe of orderly tree-lined streets and air-conditioned buildings seemed remote and barren when compared with the favelas I knew only from Nieta's descriptions, now suddenly come alive in my mind as the magical enclaves where carnival could be imagined and then made flesh. The peopled hills were everywhere—there was one only three blocks from my apartment building—and I spent months staring at the jumble of shacks pitched so artlessly across the steep slopes, imagining the hot, crazy life within. But it was a long time before I could find an excuse to get close.

The hills define Rio, highlight and bound it. Their admonitory profiles among the city's liquid blues and tropical greens give the landscape tension and transcendence. Yet despite the breathtaking views from their heights (the charming disorder of the Old City at one's feet, a sweep of bay and, receding toward the horizon, a stately procession of other mist-enshrouded outcrops floating out to sea), the hills were never part of any real estate boom. The solid granite bedrock makes it impossible to sink foundations on them, and their near sixty-degree incline prevents commercial traffic.

None of this stood in the way of the impoverished black population in the closing years of the nineteenth century. Newly freed from slavery, lacking industrial skills, savings, literacy, property or any form of reparation on the part of the lackadaisical Brazilian government, the blacks must have wanted first of all refuge from the rigors of freedom. If during slavery runaways protected their liberty in palisaded villages in the wild, they now fled to the numerous steep hills that ring Rio's downtown district and divide the city roughly in half: the prosperous (white) south, and the darker, poorer north. Joined by discharged soldiers back from extinguishing a religious revolt in Canudos, and by members of the poorer fringe of white tradespeople and artisans, Rio's poorest blacks rummaged crates from the docks and zinc sheeting from the warehouses and began life uphill. They descended to the city to scrabble a living out of occasional odd jobs, backbreaking labor at the docks, domestic employment, street vending and, increasingly, petty crime and prostitution. For a sense of order and dignity they turned again to the two things slavery had not confiscated and used against them: samba and candomblé—music and religion, the end products of centuries of clandestine worship of the African gods. During the slavery period the Portuguese had banned African religions among the blacks they imported to their colony in Brazil, but for the most part they tolerated the all-night sessions of drumming, singing and dancing that often took place in the slave barracks. They never really understood that the dancing and the worship were indivisible, and that the Catholic saints the slaves prayed to were gods from the old continent who had disguised themselves in order to enter the barracks. The African war god Ogun became St. George, the ocean mother Yemanjá made her appearance dressed in the Virgin Mary's blue and white robes. After the abolition of slavery in 1888, the African rituals sprang back: hybridized adaptations of Nigerian, Dahomean, Angolan and Portuguese traditions, they became Brazilianized under the names samba and candomblé, and their power was undiminished.

Just as regularly as the rains washed away the shacks pitched askew on the hills, police expeditions ventured up the slopes to stage raids on candomblé ceremonies and on the samba parties that almost always followed them. "Samba lovers had to make sure to sing their songs far away from the police," one survivor recalled, and sambistas' memoirs are full of bitter complaints about the persecution of their music and religion. But they had it wrong: it wasn't samba or candomblé the police were after; it wasn't the maddening pounding of the batuque drums they wanted to eliminate; it was them. The proliferating underclass on the hills posed a problem requiring far more political imagination and strength than the newly empowered bourgeoisie possessed. Absent a policy, the police were always at hand, and they were sent uphill almost on whim—a sort of mega-flyswatter, and just as effective.

The rains and the raids continued, year after year, and so did the hill communities, rendered immune to both through their absolute lack of alternatives. In time, the name of one hill—Favela—became the generic term for all the communities that even today cluster so charmingly against the slopes, their light bulbs twinkling merrily at twilight on an outcrop that seems to plunge directly into the darkening ocean in residential Leblon, on another that impertinently slides down into the center of Ipanema itself, or on the isolated hills ringed with darkness that spring up here and there, like afterthoughts, as the North Zone landscape flattens out toward the edges of the city.

Dona Marta hill lies on the edges of the South Zone, almost hidden from view from most angles by expensive apartment buildings with names like The Prince of Wales and The Paul Klee. In mid-1987 the favela on this hill surfaced in public consciousness as a result of a confrontation between rival drug traffickers—an event that was shocking and frightening to the people of the South Zone even though similar incidents were then common in the north of the city. There was even a samba about it, in which the singer announced, to a background of whistling pistol shots, that anyone who threatened his control of the top half of a hill "will turn into a corpse." What had happened on Dona Marta hill on the weekend of August 22 was that Cabeludo, a descendant of Italian immigrants and a native son of Dona Marta, declared war on Zaca, a black upstart who had challenged Cabeludo's control of the drug traffic in this favela, so enviably located in the middle of the cocaine consumer market. After an initial exchange of machine-gun fire between the two rivals, terrified residents of the nearest apartment buildings flooded the media and the government with phone calls, an exodus of frightened favelados set up camp in a nearby park, and phalanxes of military and investigative police screeched into battle positions at the foot of the hill and then did nothing, deciding wisely that the best thing was to wait for the two gangsters to fight it out.

Because of this news event I was able to make my first visit to a favela. With another foreign reporter I joined the local media crowd at their observation post halfway between the last police van and a beer shack called The Warrior, where Cabeludo's men had set up their first checkpoint. We didn't have to wait long. Cariocas are outstandingly gregarious and Cabeludo's troops were no exception. Soon we were invited up to The Warrior and asked to contribute funds for what I ludicrously believed was a round of soft drinks. It turned out to be a cocaine-sniffing demonstration, staged for our benefit by a half-mad teenager with a nine-millimeter gun who, like his comrades, was dressed for battle in a delirious approximation of guerrilla mufti: combat boots, a face mask and a knapsack. The kid groomed himself for our photographs. He smoothed down the knit cap that covered his head, wiped his grimy face, fuddled through his knapsack and at long last found what he wanted: a spray deodorant, which he applied to one armpit and then, on inspiration, to his entire body.

Presently, Cabeludo sent word that he would like to be interviewed. We followed our guides up what is probably the steepest of all the sharply inclined favelas of Rio, sewer water purling about our heels as we walked. The leader's headquarters was a compound of cement and flatboard hovels; a refrigerator had been knocked sideways to serve as a parapet, and half-eaten plates of food lay everywhere on the bare concrete floors. Here we were received by Cabeludo's two aides-de-camp, genial, coked-up outlaws—*malandros*—who made a sincere effort to focus on our inquiries through the blur of their weariness and tension. We asked the obvious questions and they provided some interesting answers: the war had broken out because Zaca wanted the whole hill; the police were reluctant to attack because so many of the members of the local garrison were on Cabeludo's payroll; the feud had started over the alleged rape by Cabeludo of a minor, but they could testify that their leader did not like little girls. Yes, they liked samba; there was a carnival club that Cabeludo helped finance, and weekend samba parties "for the *malandros* and the *malandras*." At this last revelation they both cackled, immensely cheered by the thought of the funky weekend dances.

Eventually we talked to Cabeludo himself, who proved to be far less *simpático* and forthcoming. He was a leader on the hill, he claimed, and cast himself in a warrior's light. There was a long, confused monologue about society and how it had deformed him, and about the favelados and the sad but stirring fact that he was dedicating his life to their cause. He seemed uncontrollably irritable and later, when his rival (having failed to get his claim for equal time through to us, the foreign press) had his photograph and an eloquent interview published on the front page of the local papers, I thought Cabeludo didn't stand a chance against the personable, photogenic Zaca. At the time, though, I found Cabeludo merely frightening and pathetic in equal measure. Cutting his monologue short, I asked what he would have chosen to be if society had not transformed him into an "outcast," as he kept putting it.

He studied me disdainfully, taking in my eyeglasses, raw-silk workshirt, designer jeans, Italian leather lace-ups, notebook. "An intellectual," he finally sneered.

A few days later, I went to a North Zone favela for my first visit to a samba school. It was springtime in Brazil, when the weather in Rio is loveliest: washed clear of rains, the sky turns a cool and peaceful blue. The nights too are soothing, spattered with clean bright stars and edged with promise. Spring signals the beginning of the carnival season, which starts up in September with nightlong rehearsals designed to set the festive sap running for the real event. Year-round planning for the parade also shifts into full gear with weekly meetings at which samba school directorates define their strategies and assign tasks.

The taxi crossed the tunnel under Corcovado hill, which links Ipanema and Copacabana to the North Zone; skimmed past the massive shadow of Maracanã Stadium and the concrete wastelands of the state university; and stopped at the edge of a favela that chunnels precipitously from one particularly tall hill right down to the pavement itself. This was Mangueira.

The directors of the First Station of Mangueira Recreational Association and Samba School were holding one of their weekly planning meetings, chaired by the school president, Carlos Dória. With the other school directors—mostly black, mostly middle-aged to old—Dória discussed the coming parade, which was to commemorate the hundredth anniversary of the decree that abolished slavery, signed by the Brazilian Crown in 1888.

Like the other schools, Mangueira had already begun its samba harvest; a process of winnowing out competing sambas composed around the official parade theme, until one is selected to be sung in the Sambadrome by the school's fifty-three hundred members. There was general enthusiasm for the theme, and agreement that the competing sambas offered a rich crop, but some members of the directorate were unsatisfied with the costumes and the floats: they were too frilly, and they did not convey enough about the present situation of blacks in Brazil or about their past hardships.

I hung around the edges of the meeting and at the end spoke briefly with Dória, a burly man in his mid-forties with a paunch, thick gold jewelry, a moustache and an unfriendly air. I told him I was a reporter and said I would like to follow Mangueira through its process of making carnival. Roughly, he told me I was wasting my time. I was persistent, but he was mean; he was a member of the state military police, and the hostility in his manner was both professional and frightening.

After we had reached an impasse, a young woman listening to our conversation interceded and took me aside. Nilsemar was very pretty, with the modest, precise gestures of a skillful nurse. She had been sitting at the directorate table with other women to whom she now introduced me: her grandmother Dona Zica, widow of Cartola, one of the founders and outstanding composers of the Mangueira samba school; her friend Marilia, a white sociologist; Dona Neuma, daughter of a founder of the school and an all-time sambista; and Neuma's daughter, Guezinha. The women were as friendly as Dória was brusque. They listened to my questions and invited me to attend the harvest dance the following Saturday. "Don't worry," Nilsemar said softly, when I said Dória might not approve of my presence. "He's gruff, but we'll convince him to let you see what you want to see."

Part One

HARVEST TIME

1　*A Samba Night*

Samba: A musical composition based on a two-by-four beat.

Samba: Dance(s) the samba (second and third person singular present of the verb *sambar*).

Samba: A gathering that takes place specifically to dance the samba.

Bamba: A person wise in the ways of the samba world.

Escola de samba: Samba school; an association of individuals who unite for the exclusive purpose of parading together during carnival, wearing costumes in the school's official colors.

Palácio do Samba: Samba Palace; the headquarters for the Mangueira samba school.

The turnstiles were green, the rest of the façade glaring pink. A man in a pink T-shirt waved me through the turnstile of Mangueira's Palácio do Samba into the bright pink-and-green space beyond. It was shortly before midnight, and the harvest was not scheduled to start until one. The huge central dance space was empty and only a few of the red folding tables around it were occupied. A man in a pink-and-green crocheted muscle shirt, another in a pink felt hat, women in pink shirts and green dresses leaned casually against the green and pink walls. Banners hanging from the metal roof structure advertised the support of Xerox company and Ypiranga Paints for the Mangueira cause. Ypiranga's contribution was evident: other than the metal tables emblazoned with the Coca-Cola logo, not an inch of space was painted any other color than the two Mangueira favorites.

At the opposite end of the central area a few children were scrambling onto a green platform twelve feet high. When they reached the top, others handed them sticks, drums as tall as they, smaller metal objects that jangled. Soon the platform was full: some twenty small boys and their director, a wiry young white man in a Hawaiian shirt. It was 11:58. The boys, skinny and solemn-faced, fidgeted, fiddled, adjusted their shoulder straps, their shirts, their faded baggy shorts and hit the drums. The sound wave began.

It was what one tied to the railroad tracks might hear as a train hurtles immediately overhead: a vast, rolling, marching, overpowering wave of sound set up by the *surdos de marcação*—bass drums about two feet in diameter in charge of carrying the underlying beat. Gradually a ripple set in, laid over the basic rhythm by smaller drums. Then the *cuica*: a subversive, humorous squeak, dirty and enticing, produced by rubbing a stick inserted into the middle of a drumskin. The *cuica* is like an itch, and the only way to scratch it is to dance. Already, people were wiggling in place to the beat, not yet dancing, building up the rhythm inside their bodies, waiting for some releasing command of the drums. As the children drummed on with all the solemnity of a funeral band, husky morose men climbed the platform, hoisted their instruments and joined in. There were more *surdos*, another *cuica*, a clackety metal *agogô*, a tambourine and something that looked like a Christmas tree and sounded like a shiver—the *chocalho*.

For long minutes the wave rolled over us, a formal presentation of the *bateria*, the rhythm section that forms a school's core. Without a *bateria*, no school can parade, no school can exist. These percussionists are recognized as the hardest-working members of the samba world. While everyone else is having a good time, they are raising bloody welts on their shoulders from the drums' heavy straps, tearing the callused skin on their hands with their ceaseless beating and rubbing of the metal instruments. Others enter and leave rehearsals as they wish; the drummers anchor a samba from the beginning.

They are a paradoxical aristocracy, sweat-drenched princes who are among the poorest members of the school. By inheritance and tradition, most of the *bateria* make their living as day laborers in the Rio dockyards. They never smile.

The *bateria* director brought his arms down sharply. With a final shudder and slam the wave came to a halt. The samba harvest was open.

The *quadra*—or samba building—had filled up quickly. About five hundred people were now milling about, lining up for beer, occupying the tables or marking off private spaces for themselves along the edges of the *quadra* by setting their beer bottles in the center of where they intended to dance. There were groups of middle-aged women out for a night on the town, and whole families sitting at tables crowded with beer, soda pop and, here and there, sandwiches brought from home. A birthday party was in progress at one end of the *quadra*. Lounging at the opposite end were a handful of young men in slouchy felt hats, long T-shirts, Bermudas and hightops. I spotted Guezinha and the sociologist Marilia at one of the front-row tables, and then, as I stood in line for a soft drink, Carlos Dória. I smiled in greeting and he turned away. Shortly afterward, he left.

The dance space itself remained empty, separated from the tables by metal parade barriers. Eventually two older men strolled into the inviolate space, slowly and with authority. One was short, stocky, heavily moustached and slightly stooped. He wore an assortment of whistles around his neck and something of the tired, impatient air of a boxing referee. The other was improbably tall, with a hatchet face crowned by a narrow-brimmed straw hat. He was as long-legged and deliberate as a praying mantis, and as brightly colored in his grass-green suit. His head rotated on an axis as he paused for a moment and inspected the *quadra*, chewing on a piece of gum with toothless jaws. Slowly his head returned to center and he resumed his crossing. As if the two men's presence were a command, several other men climbed onto a singers' tower placed at right angles to the drummers' platform, on which they were soon joined by Beto End-of-the-Night. Beto Fim da Noite, energetic, bald and very black, announced the evening's events over a foggy microphone that stirred his words into the general soup of noise and confusion and only sporadically let some meaning through: "The harvest now commences . . . best team win . . . great Mangueira nation . . . this night memorable . . . end of the evening three finalists . . . competing for the glory of carrying our school to victory at carnival . . . now sing the Mangueira anthem . . ."

The drums slammed into action, there was a piercing short whistle, and as if released from coils the dancers bounced into the air. At the center of the dance space stood Alberto Pontes, the heavy-shouldered man with the whistles, looking now more like a gladiator ready to take on all the Colosseum's lions. He crouched menacingly and blew sharp commands on his whistle, and as a stream of hyperkinetic women charged onto the dance floor he growled, gestured, stamped his foot and pushed the herd away from the center of the floor and back toward the barriers. Unheeding, the women jumped and swayed and broke into frenzied little circles of movement, hips and jewelry flying in every direction; they surged forward and grabbed all the available space while Pontes cursed and ordered them back again with a righteous forefinger, Moses compelling the waters to retract, God expelling a thousand Eves. The samba pounded on and the women multiplied, but Pontes did not interrupt his labors.

"The shepherdesses," Marilia shouted over the commotion when I sought her out in the crowd. "They're called *pastôras*," she repeated. "By tradition, only women are allowed to dance in the central space during real rehearsals." But in fact it was Pontes who seemed more like their sheepdog, herding his flock away from their Dionysian instincts and back to a world of order and sobriety.

A skinny little man approached the central space, giddily drunk and full of gay mannerisms, dance bursting out of him. Swiftly he was scooped up by two youths in pink "Mangueira Security" T-shirts. It was not time for him to dance yet. It would not be time until the end of the harvest, when Mangueira began its more commercial round of "rehearsals" designed to fill the school's coffers. Then the dance floor would be open to all.

Meanwhile the men danced on the edges of the *quadra*, between the beer counter and the tables. The real bambas danced in all-male groups, whipping their legs in circular movements over the beer bottles set on the floor, knifing out with one leg to upset the balance of another male dancer, shifting from high to low movements and from sitting to standing to spinning positions like break-dancers.

Couples danced too, provocatively. A teenage girl sheathed in a tight white strapless dress circled her hips slowly to the floor in front of her enthusiastic middle-aged partner and then slid straight up again, her pubic bone pressed to the man's thigh. Eventually the man offered his place to a little boy who had been practicing samba off in a corner on his own. The boy kept his distance from the girl for a few seconds with elaborate dips and bops, a little out of breath with shyness. He stood still, hesitating, before diving into the space between her thighs. Chest level to her hips, he grinned awkwardly while she pulsated against him. Then he leapt away, laughing and proud and cheered on by a circle of observers.

A chunky gray-haired woman in a plain cotton shift and slippers stood at the center of a group of teenagers. Too old to jump or spin, she faced her adolescent partner and wiggled as hard as she could, bursting into great roars of laughter every time she managed to set her entire body shaking. "Vovó," the kids called her, "Granny." But she explained that she had no children of her own, and that the teenagers who had brought her here were children she had helped raise in her suburban favela.

Through the mad crowd that had formed at the center of the rehearsal space a serene dancer emerged. The flag-bearer and the majordomo, a royal pair, head the dancing section of every parade, and a candidate for the flag-bearing position was now just beginning her practice. She was very young, shy and hesitant. For a second she seemed to be floating alone, but out of the crowd her partner appeared, scything the air with his long bones, folding his limbs at the joints and then stretching them out again to full, preposterous length; Delegado, the green-and-brown praying mantis. Together they dipped and spun and circled for a few seconds, and then Delegado turned the flag-bearer over to her teenage coapprentice. The women marched behind, tirelessly, over and over, while the sound wave broke and shattered against the wall.

By now it was almost one in the morning. The song we had been listening to, someone said, was the samba from the previous carnival parade, in which Mangueira had won first prize. The contest for this season's samba had in fact not yet begun, but now that the song had come to its abrupt end the composers and singers on the tower shifted and cleared their throats and consulted. There was a great flurry of activity down in the table area, where Marilia and Guezinha and several other members of the directorate were sitting. A hopped-up, nervous young man named Rody came up and with a superb smile handed me a slip of pink paper with the mimeographed lyrics of his samba, a heavy crowd favorite. He had written it together with

Verinha—a woman composer—and Bus-Stop Bira; the three made up a team that had written the previous year's winning samba. He shook hands earnestly with everyone in sight. "Give me a little strength," he asked Marilia, but I knew his fate was sealed. "We in the directorate are rooting for Helinho's samba," the women had said on the night I met them.

This is what Rody's song said:

> The black race came to this country,
> Bringing their strong arms and their roots.
> They planted their culture here,
> Yoruba, Gêgê and Nagô.
> In the refineries, mines and fields,
> Blacks were always oppressed,
> And in the rebel enclave of Palmares
> Zumbi our leader fought for freedom.
>
> Finally light dawned,
> Reason prevailed,
> And Princess Isabel
> Abolished slavery.
> Or did she?
> Is it true, is it a lie?
> Because to be born with a black skin
> Has not given us the right to equality.
> One hundred years of liberty:
> Is this reality or illusion?
> Let's all wave our white handkerchiefs
> And with Mangueira ask
> For an end to discrimination.
>
> Throw off the ties that bind!
> Please give people their freedom!

Rody's song ended, another samba began. A messenger broke through the dancing crowd, breathless and tragic. The music stopped, there was a moment of silence, and the singer at the microphone announced that Carlos Dória had just been murdered.

* * *

The news sent people whirling centrifugally toward the exit doors, concentrically into each other's arms. The Samba Palace emptied out. I stood on the stairs leading to the mezzanine and the directorate offices and watched Dona Zica being carried out in a half-faint. Marilia gathered her ten-year-old daughter and her friends off the dance floor and headed down the road for Dona Neuma's house. The school vice-president staggered by, clutching at his chest with one hand. A large, fortyish woman, considerably drunk, screamed *"Meu presidente! Meu presidente!"* and flung herself repeatedly against a standing column at the foot of the stairs. A man climbed up to the directorate offices—slender as a knife, of indeterminate age, wearing a bright pink leather jacket and pitch-dark glasses at four in the morning, surrounded by bodyguards. He emerged again, sliced his way through the clots of hysterical bystanders on the stairway, paused at the landing to announce, "A lot of blood will run for this," and was gone. The last stragglers left. The *quadra* shut down.

Dória had been sitting in his car a short drive north from the *quadra*, waiting for the garage door in his apartment building to open, when someone came up and shot him four times through the head and chest. His murder was never solved. The few Mangueirenses I had met were not forthcoming on the possible causes or culprits, and I had to rely on the Rio papers, where the murder made the front page and then filled the crime section for almost a week with the latest speculations on the assassins' motives: that Dória had been involved with a drug group and was killed by a rival gang; that he had participated in one of the Rio police corps' notorious death squads and had been singled out for revenge by a victim's friends; that the entrenched leadership of Rio's League of Samba Schools had had him murdered after he threatened to set up an independent association. This last became the official Mangueira version, volunteered to all and just as vigorously denied by the League leaders. In any event, Mangueira never resigned from the League, nor did the school or Dória's relatives ever press charges. Over the months, as carnival activity spread beyond the favelas and took hold of the entire city, the case faded from public attention.

In the wake of the murder Mangueira's carnival prospects were assumed to be nil. The samba harvest was suspended for two weeks. There was a funeral and then, eight days after the murder, a mass for the resurrection of the soul of Carlos Dória.

2 *A Little History*

There were few tears during the resurrection mass for Dória. The young foreign priest from the church down the road set up an improvised altar in a corner of the nearly empty *quadra*, led his uncertain parishioners through the church rituals and spoke about crime and the difference between forgiveness and justice, hinting broadly that those who knew who had killed Dória might absolve the culprits in their hearts but let the criminal justice system know exactly who it was they had forgiven all the same. The priest seemed realistic about the limits of his moral influence and kept the sermon brief. Shortly after he finished folding the altar cloth he was out the door.

The sambistas lingered in the drafty *quadra* until well after nightfall. There were people here who did not meet in the course of daily life except at rehearsal time, when the din of the *bateria* made real conversation impossible; but on this chilly evening, made nostalgic and vulnerable by the presence of death, they clustered together for comfort and in the congenial silence soon found themselves laughing at old stories, singing forgotten samba verses quietly to each other as they remembered this or that carnival or party. They talked about Dória and his brief tenure as Mangueira president, about his violent temper and his devotion to the school, and because the future was looming in the shape of an upcoming carnival with no president to lead it, they talked about the past, with special emphasis on the moments of glory.

"Mangueira was the first of all the schools to come out with a story samba," a trim old man said, to murmurs of agreement. "Other schools keep claiming that honor, but they know the truth." The speaker, Carlos Cachaça, was the last surviving founder of the Mangueira school, having outlived almost every other bamba of the period when samba first became popular and led indirectly to the invention of the samba schools. "Story samba" is the proper name for the song that sets forth the theme of a school parade, easily distinguishable through its speed and emphatic marching beat from song samba, counterpoint samba (known outside Brazil as "bossa nova") and the earliest form of the genre, call-and-response samba. Cachaça liked to remind people of Mangueira's historical if much-disputed claim to leadership in the field of story sambas because, as it happened, he had invented the subcategory himself back in 1933, when samba—the whole broad genre of highly ornamented two-by-four rhythms—was just establishing itself as Brazil's national music. Cachaça was in his early thirties then, Mangueira was a miserable stop on the suburban rail line, and Brazilian carnival was about to witness its great flowering, brought about by the fusion of black and white carnival cultures in the crucible of the newly created samba schools.

Brazilian whites today readily admit that carnival would not have amounted to much had it remained in their hands. The Portuguese colonizers' idea of enjoyment during the week before Lent was to spray each other with syringes filled with water, foul-smelling liquids or worse. In the mid–nineteenth century someone came up with the only slightly better idea of beating a very large drum while a crowd followed him around the neighborhood. Carnival life began to improve only toward the end of Emperor Pedro II's progressive regime, when a restless new urban elite championed the abolition of slavery, which the emperor also favored; republicanism, which the emperor, understandably, was against; and a more sophisticated, "European" form of carnival to which Dom Pedro, as far as the evidence shows, did not object. Patterned on the elegant celebrations of Paris and Venice, elaborate costume balls quickly became the rage. "Carnival societies" were formed to parade through the main streets of the city dressed in complicated allegorical costumes, often designed to satirize the old regime and promote the liberal agenda. One of the better-known of such societies, the Devil's Lieutenants, suspended its carnival parade one year and used the funds for the manumission of slaves.

The law promulgating freedom for slaves, which Mangueira was about to commemorate in its parade, was signed in 1888 by Pedro's daughter, Isabel, acting as regent for her father while he was away on an extended visit to Portugal. In instructing his daughter to sign the decree, Dom Pedro not only was acting out of a lifelong desire to bring Brazil into the modern world but was under great pressure from Europe, notably from England, which held most of Brazil's foreign debt and ran its sugar mills in the Caribbean with paid labor. The end of slavery made Brazil's sugar-production prices competitive with Europe's, but it also quickly forced the empire into conflict with the landed gentry and the military. Pedro II was overthrown and his daughter joined him in exile in France. Brazil was to spend much of the next hundred years in political turmoil, throughout which carnival would remain a constant, divorced from its liberal political origins but permanently linked to a gauzy vision of European elegance and sophistication.

The newly free blacks were a constant source of irritation for the conservative elite defeated in the fight over slavery, and at no time more so than during carnival, when their boisterous presence on the streets amounted to a provocation. By the turn of the century carnival had become the staging ground for a new battle fought between the proponents of a "civilized" celebration and the recalcitrantly "African" blacks. A flurry of police regulations and restrictions sought to limit or eliminate the black influence on carnival. African drum sessions were prohibited. With an eye to keeping black revelers up on the hills, many regulations specified that only "certain types" of carnival associations could parade down Rio's principal streets. Palliatives, sniffed the elites. What was needed was decisive action. In 1901 a reader wrote to the *Jornal de noticias* of Bahia: "I am referring to the great celebration of Carnival and the abuse being made of it . . . and also to the way this celebration of Civilization has become Africanized among us. . . . I find that the authorities should prohibit those [African drum sessions] and *candomblés* that in such quantity are overflowing on our streets these days, producing such great cacophonous noise, as well as those masquerades dressed in [typical black costumes] singing their traditional samba, because all of that is incompatible with our current civilized state."*

It might have afforded the letter writer some comfort to know that whites like him weren't the only ones longing for a different black carnival. The emerging class of black artisans, skilled laborers and professionals were also being visited by European daydreams: not only did they want to distance themselves from the drums and the chants and all the native music's tribal connotations, they also wanted to move beyond the Catholic rituals to which their celebrations had so often been confined. For centuries, blacks had chanted and danced in the innumerable church processions that constituted the main form of public amusement in colonial Brazil. When priests paraded the blue-and-white statue of Our Lady of the Lamps on her feast day in February, blacks sang her praises and secretly dedicated them to Yemanjá, the African mother of the oceans who welcomes offerings of white flowers. On January 6, when the Catholic Church celebrates the visit of the Three Kings, or Wise Men, to the infant Jesus, blacks joined the processional in a Rancho de Reis, or Kings' Promenade, complete with cardboard-and-tinsel-crowned kings and singing shepherdesses. These were the customs the more prosperous blacks wanted to transcend, but they were also the cultural wellspring they had to draw from. On a memorable February evening in 1907, on the return trip from a picnic on an island in Rio's Guanabara Bay, a group of skilled artisans and laborers of black, white and mixed blood decided to incorporate into a new type of carnival association called, simply, a "promenade." There would be singing, but no African chants; there would be drumming, but as background to flute solos; there would be shepherdesses, but dressed in the latest European fashions. The group christened itself Delightful Myrtle, and its bid for respectability was warmly received by the carnival elite; in the following years the media consistently praised the group's presentations—"the music, the poetry, the luxury and splendor of their original and harmonious conception"—and the ambitious themes it took on—Asian court life, the planetary system, the brotherhood of nations. Here at last was the civilized black carnival the white world had been waiting for, and even a president of the Brazilian republic, Marshal Hermes da Fonseca, felt compelled to en-

* Nina Rodrigues, *Os Africanos No Brasil* (São Paulo, 1977), p. 177.

courage the trend by presiding over one of the promenade's parades.

Notwithstanding, samba continued to remain off limits for many years, even if some of its most talented creators were founders and followers of Delightful Myrtle. There was, for example, the promenade's rehearsal director and principal dancer, Hilario Jovino, a former lieutenant in a somewhat disreputable militia in northern Brazil. He was held in high esteem by the Carioca carnival crowd because he came from the north, from Bahia, the breeding ground for native Brazilian black culture, and also because as a sambista "he was so good he deserved a statue." But for Delightful Myrtle he rehearsed lyrical songs and courtly dances. Then there was his friend and sponsor, Aunt Ciata, a pretty, vivacious member of the well-to-do black community whose lavish hospitality was made possible by her husband's income as a doctor. In Aunt Ciata's spacious residence on the outskirts of the Old City there may have been formal dances in the parlor, but there were African drum sessions in the backyard, and when the party got hot, there was samba. Her house soon became a meeting ground for sambistas from the hills and professional musicians, and for those who had made the transition from one to the other. Sinhô, the earliest master of the samba form, was a regular. So was Donga, one of the first samba composers to tour in Europe. The samba chronicler Cold-Feet Turkey never missed a session. It could be argued that it was from Aunt Ciata's house that samba itself made the final leap to respectability.

Despite the ragings of the letter writers, it was becoming hard to persecute sambistas for playing the music that all Rio society was by now dancing to. The whites' official loathing of black culture had always masked a secret attraction, and if those who had persecuted tribal rites in the plantations were not above asking for some black magic on the side, this century's Cariocas could hardly be expected to refrain from putting on a little black music when they were feeling naughty. Indeed, white love of samba emerged from the closet thanks to gramophone records, first introduced to Brazil in 1900. Two years later, Casa Edison recorded the first Brazilian song, a *lundu* sung by the famous Baiana: "Winter is rough, / My grandmother always said. / Those who sleep together are cold, / Imagine when there's only one in bed." By 1912 Casa Edison was able to rack up sales of almost a million records, largely in Brazilian music. Demand for a samba recording grew.

Then, one inspired evening, the regulars at Aunt Ciata's who used to improvise call-and-response chants in the early samba mold came up with this verse:

> *The chief of police rang me up*
> *Just to let me know*
> *That there's a good roulette game*
> *In Carioca Plaza.*

This miniature of city life was paired with a traditional call-and-response chant:

> *Look at the swallow,*
> *My Lord, My Lord.*
> *She's got all tangled*
> *In our love's knots.*

A few months later this samba, "On the Telephone," was recorded by João da Baiana under a copyright claimed by Donga and Cold-Feet Turkey. The song was a complete success, even though for the 1917 carnival it was cleansed of any allusion to corrupt officials. ("The chief of police sent me a message / That everyone is free to jump and dance".)

The lyrics of "On the Telephone" say a great deal about the new age of détente between the black community and the law, and for sambistas the recording itself was something of a political triumph. Donga saw this clearly, and in an interview long afterward recalled how the police used to make a point of persecuting "what they called the jungle follies," and how police would raid sambistas' homes in order to confiscate their guitars. The change, Donga believed, started with the professionalization of the justice system. "Law graduates were appointed to the office of police commissioner," he noted, and "persecution of sambistas diminished little by little. We wanted to introduce samba to Carioca society. . . . In 1916 we started to lean on Odeon Records to record a samba. That's when they recorded 'On the Telephone.' "*

---

* Interview with Muniz Sodré, quoted in Dulce Tupy, *Carnavais de Guerra* (Rio de Janeiro, 1985).

In 1923 the Brazilian government set up the country's first radio station. Bowing to public demand, it broadcast the most popular music of the day. The Samba Era had arrived. Blacks' music acquired a national following. Their presence in carnival was legitimized by the fashionable promenades. The way was clear for the transformation poor blacks were about to effect on Brazilian carnival, but no one who saw the change take shape was at the time aware of its transcendence, least of all its principal architects.

The seeds for the coming revolution were planted in a favela on São Carlos hill, which overlooks what used to be known as Little Africa, the bustling commercial enclave where Aunt Ciata lived and where most of the black carnival celebrations took place. One day the bambas who gathered regularly on São Carlos hill to improvise songs and pass the time of day reflected bitterly that only middle-class blacks and whites had the privilege of parading down the main avenue of Rio de Janeiro at carnival time dressed like lords and princesses. Young women joined these promenades and did not consider it a dishonor, while up on the hills mothers would never let their daughters out to parade with the rowdies who formed into *blocos de sujos*—"dirty blocks"—to march around the hill drinking, dancing and scrapping for a fight during carnival week. The São Carlos sambistas decided they could do better. They too could parade with the style and elegance of the respectable people, come out with proper costumes and their own theme songs.

But what would this new association be? It was too poor to be a promenade but definitely represented an evolutionary leap from the "dirty" image. In an interview before he died in 1975, the great São Carlos composer and all-time bamba Ismael Silva explained how the term "samba school" had come to him. The sambistas used to rehearse in an empty lot near a teachers' college, Silva recalled. "And people always said, 'That's where the professors come from.'" The São Carlos sambistas decided that while teachers' colleges and universities might be out of their reach, nobody knew more about samba. "People started saying, '*This* is where the professors come from,'" Silva remembered. "That's how the idea of a samba school came about."

And what would they name the school? They were lumpen, known as thieves and pimps to the white world; they would call themselves Deixa Falar—"Let Them Talk."

On the crest of a wave of empowering enthusiasm on São Carlos hill, the members of the Let Them Talk samba school took up a collection, invited women to the rehearsals and composed marching sambas especially for the occasion. In imitation of the vanguard promenades, Let Them Talk also boasted an "opening commission" of favela elders, a female flag-bearer and her partner, the majordomo. During the 1929 carnival Let Them Talk dazzled all the other sambistas from the favelas and suburban factory towns. Two bambas from Mangueira, Carlos Cachaça and his great friend and song partner Cartola witnessed the São Carlos debut and knew they had been bested. The following year five other black communities, including Mangueira, came out with their own samba schools at carnival time.

Mangueira was one of the first favelas, its growth fueled by soldiers discharged from the departed emperor's barracks, immigrants from the arid Northeast and refugees from twentieth-century urbanization programs in downtown Rio. From the apex of the hill, the view is commanding: the city's flat northern expanse lies to one side, the downtown docks, the hills and Guanabara Bay to the other. Just behind Mangueira are the park and the former residence of the Portuguese emperors, who in their flight from the Napoleonic invasion transferred their capital to Rio de Janeiro in 1808 and brought the city to its late-colonial splendor. Yet none of these glories forms part of the average Mangueirense's landscape. Community life here started at the bottom of the hill, in a narrow indentation known as the Buraco Quente, the "Hot Hole," where the more prosperous Mangueirenses are still proud to live. The Hot Hole opens out on a grim viaduct that starts on the edge of the Old City and runs parallel to the suburban railroad, passing Maracanã Stadium and the state university before skimming along the edge of Mangueira hill. By the late nineteenth century the railroad linked first the sugar refineries and then the working-class suburbs to downtown Rio, and a popular misconception holds that the samba school's name, First Station of Mangueira, refers to the fact that Mangueira was the first suburban stop on the line. "Of course not!" Cartola exclaimed in an interview in the 1970s. "The name refers to the fact that we were the first station to have samba!" Let Them Talk might have been the first samba school, but Mangueira, in its name, claimed its own first place in history. Cartola recalled the beginnings:

We had a dirty block. And [other people on Mangueira] had blocks. Those were organized. We were disorganized, we came out any old way. So we decided to organize ourselves properly, into the Rowdies Block. That block was made up of the worst kind of crowd, real low-lifes, good-for-nothings, that species was! It didn't come out at carnival to play, it came out to fight. To fight, get beaten up, beat up, get thrown in jail. So much so that all the other personnel in the neighborhood, in the other blocks, didn't accept us one bit: "Those are bad elements!"

We had very good tabor and tambourine players, but we couldn't come out with the family-type blocks. The personnel there watched out for their daughters and didn't let us come out with them.

So we decided to get organized. Me, the late Marcelino, the late Zé Espinelli, Pedro, several others. We got together:

"Shall we get serious, then?"

"Absolutely!"

Cartola chose the Mangueira school colors. The other schools had settled on conventional color combinations: São Carlos was red and white, Portela blue and white, Império Serrano green and white.

When I was nine years old, my family moved to Laranjeiras. There was a promenade there, called Gooseflesh, and it was pink and green. . . . I liked Gooseflesh. . . . My father and my sister came out with it; my father played the tambourine. I never got to come out [with them] . . . but I really liked those Gooseflesh colors. . . . When I was eleven, I came here to Mangueira, and those colors just stayed in my head. I don't know what it was, but I really was crazy about that pink and green. When the First Station school was founded, I chose the colors, pink and green.*

* Maria Julia Goldwasser, O Palácio do Samba (Rio de Janeiro, 1975), pp. 26–28.

Pink and green, the colors of the mango tree that is Mangueira's namesake, was Cartola's daring choice, and pink and green Mangueira has remained.

To Carlos Cachaça's enduring chagrin, an appointment with a woman from another hill kept him away from the historic first founders' session, but he was soon at the center of the school's life, writing story sambas with Cartola, sharing with the other founders the various administrative and artistic responsibilities: collecting funds for the parade from the Portuguese dry-goods and beer-shack owners on the hill, rehearsing the shepherdesses, honing the *bateria*'s sound to the proper degree of crispness. For the 1933 carnival the school decided to honor the city of Bahia, and to complement a song by Cachaça that mentioned famous poets born in the city, their portraits were painted on posters and displayed in the parade. The following year the other schools imitated this successful innovation, linking the lyrics of their marching sambas to the general parade theme. The central theme became known as the "story" or "script," and the parade song, by extension, as the "story samba."

By the end of its first decade, the Mangueira school had several hundred members, and its parades were at the center of the community's life. Fixed rules had been established for the samba schools in 1935 by the city carnival commission, including the somewhat arbitrary ban on musical instruments other than the percussion elements of the *bateria*, and the mandolin that accompanies the "samba puller," or parade singer, and another ban on "non-Brazilian" carnival themes. In the short decade since their creation the samba schools had become a structured, accepted part of the Rio carnival tradition, but they were still far from being at its center.

Not so samba music, which had made far greater strides. There were samba radio programs and samba recording stars, and the kind of fashionable slumming to samba parties that Harlem blacks of the same period would have recognized. Donga toured Europe and returned chuckling over how the French had raved over his *"sambage."* A wisecracking Portuguese-born chippy with a talent for mind-boggling headdresses and a singularly unsexed screen presence traveled to Hollywood and was soon adopted there, a symbol of the cuddlesome Good Neighbors the United States liked to imagine it possessed south of its borders. "Aiaiaiai, I laik you verry moch," Carmen Miranda sang, and Cartola and Carlos Cachaça, unaware of the ironies, recorded the transition of their music in a story samba. "It's no longer backyard samba, / It's graduated from the streets, / And in the voice of genius artists / It's gone to visit foreign lands."

The "genius artists" were not Cartola or Carlos Cachaça or Ismael Silva—at least not in the white public's eyes. If Rio society was crazy about samba, it was less comfortable with its disreputable creators. A slew of middlemen sprang up, well-dressed, smooth singers who interpreted in the salons the rhythms of the funky inhabitants of the hills. Lacking the true sambista's fertility, the professional singers and song publishers simply copyrighted the songs they liked, made them famous and kept the profits. Francisco Alves—"Chico Guitar"—became particularly known in the favelas for the skill with which he authored songs uncannily like the ones that had become popular on the hills only days before. He devised a system still in use today. Cartola recalls:

Clovis [a fellow sambista] came and told me that [someone called Mário] wanted to buy one of my sambas. I told Clovis I wasn't about to sell a thing . . . that Mário must be crazy. What would he want to buy a samba for? And Clovis said, "Oh, they buy them to make recordings, things like that." But I didn't feel like selling anything. Finally Clovis insisted so much that I went to meet Mário. I sang a samba that Mário already knew—he must have heard it somewhere—and he asked me how much I wanted for my music. I said I didn't know the price. I whispered to Clovis, "I'm going to ask for fifty contos [about ten dollars]. He said, "No way! Ask him for five hundred; he'll give it to you." But I couldn't believe that, so I asked for three hundred. And he gave it to me."

With this first purchase, Cartola entered the limbo to which many black samba composers are still confined. Like Mário, Chico Guitar became a regular customer of Cartola's sambas and passed them on to other establishment singers, including Carmen Miranda, who before leaving for Hollywood recorded Cartola's "I Have a New Love." But Cartola remained unknown and dirt-poor for the greater part of his life; he died in Mangueira, where Carlos Cachaça still lives in a small cement-block house that is certainly respectable by hill standards, but hardly reflects the profit other entertainers have made off the music he helped create.

Cachaça is a sweet-tempered man, not given to rancor or regrets, but among the younger generation of bambas there is a resentful awareness of what has happened to their birthright. At the resurrection mass for Carlos Dória, a voluble conversationalist with an Assyrian profile and a sculpted beard to match talked to his friend Marilia, the Mangueira sociologist, about this very issue. He was bitter about many things—about how *Time* magazine had once used him on its cover and how he had concluded there was no point in asking the publication for money because in the photograph his face was hidden under a carnival mask. "How could I ever prove it was me?" Djalma asked. "But just imagine how many copies that issue sold, how much money *Time* made off me!" The conviction that sambistas lived at the mercy of entrepreneurs far more powerful than they colored his vision of life and gnawed at his sense of its fairness, for samba was everything that made his life worth living. He belonged to the much younger samba school of Vila Isabel, and had come to Dória's mass to pay the respects due to a school considered by many the last holdout against encroaching commercialization. "Because look here, the schools are dying. Do you know what some big companies are trying to do this year? They want the float pushers—the only school members who are not in costume—to wear T-shirts with the company logo on their backs, just like racing-car drivers. The day is coming, I want you to know, when one school will belong to Coca-Cola and another to a supermarket chain. It's the same thing that happened to the soccer clubs, and I want no part of it. I'm a bamba to my very soul, I live and die for my school, but for me the schools are the people on the hills, and watch out: the day the companies take over, I'm out of here."

It was getting late. The mass had ended hours before, and someone in the control room flashed the *quadra*'s lights off and on impatiently. Djalma had much more to say about the current state of samba, and the other groups of stragglers were also in no mood to end the evening. Someone suggested the party move down the road to Dona Neuma's house, whose doors remained open at all hours of the day and night. She had not attended the mass, and Djalma thought it would be a good idea to stop and pay his respects to her as well.

Dona Neuma was the daughter of a school founder who had died of tuberculosis and poverty many years before. Her husband had worked as a carpenter until his death, and Dona Neuma and her family had almost always lived in a brick-and-wood shack on the same spot where their house now stood. One of the daughters, Chininha, had married well, to an airline attendant. Another, Ceci, had a government job with which to support herself, her daughter and granddaughter, while Guezinha, married to a car salesman, also worked off and on at a store or at other clerical jobs. The family's combined incomes and a little money from carnival-related activities had built the house, which was magnificent by hill standards. Its retaining wall climbed straight up off the viaduct to a concrete porch and beyond that to a two-story edifice with an outside staircase leading to a veranda and the suite of rooms where Ceci and Guezinha lived. A floating population of family friends shared the sisters' rooms or, as space grew scarce and the heat rose around carnival time, slept on the cool tile floors of the front room or even camped out on the porch. "There's always more room, child," Guezinha liked to say. "There's the veranda upstairs, there's the roof. . . . You put a little more water in the soup and it's ready for company." The house had been the first on the hill to acquire a telephone—a still scarce commodity—and this was an additional cause of traffic, with Mangueirenses perpetually bursting into the house with urgent pleas to use the phone to call a doctor, or a sick relative, or someone rumored to be looking for a servant or a bricklayer.

Dona Neuma presided over the household and the female divisions of the school with similar style. Irascible and autocratic, she was also completely vulnerable to pleas for help, which is why so many temporarily homeless people ended up at her doorstep, and why all complaints of injustice and wrongdoing in the school were eventually addressed to her. No one was turned away, the same price being extracted from all: unswerving loyalty and wide-eyed attention when Dona Neuma spoke.

On this solemn evening she was in a speaking vein and in one of her moods. Djalma, who had been impeccably reverential in his role as ambassador from a sister school, got the worst of it.

"I hate communists," Dona Neuma was saying, in what seemed like a non sequitur. "Communists are the filthiest creatures on earth. They would all be better dead. What do they do? Call strikes. They always want to strike, and what's the result? People out of work. Good, honest people who have a right to earn their living, prevented from working. And who suffers? We do. Communists disrupt transportation, take the food out of our mouths, bring the police into every situation. They make me sick!"

As it happened, Djalma's school, Vila Isabel, had just recently voted out its longtime president and sponsor, a former captain in the state secret intelligence service, and elected a white woman member of the Communist Party in his stead. Djalma, who understood that the preceding speech had been made for his benefit, was desperately eager to change the subject. "What a good smell you have coming out of the kitchen!" he said anxiously, but Dona Neuma instantly snatched back the conversational ball. "Good smell nothing!" she said, rocking her round body forward for emphasis. "I spent the entire day scrubbing clothes, with my arms elbow-deep in soap suds, bent over a sink, with my back aching, not the kind of work a sick woman like me should be doing, and you'd think someone around here would show appreciation by having a proper meal ready at the end, but what do I get? Rice and beans and scrambled eggs! People work in order to eat decently, but if we were living in communism they'd starve us all!"

Her low, hoarse voice was exploding with indignation, and Djalma made his soothing. "But even rice and beans taste good when you've worked up an appetite, Dona Neuma!"

"Rice and beans? *Rice and beans?* I didn't live off rice and beans even when I was poor. We always managed to have a little beef, a little ham, a little stew. It was a question of dignity. And now that I've raised three grown daughters with the sweat of my brow, do you think it's right for someone from the First Station of Mangueira to live off rice and beans? I don't see things that way at all. I like my food. I like to eat a lot, fill my belly with tasty things. That's what life is about: eating a lot, crapping a lot, farting a lot!"

She ambled off to air her vexation in the front yard. "Poor thing," someone murmured. "Dória's death has everybody's spirits so altered." But a communist woman president of Vila Isabel seemed much more on Dona Neuma's mind, and Djalma, sensing that the evening would not improve, said good night. Dona Neuma nodded to him curtly as he walked out the door.

With Dona Neuma cooling her temper out in the yard, the household resumed its usual bustle. Half a dozen people sprawled on a couple of worn, fake-leather sofas, watching television. New family members constantly emerged from back bedrooms and joined the others on the couch. Someone made coffee. Beers were poured. Guezinha stored the week's shopping—beans, rice, macaroni, detergent, toilet paper and gallons of cooking oil—in a carved wood highboy that matched the rest of the fancy and uncomfortable dining room furniture. I fidgeted, feeling both out of place and eager to linger in the household's chaotic warmth. Guezinha gave me an amused look. "You're here to learn, aren't you? Come here, I'll show you something." She led me to the huge kitchen, where an excited group of women was studying a sketch of a woman in a feather-topped turban, sequined bra and ankle-length, below-the-navel skirt, seductively draped and slit thigh-high up the front. The outfit looked like something the chorus girls at the Crazy Horse in Paris might wear for their presentation walk-on, but Guezinha said it was supposed to be a parade costume representing an *orixá*, or African goddess. Looking at the sketch I understood why the Portuguese word for costume is *fantasia*—"fantasy": all my life, I had wanted to look like that, if only for a few minutes, a few seconds.

"It's for my wing," Guezinha explained. "I have an all-woman wing, fifty of us, and this is the costume we'll wear. Do you like it?" I said I did. She gave me a sidelong glance, then looked around at the other women. "Well, how would you like to join my wing and parade with us at carnival time?" I said I would like that very much indeed. "But first," Guezinha said, with hardly the shadow of a smile, "you have to learn to samba."

One of the subtler forms of amusement for blacks at carnival time is watching whites try to samba. White people have had nearly the whole century to work it out, and most of them still can't quite get it right. It's not that blacks mind; that whites look clumsy while they're trying to have fun is a misfortune too great to be compounded by mockery, but it's also a fact that can't be denied. Whites are certainly given points for trying, though, and in the Samba Palace the ones who got up to dance seemed to be much more warmly regarded than those who tried to maintain their dignity. But I was terrified of what I might look like, and in the weeks before carnival, after lurking in the corners of the *quadra* at almost every rehearsal, I went home and practiced samba grimly and in secret.

HOW TO SAMBA (WOMEN'S VERSION)

1. Start before a mirror, with no music. You may prefer to practice with a pair of very high heels. Though samba is a dance that started out barefoot, and can still be danced that way, high heels will throw your spinal column out of whack and give your pelvis the appearance of greater flexibility. Platform shoes with relatively wide heels provide the best combination of stability and shock absorption.

2. Stand with feet parallel, close together. Step and hop in place on your right foot as you brush your left foot quickly across. Step in quick succession onto your left, then your right foot. Although your hips will swivel to the right as far as possible for this sequence, your head and shoulders should remain strictly forward. Otherwise you'll start looking like you're doing the *hora*. Practice this sequence right and left until you can do it without counting.

3. Test yourself: Are your lips moving? Are your shoulders scrunched? No? Are you able to manage one complete left-right sequence per second? Good! Now that you've mastered the basic samba step, you're ready to add music. Choose Zeca Pagodinho, Jovelina the Black Pearl, Neguinho of the Hummingbird or any other sambista you like and start practicing. The key thing at this stage is speed: when you are up to two complete sequences per second you are well on your way to samba. Aim for four.

4. A samba secret: Add hips. They're probably moving already, but if you are trying to hit required minimum speed they may be a little out of control. You want to move them, but purposefully. When you step on your right foot your hips switch left-right. When you step on your left they switch again, right-left. Two hip beats per foot beat, or about twelve beats per second, if you can manage.

5. Stop hopping! Keep your shoulders down! Face front! The magic of samba lies in the illusion that somebody is moving like crazy from the waist down while an entirely different person is observing the proceedings from the waist up. Keep your torso detached from your hips and facing where

you're looking, and practice with a book on your head until you can stay level at full speed.

You've mastered the mechanics of samba. Now you're ready to start dancing. If the following essentials seem a little daunting, don't be discouraged. Remember, you've come a long way from your beginning days. Dress appropriately for this next stage. Preferably something that emphasizes the waist, so that hip movement is maximized. Go for shine. Twelve hip beats per second will look like a hundred if you're wearing sequins.

Arms: If you are up to two to four sequences per second with a book on your head and your hips swiveling at least forty-five degrees in each direction away from the wall you're facing, you're ready to ornament your dance by holding your arms out and ruffling your shoulders as you move. Think of a fine-plumed bird rearranging its wings. Keep the movement flexible and easy. Reach out with your fingertips. If you can't shimmy without looking scrunched or panicky, drop it.

Smile: The key rule is, don't make it sexy. You will look arch, coy or, if you are working really hard, terribly American. Your smile should be the full-tilt cheer of someone watching her favorite team hit a home run. Or it should imitate the serene curve of a Hindu deity's. The other key rule: There is no point to samba if it doesn't make you smile.

Sweat: Obviously, you will produce lots of it. You will soon discover that it looks wrong when it is dripping off the tip of your nose. Don't let this upset you. Perseverance and practice have got you this far; keep at it. Practice. When you find that your body is moving below you in a whirlpool frenzy and your mind is floating above it all in benign accompaniment; when your torso grows curiously light and your legs feel like carving little arabesques in the air on their own for the sheer fun of it; when everything around you seems to slow for the rush that's carrying you through the music, you'll probably discover that sweat is clothing your body in one glorious, uniform, scintillating sheet, flying around you in a magic halo of drops, and you'll know that you have arrived at samba.

* * *

Two weeks after Dória's death, on a wet, cold Friday evening, the Mangueira samba harvest resumed with the selection of the story-samba semifinalists. Dória's murder had had a number of devastating consequences, not the least of which was a nearly empty *quadra* that mid-October night. Bereft of crowds, the Samba Palace looked garish and lonely in the late-night drizzle. Garbage overflowed a dumpster between the *quadra* and Dona Neuma's house, and pigs and dogs rooted about in the soggy mess. The few hundred people from the hill who did show up looked chilled and uncomfortable among the puddles in the dance space. The sound system ground the music into mush, the singers repeatedly wavered off key and the *bateria* did the worst thing possible: it lost contact with the singers and went off the beat. When this happens during the parade the result is unsalvageable ruin; caught between the competing rhythms of the marching drummers and the singers, who travel separately on a sound truck, school members wander off on their own, and the parade's tight ranks soon dissolve into chaos. When this "crossing up" occurs in the course of a rehearsal, the result is simply to make the music unbearable.

Sometime around two in the morning I stopped by the table where Guezinha was sitting with her sisters and a few friends, looking close to tears and very slightly drunk. We stared for a while at the dance space, where the shepherdess-herder Alberto Pontes was halfheartedly chivying a handful of women. "The samba is really hot tonight, isn't it?" Guezinha said, smiling at me like a television announcer. I said that it certainly was, and we sat together wordlessly for a while, listening to the *bateria*'s excruciating hammer. Guezinha pushed back her chair. "I'm going to bed," she announced, and went home.

The school's situation was no better in the daytime. When Mangueira was mentioned in the press, it was in the context of police interrogations and speculations on Dória's off-duty life: *Had* he participated in a death squad? *Was* he involved in the drug trade? Dona Neuma and Dona Zica, the two "First Ladies" of Mangueira, were interviewed by the press not on the usual colorful subject of carnival's early days but on the question of who had murdered their president. "If I knew, I would have chased the culprit all the way to Japan," Dona Neuma avowed, and tried unsuccessfully to get her questioners interested in the wonderful theme for the coming carnival.

Comment on the misfortune was generally avoided around the samba school, as if reference to it might attract additional bad luck. "Dória is dead but the school lives on" was one standard answer to questions about the current adversity. And it was a sign of how bad things were that the most devastating consequence of Dória's murder was the one that was never mentioned. Mangueira had won first place in the carnival parade for the previous two years running. With a striking theme and a first-rate story samba this year, there had been little doubt in the community's mind that the school could win a third time in the upcoming carnival, an achievement that only two other schools could boast of and that was permanently associated with their names. That Mangueira, bereft of leadership, was no longer in the running for a triple championship was the great unstated fact casting its miserable spell on the harvest evening that followed Dória's murder. "Mangueira is going to have to parade any old way," Vila Isabel's Djalma had commented sorrowfully on the night of the resurrection mass. "And I, for one, am not looking forward to watching what will happen. It's going to be a very sad thing." The disastrous semifinal rehearsal was evidence of the school's depression and disarray. Now, less than twelve hours later, the *finalissima*, or final contest night, loomed ahead.

When I walked in at midnight, the Samba Palace was unrecognizable. The walls looked scrubbed and the floor was dry and spotless. Every table in the house had been set out and all were full. A huge crowd threaded its way among them, dodging radio reporters and school members busing trays of fancy appetizers to a section of tables that had been cordoned off for VIPs. The master sambista Delegado had clothed his long body in a hot-pink suit. Pontes the shepherdessherder had an extraordinary array of whistles bouncing off his chest. There was a phalanx of flag-bearers: old ones, new ones, apprenticing adolescents. Guezinha, a woman I associated with hard work and practical clothes, stood smiling at the center of the dance area, enclosed in the halo of her own sexuality, dressed in a strapless sheath someone must have stitched directly onto her body, exhaling perfume with every movement, unapproachable as a shrine. "What happened?" I asked, bewildered. The goddess, remote and knowing, only smiled.

"What happened?" I asked another member of the directorate. He smiled too. That morning, he said, people had recognized that things looked bad and that a final harvest session like the previous night's would be fatal. A cleanup brigade was organized. Emissaries were sent to the radio stations with pleas for a little promotional help to get Mangueira back on its feet. The hill membership was asked to turn out in force. Dona Neuma and her family brigade worked overtime cooking up platters of special tidbits for the press and the VIPs. In short, Mangueira drew on the habits, discipline, infrastructure and reflexes that wealthier and younger schools covet and cannot reproduce. After all, what sambistas call tradition is often simply the training provided by years of endurance.

The walls were aglow with paper banners in magenta and green for Helinho Turco's team—the school directorate's favorite—and green and yellow, the Brazilian national colors, for the other finalists. This was the team made up of the composers Ivo, Otacilio and Sinval, and their song was a favorite with the *bateria*, especially because it included a catchy little drum riff in the middle. A huge white banner hanging from the metal rafters depicted this team's logo: a bare-chested black man with arms open in a victory sign. The directorate had in fact settled on the samba they preferred practically at the beginning of the harvest, but the teams whose songs were popular with the audience had continued lobbying among school members, hoping to overturn the decision with a display of enthusiasm on the dance floor. They had a lot at stake. The display of flags, the photocopied handouts of each samba's lyrics, the singers hired for the night to present the song, all cost money—perhaps as much as two or three thousand dollars in the course of the season. The school contributed some of the funds, but a composer who believed his samba was likely to win would invest as much as he could rummage, because the royalties for a winning samba would solve his financial worries for a healthy period of time. Now, caught up in the excitement, the claques for the two finalist teams shuttled between tables, egging their supporters on, flashing victory signs at each other, handing out bags of confetti to be thrown into the air at the appropriate moment. Even the sound was clean, and as the loudspeakers broadcast recorded sambas from the current hit parade the crowd was on its feet and dancing, wired so tightly to the music they seemed to anticipate and create every riff and flourish. Friends called greetings to each other across tables. The slouching young men in Bermudas looked alert and bright-eyed. On the mezzanine, the VIP balconies filled with men in white linen suits and women in skintight spandex halter tops and miniskirts. Through the gap between the *quadra* walls and the corrugated metal roof suspended high overhead, the favela was visible, and in the houses that bordered directly on the Samba Palace spectators hung out of windows for the best view of the action below.

At a table near the VIP section an old woman who had been sitting with a group of young white men got up and began to dance. She was tall and ruined by age. Her hair was pulled back in a scrawny ponytail, and her generous grin showed few teeth. She wore thick glasses and a faded T-shirt over a pair of patched, much-washed blue jeans, but when she rose from her chair, the groups at the surrounding tables turned to her expectantly. Leisurely, she began her dance: Shuffle to the left, shuffle to the right, circle all around and wiggle on down. Shuffle again, do it one more time, put your hands on your hips and shake them down the line. . . . The men at her table were grinning with her, waiting, clapping in time, egging her on as she smiled down on them. Standing in place, immobile, she began a shiver that climbed slowly from her heels to her calves, crawled up her thighs and settled in her haunches, dividing the samba rhythm into a hundred faster particles without ever losing a beat. Then, with her hips trembling in isolation from the rest of her body, she produced her pièce de résistance: bunching up her fingers, she blew a bouquet of kisses on each one and bestowed them on her admirable behind, first on her tremulous left buttock and then, with a second appreciative smile, on her right. Her audience went wild, and the woman, delighted, doubled over with laughter. When she saw me staring in captivated amazement, she performed the routine all over again and raised her bottle of beer at the end in a mischievous toast.

"That," said Marilia, "was Dona Nininha Xoxoba, one of the great Mangueira flag-bearers."

A burst of rockets interrupted her explanation. In the great open space between the *quadra* walls and the roof, the view of the favela was momentarily erased by a curtain of fireworks, exploding in constellations of silver, green and gold. The *bateria* rammed its sound wave into the night, a huge cheer went up, and on the singers' tower Ivo, Otacilio and Sinval's team raced into its samba, pursued by the drums. "Black men are outcasts, / But they're the kings of the parade!" they sang, and later, Helinho Turco's team answered, "They are the kings, / pink and green, / of all Mangueira!" And, "Has freedom really dawned / Or was it all an illusion?" To which Ivo's team answered, "It's going to change, or isn't it? / It's going to change, or isn't it? Who knows. . . ." The dance space filled to overflowing for both teams, the women sweating and pushing the samba on. Nininha stood up once again to dance. Guezinha made her way onto the dance floor, and Dona Zica, in her granny glasses and white hair, led the river of women, escorted by the preening Delegado. Both sambas were hot, the drums were brilliant, confetti filled the air, there was no stopping the dancers.

Beto End-of-the-Night announced the winner at dawn, and as light filled the *quadra*, a hoarse white man, Percy Pires, acting as rehearsal coordinator, evoked Dória's name and Mangueira's past and assured the happy, sweaty crowd that another school victory was on its way. His speech did not sound hollow. As the Mangueirenses streamed out through the turnstiles into a hazy, unclouded day, someone ventured a cheer: "Mangueira Triple Crown!"

3 *Baianas I*

Catholicism LT, foreigners, etc
Protestantism
Regionalisms

A young woman named Eurides led me through a maze of alleyways up to the home of Dona Nininha Xoxoba, the former Mangueira flag-bearer. I'd met Eurides on my first visit to the hill; a chain-smoking, nonstop talker who lived in a small room near the *quadra* which she shared with the serious-minded Lilico, who doted on her, worked hard in the shipyards when he could find a job, and rarely said a word. Eurides worked on and off as a housecleaner and manicurist, more often as a volunteer distributing municipal milk coupons at the hill's neighborhood association. Eight months of pregnancy had in no way diminished her remarkable energy—perhaps because the belly was too tiny to get in her way—and her enthusiasm for Mangueira's history and the intricacies of its community life carried me through the initial awkwardness of making a nuisance of myself on the hill. Now, as we zigzagged rapidly up a footpath past shacks and beer stands, bare-brick houses and a miniature shrine with plastic flowers on the altar, she talked about the dancer I had seen at the final contest night, the oldest of Mangueira's surviving flag-bearers.

"Dona Nininha isn't what she used to be," Eurides said. "She was the most sensational-looking woman Mangueira ever saw. That lady was *big*; not just tall, but built. And she had this enormous savings, so when she did her special step, the one you saw, the Xoxoba, that savings would shake like anything." Savings? "You know; her behind. She doesn't have much left now, but when she was young, men sighed over her, they really did."

"Dona Nininha!" Eurides yelled at the door of a small brick house. "You have a foreign girl here to see you."

Dona Nininha shuffled to the door, peered at us and waved us into her cluttered room with no particular gesture of friendliness. She sat us down and searched the table, the sprung sofa and the jumble in her handbag until she found her eyeglasses and put them on. Then she flashed a gigantic grin of recognition and I explained the purpose of my visit: "I wanted to see you dance again, Dona Nininha," I said. "But you seem to be having trouble with your legs." She looked down at the bandages wrapped tightly around her calves, freshly stained with a seeping yellow liquid, and shook her head. "I don't know what's the matter with these legs. The veins burst no matter how tight I bind them up. Look at this! I changed the bandages this morning and they're wet already. But that doesn't mean I can't dance!" She stood and produced a few steps, grimaced, sat down abruptly. "Not all that much," she acknowledged. "But I can dance."

Nininha ("Don't call me Dona, girl, it makes me feel *old*") was born in Mangueira in 1923, the only surviving child of a family that never strayed from the hill or from the twin paths of samba and *candomblé*, music and religion. Her mother's singing was famous in Mangueira. Maria the Sieve, her mother was called, because the family was poor and Maria's husband wore hand-me-down trousers that were often too big. The neighborhood children called him Sieve and turned it into Maria's married name. Maria the Sieve specialized in a call-and-response musical form that preceded samba:

> *Jongo* is what my mother used to sing. It was all improvised, and you'd make up songs out of any old thing. When my mother agreed to marry my father, for example, people made up a song, because she was this great big healthy woman, and all the strongest, hardest-working men around here would come around and pay court, and she'd turn up her nose. So when she started paying attention to my father someone improvised a verse like this: "A horse went over the bridge...," to which everyone was supposed to answer, "And the bridge

didn't even shake!" And the the lead singer would go, "An ox-drawn cart went over the bridge . . . ," and everyone would answer again, "And the bridge didn't even shake!" And then, because my father was this little bit of a man, really nothing to look at, the lead singer would go, "Then a mouse went over the bridge . . . ," and everyone would answer, "And the whole bridge started to tremble, the whole bridge started to tremble!" And the drums would begin. That was their courtship song.

Maria the Sieve had twelve children before her husband died of cirrhosis (as Nininha's husband would also, much later). Nininha thinks her own survival was probably guaranteed when her mother dedicated her to St. Sebastian/Oxóssi, who in his Catholic manifestation is the patron saint of the city of Rio de Janeiro de São Sebastião and in his African aspect is the reclusive god of the forests and the hunt. Every January 20, on the saint's day, Maria the Sieve would walk his statue through the neighborhood, singing his praises in her carrying voice to thank him for keeping her daughter alive. The small plaster figure of St. Sebastian tied to a tree and pierced by arrows still lives on a table in Nininha's jumbled front room, and when floods or other natural disasters strike the Mangueirenses they go to the church down the road and ask the affable Italian priest there to take the saint in procession around the hill once more.

There are other plaster-cast figures on the table. St. Barbara, who is the war goddess Iansã; St. George, who is Ogun, the fierce god of metals and rage; St. Cosmo and St. Damian, who are the mischievous child Ibeji, or divine twins. I had seen all of them before at the religious-supplies stores—entrancing shops filled with strangely buxom Virgin Marys and leering red devils clad in the pornographer's black shoes, socks and trunks. The dark corners of these stores are piled to the rafters with dried herbs and magic lotions and strands of plastic beads in the gods' colors (blue and white for the oceanic Yemanjá, carnelian red for warring Iansã, blue and green for the leafy Oxóssi), but I was riveted by the front shelves, by the rows of blond, pink-cheeked plaster babies with the ever so slightly weird glint in their blue eyes, by the eternally suffering St. Sebastians and the diseased St. Lazaruses, always depicted with dogs licking at their sores. Why, among the pearl-fleshed saints, were only the devil's features recognizably black? What were all those evil children up to? And who, again, was the strange black woman with blue eyes and a gag across her mouth?

Nininha thought the gagged woman I'd seen was probably someone called Anastácia, and her understanding was that this was a slave who in the old days had refused to submit to her owners. She didn't have a statue of Slave Anastácia on her table, but she spoke of her with respect. As for her own resident divinities, Nininha seemed unaware of the meticulous classifications and divisions set up by some anthropologists between deities from the *candomblé* pantheon and those belonging to Brazil's fastest-growing religion, *umbanda*, which is an urban mix of the basic African beliefs of *candomblé* with the nineteenth-century spiritist notions of a Frenchman named Alain Kardec. There is an influential school of anthropologists with close ties to the *candomblé* community who present the older religion as "better" because more pure and *umbanda* as more decadent, primarily because the latter regularly incorporates whites into the cult and draws freely from every religion known in Brazil, but also because it took the initiative in representing Exu, the *candomblé* messenger between heaven and earth, as the devil. It's not difficult to see why: Exu, an unpredictable, not quite divine being whose intercession is essential when humans want to communicate with the gods, is partial to the transitional world of cemeteries, where flesh becomes spirit. But he also likes crossroads, because they represent an opening of possibilities, and possibilities are what he deals in. Exu likes to work mischief, is sexually insatiable and communicates regularly with the dead. When the time came to look for his equivalent in the Catholic pantheon, the unavoidable conclusion must have been that the only entity with comparable characteristics also happens to wear horns. The pro-*candomblé* anthropologists complain that the Catholic concept of evil has thus been imposed on the priapic Exu, but it seems to me that the concept has been at least as imposed on the academics themselves, that the type of evil they see in the horned figure is not necessarily there for his worshippers. The storefront devils contemplating the offerings of money, cigars and firewater at their feet are creatures one could strike a deal with: I'll keep you in firewater, you get me back my man. Lecherous they may be, but they are no more threatening than the murderous Ogun, or more vengeful than the silly, flirtatious river goddess Oxum, and certainly no more arbitrary in their dreadful powers than any of the other gods imagined by humans.

Nininha admitted—only long after I first met her and with some reluctance—that she herself had been claimed long before as a "daughter" by Bombogira, one of Exu's more mischievous manifestations. As for whether she belonged to *candomblé* or *umbanda*, she ignored the distinction and said vehemently, "I belonged to *macumba*!" This is the word many blacks use for Afro-Brazilian religious practice in general. But she spoke in the past tense because, she said, the old gods were growing weak. She remembered going as a child with her family and fellow worshippers to the forests then still close on the outskirts of Rio, and helping to sweep a clearing clean where the gods—who when they are being African have no physical representation but reside rather as forces in a tree, a river or a stone— could be convoked by the drums and welcomed. And she remembers the drum sessions starting at dusk and going on for hours around a fire, until the St. Anthony statue brought from Mangueira bristled with life, stood up, tromped down the steps of his altar and marched stiffly around the circle of worshippers, staring each one harshly in the eye before clomping back onto his platform, spinning around and turning to plaster.

There were other miracles:

We would get hungry after so much worship. And the man who led us would step into the center of the circle, and stamp the ground, and a banana tree [*macondo*] would sprout, and grow, and flower and bear fruit. And when it was ripe we would all eat and not be hungry. Afterward, in the morning, when the fire had died down, I used to go to the spot where the tree had stood, and tap the ground and feel to see if there was any bump, or a hollow. And there was nothing, the tree was gone. But the religion isn't so strong anymore. That doesn't happen now, or I haven't heard of it.

The saints may be weaker but they continue in residence on Nininha's table. They are part of what makes her unmistakably "root"—an embodiment of black tradition. It's in the spare, sharp-angled way she moves, in the way she relishes a breakfast of plain boiled manioc root, in her undivorced relationship with gods who even in their prime neglected to show her great favor. And it's in her dancing, so unlike the ornamented, light-footed style of today. Nininha stands firmly rooted on bandaged legs to illustrate what her mother's *jongo* dancing looked like, and in a few gestures she has sketched the entire *roda de samba*—the samba ring: the upright stilt-legged figures standing in a circle in the late, late night, flattened palms beating together to underscore the chant; the lead singer improvising another verse for the chorus to memorize until it takes on the full shape of a song; the lone dancer spinning toward another to anoint him with the *umbigada*, or "navel touch," known in Angola as *semba*, a fertility gesture that passes the torch of dancing from one member of the circle to another. The secret of Nininha's rootness is that her ancestors travel with her and she can make them present at will.

The favela concept of "root" is all about the past buried beneath the visible surface. Favela blacks, with not a single history textbook to claim as their own, or one hero of theirs mentioned by name in white textbooks, with hardly the literacy required to get through whatever rare academic studies are available on black culture, are obsessively concerned with their origins. Unlike white Cariocas, whose conversational references to the past rarely extend beyond the previous week, blacks like Nininha can scarcely mention an event without explaining where it came from, how it got to be that way. Sambistas write songs about earlier sambistas so they won't be forgotten; carnival scripts frequently focus on specific historical events; Eurides describes a neighbor and automatically includes a reference to the person's parents. Perhaps this is because so little of what a person can know about his past is known in the favela. Hardly anyone has baby pictures. Many people are confused about the exact date of their birth, or their name. Cartola discovered that his given name was Angenor and not Agenor only when he was in his late fifties and went to the civil registry to marry Dona Zica. Many children's names don't make it into the civil registry at all. City officials recognize that an undetermined—but high—number of favela births never get recorded. As for history: seventeenth- and eighteenth-century accounts of black life are almost impossible to find in print. And in the nineteenth century, when blacks became a political issue, a leading abolitionist ordered the government slave registers burned to avoid paying indemnification to the former owners. Still, favelados say proudly, "I am root," meaning, "I belong to my past."

The words used are "root" and "black" and "past," in the singular, as if there were one history, or one color, or a single place or time from which Brazilian blacks had emerged. One might as well refer to "Europeans" when speaking of the successive waves of English, Scots, Italians, Norwegians, Germans, Portuguese and Lithuanians who eventually populated the United States. By the time of abolition all sorts of non-Europeans had been carried forcibly from Africa to Brazil, and mixed and allied there to create an even greater diversity. There were the thoroughly Brazilian descendants of the initial sixteenth-century influx of slaves from Guinea; the children and grandchildren of subsequent shipments from Angola and the Congo; the descendants of slaves brought over during the eighteenth-century Dahomey wave; and the first generation of Yorubas brought over from Nigeria and Benin during the final period of slavery. By 1888 the black population of Brazil included the slave descendants of generations of slaves, and young children born in liberty under the 1871 "free womb" law. There were former slaves granted their freedom in their owners' wills but also blacks born in Brazil and reduced to a state of passive submission by their second-generation education in slavery. Ibo princes and priests, defeated and sold in the course of internecine warfare in Nigeria and Benin, were brought over in large numbers during the last wave of trade and became runaways and rebels. There were black Portuguese-speakers and black Yoruba-speakers, Muslims and animists, old freedmen and -women and young slaves, Nagô priests and Brazilian water carriers, beige-colored house slaves and dark brown doctors. Nininha was descended from all of them. Her lack of access to a "real" history had made them all available as the mythical root she embodied and could not see.

I did see the diversity of Nininha's roots made visible once, in photographs. In the second half of the nineteenth century the photographer Christiano Jr. set up a studio in the old commercial section of Rio de Janeiro, where he made the usual portraits of little boys in sailor suits and young couples on their engagement day. But because they had become the rage he also took pictures to be printed as souvenirs, and because the souvenirs that people wanted to receive from exotic Brazil were ones that showed its exotica, Christiano Jr. took photographs of slaves. The collection was published in book form on the occasion of the abolition centennial, and that is where I found the people of Nininha's past staring out at me in a bookstore one afternoon, every one of Christiano's subjects looking at or away from the camera with an expression of arresting blankness. Had the photographer encouraged such unsmilingness to make his subjects look more slavelike? Or had the models themselves decided to pose thus, ordering the camera, in effect, to register not the willingness to laugh and banter that Brazilian blacks have in common with Brazilian whites, but the essential truth of their lives?

The identical hollow gaze had many different faces. There was a delicately beautiful woman still wearing her tribal robes and jewelry, posed with her child, dressed in lace-trimmed Christian clothes. Nigerian? I wondered. Was she a Yoruba, then? Or did they wear clothes like that in Angola? In Brazil, Yorubas were held to be more intelligent than the people of Angola and Dahomey (perhaps because it was Yorubas who controlled the slave traffic from the Benin coast), and they were often reserved for housework. The tall, thin woman with the elegant neck did not look as if she worked in the fields. But here was a man who looked as though he might have: his expression was not blank but thoroughly bewildered and brutalized; a recent arrival, perhaps, he was shown bare-chested and in close-up in order to display the tribal scars on his face. And here was someone with an elegantly pointed beard, in a hand-me-down white suit with a handkerchief stuffed in the breast pocket, wearing a bowler hat and carrying an umbrella. One might take him for an ordinary Brazilian but for his bare feet: slaves were forbidden to wear shoes—even for photographs. He was most likely a "black-for-profit," one of the privileged caste of urban slaves who were sent out every day by their owners to sell flowers, bread, chairs, haircuts, paint jobs—the gamut of urban goods and services.

Blacks-for-profit were allowed to keep whatever they earned beyond a basic quota, and this eventually allowed many to buy their freedom and join the growing black urban class of petty artisans and merchants. Their first purchase was almost invariably a pair of shoes, and the wood-and-leather slippers they could afford were most fashionably worn a few sizes too small, perhaps in an attempt to disguise the broad contours feet acquire in a lifetime of barefoot heavy labor. Free and shod, they gravitated toward the backyard religious temples that had begun to spring up in the atmosphere of relative tolerance provided by the cities: in the waning days of slavery the African gods were surfacing again. Mostly they were Yoruba deities, because their worshippers were the slave trade's most recent arrivals, but in the uprooting and displacement of slavery Africans intermixed as they would not have at home, and so did the gods. When the first centers of worship were set up in Rio de Janeiro in the 1870s, the drums beat for an amalgam of Nigerian, Angolan, and Dahomean religions that owed much to Africa but also had a peculiar relationship to Catholic saints and a Brazilian name—*candomblé*. The most outstandingly African characteristic of this syncretist religion was the ritual of "possession": of dancing oneself into a trance state that permitted the deities to "descend" and occupy the bodies of their chosen "sons" and "daughters."

The *candomblé* temples of Rio de Janeiro were set up by women, freed slaves who had emigrated from Bahia and brought the cult with them. A law passed in 1885 had granted freedom to all slaves over the age of sixty, but few men survived the rigors of slave labor that long. The freedwomen were often former blacks-for-profit, vendors of sweets and dumplings whose perfumed, starched, frilly clothes and flirtatious ways were described in the novels of the time. The women from Bahia were special in other ways: because commercial traffic with the slave ports of Nigeria and Dahomey had continued long after the end of the slave trade, Bahia was a center of constantly renewed African tradition and religious practice. The women who set up the first *candomblé* temples in Bahia wore shawls and turbans woven in Africa, sold black-eyed-pea dumplings identical to those offered in the markets of Lagos and were in regular contact with "fathers-of-saints" from the Yoruba cults. When the Bahianas arrived in Rio as part of the great wave of migration that followed the end of slavery, their special relationship with the old continent was immediately recognized. The "daughters-of-saints" sold sweets in the daytime, and in their backyards at night they sponsored *candomblé* sessions for the gods and samba parties after for the people made joyous in their worship. The women from Bahia were addressed respectfully as "aunts." They knew the religion, they had "samba in the foot," they had survived, and they kept the culture going. They were root. To this day all samba schools, no matter how trendy, have a contingent, or wing, of baianas in honor of these sturdy women.

* * *

Celina is a baiana. I met her one afternoon in October when a particularly belligerent sun had flattened everyone on the hill into shapes
of listlessness and exhaustion. At Dona Neuma's house, where I
stopped for a drink of water, several of the younger women and
children were dozing on the tile floor, seeking its very relative cool-
ness. Dona Neuma had just finished scrubbing a tubful of laundry,
and she was hanging it up in her front yard on the clothesline strung
parallel to the viaduct. I asked her to introduce me to some baianas.

"It's hot and my legs are swollen," Dona Neuma said. "I can't
go up the hill with you to visit. But you can find them. There's Dona
Yvette, Dona Marina, Dona Celina, Dona Deia, Dona Elsa, Dona
Daisy, Dona Giselle . . ." The names floated in the air: Dona Daisy
would be delicate and shy, Dona Yvette tall and strict. Dona Giselle?
The best dancer. But Dona Neuma was right: it was killingly hot
and the hill was steep. Dona Celina lived closest.

Between Dona Neuma's house and the *quadra* there is a little
clearing a few steps up from the main avenue. A "plaza," it is called,
and if the name is far too elegant for this accidental space it does at
least suggest its function in Mangueira community life. It has a tiny
restaurant and an even smaller evangelical temple, a shack that sells
beer and soft drinks, and a bar that opens only on festive occasions
late at night. An abandoned chunk of concrete serves as a bench
where in the late afternoon people gather to chat with those returning
from work. This is a central entry point into Mangueira. Beyond it,
alleys thread their way up the favela.

"Do you know where Dona Celina lives?" I asked a toddler who
had been staring as I tried to get my bearings. The child's mouth was
plugged with a pacifier, but she nodded yes and, setting off at a listing
trot, tucked into a dark alley so narrow it was virtually invisible.
The air thickened here, and the heat turned adhesive. A thin black
trickle of water ran down the lane, but my guide picked her way
across a series of planks and made a turn, pausing to see if I was
following. There was a broader alley, and here the sun shone on
geranium pots, a rotting mattress, a pile of rubble, a communal sink
from which water ran through a hose, and the lopsided entrance to
a latrine. Beyond the mattress the child stopped and called through
her pacifier for Dona Celina.

A slatternly woman of about fifty sat just inside the doorway of
a one-room brick house, skirts hitched up and knees wide to catch

any cooling breeze. Both she and the house looked as if they had been picked up by a hurricane and released to crash in this spot. The house was crumbling, the woman's hair stood on end alarmingly. She was chunky and unsmiling. "I'm a reporter," I said. "I'm looking for long-term baianas, and I'd like to invite you for a beer." Celina offered me the first of her many transformations. She smiled, and her face took on a rounded charm. She laughed, and the music of it filled the afternoon with bohemian prospects of lazy garrulous drinking, punctuated by stories and song. "Come in!" she beckoned. From the darkness behind her a young man emerged, offering the bony remains of a stuffed chair. "Sit down here while I finish fixing my hair," Celina urged. She grabbed a tonglike instrument from the flame of a gas stove propped against the doorway and clamped it on a chunk of hair. There was an exhalation of cooked wool, and when she removed the tongs, the hair to which they had been applied was standing straight on end. "You'll see; this won't take long."

"She's right, you know," her son said. "She's very good at it."

While Celina applied herself to her hair, we chatted. She had been a baiana for twenty years, she said, and she had never paraded with any other wing. "The other costumes are too shameless," she explained. Her son Sidney rummaged around in a drawer and pulled out several snapshots of a stunning woman in a voluminous pink-and-green dress. The costume's oceans of froth would have drowned an ordinary person, but the woman in the photograph had weight, volume, carriage and energy to spare. She had conquered the dress and turned it into a backdrop for her carefree smile, expressive arms and commanding stance. "That's her," Sidney said. I turned, and indeed it was. Standing in the hovel was the same glamorous person in the picture, smoothly coiffed, poised, smiling as if the world's stagelights were turned on her. She laughed at my surprise. "Ready!" she sang, and, patting a last strand of hair into place, struck another pose for her imaginary photographer. "Shall we go have a beer now?" Deftly she slipped on a pair of Bermuda shorts under her skirt, changed the T-shirt for a blouse, paused to sling a handbag over her shoulder and strode out the door.

We headed for the little restaurant on the plaza, whose owner was evidently active in one of the school wings; a costume sketch was tacked up on the back wall so that all who liked it could sign up. Eurides, who lived just up the hill, was sitting at one of the long tables underneath the drawing. She was the owner's niece, and now that she was pregnant her uncle sometimes treated her to the daily special—on this occasion a mountain of rice and beans and spaghetti with a strip of meat on the side. Eurides split her portion with Celina, and Celina talked about her life before carnival. She was born Celina Andrea da Silva in 1931, near Muraé, in Minas Gerais. She had eleven children, but one had died. Her grandfather, she began proudly, was a slave:

My grandmother was an Indian. She was a baby when the whites took her mother captive and brought her to the *fazenda* [plantation] where my grandfather lived as a little boy. The baby's mother was completely wild. She couldn't get used to cooked food and she died, because in the forest they ate only leaves and things like that. So my grandfather—even though he was just a boy himself—took over the baby's upbringing, and when she was twelve he married her.

My father grew up working on a *fazenda* on a sharecropping system: the owner let him work a plot of land in exchange for half of what he produced on it. We lived there until I was five. Then an uncle of mine who had moved to the city convinced my father to come here too. In the *fazenda* we ate in plenty: there was pork, chicken and even, sometimes, fresh beef. There was duck, yams, manioc, pumpkin. Each time my mother conceived she would rear a pig and eat off the fat of it once she was nursing.

Things didn't go well when we came to the city. We started out in Irajá, a suburb far away from here. My father couldn't find work, and we lived in a tiny room and went hungry. My father would go out to the trash dumps and dig around in them looking for food. He used to bring us leftover bits of salami, bacon, things like that that he found. It made him ashamed to do this, but he did, and we ate.

My mother got skinny. When she got pregnant there was no place to keep a pig in our little room. Even when things got a little better and we moved to a favela near the center of town she couldn't keep animals. She found work washing clothes by day, and at night she took in sewing. Eventually she saved enough to buy a sewing machine on credit, but then she couldn't keep up payments and they repossessed it. I think this broke her. She loved the machine, and she used to tell us girls it would be our inheritance. When they took it back she became passionate with rage. She suffered from rage so much she got sick. She didn't improve. She got skinnier. Her family took her back to the country, and that's where she died. That happened when I was eight or nine years old.

Then things got a little better. My father moved us—there were five children—to Piedade, also near the center of town. There's a rock quarry right there on the hill and he got a job cutting it, loading it onto wagons, driving the mules, that sort of thing. The owner of the quarry had a huge house on top of the hill where the workers rented rooms. We lived there, and that's where I first began coming out in a samba school. It was just a little one; it was called Unidos da Piedade.

Celina fled to Mangueira some ten years and three children later, running from a man who beat her and tried to molest the oldest of her girls:

He was a drunk. He beat me. He threatened my babies, his own children. Once when he got drunk he took Jorge, who was tiny, and hung him upside down by his swaddling clothes and swung him hard against the wall. I screamed and crawled out of the house with my baby, but I had absolutely nowhere to go. I remember it was late at night and pouring with rain, and I crawled under the floorboards and waited until my oldest girl came out and told me he was asleep. I was stupid, I had three children by him. He would get drunk and ask me for food. When I brought it to him he'd say it was too cold. When I heated it up he'd accuse me of trying to burn his mouth, and beat me. When my little girl told me he had tried to force her to do things with him I grabbed the children and everything I could and ran straight here to Mangueira.

She had a brother who lived in Mangueira, but that wasn't what originally brought her to the hill. Celina arrived on her own one night to check out a rumor that the samba in Mangueira was really of the best quality. And was it? "Of course! I stayed until dawn."

She came to Mangueira during the transitional period in the 1950s when the samba schools, after decades of minor and patronizing coverage in the media, were finally being recognized as carnival's outstanding event. But what captured her fancy that first evening was not a rehearsal, in which only marching sambas are played, but a samba party, with improvised singing in a circle around the drums, plenty of beer and dancing. Mangueirenses can spot someone who learned to dance in another school, but it is a safe bet that even with her Unidos da Piedade style, Celina excelled at samba on her debut evening in Mangueira. She still does.

Celina still lived with five of the seven children she had while she was living with a second man, who also beat her but whom she loved to distraction until long after he left her. By now the oldest of the children was twenty-eight, the youngest, seventeen. One son from her previous man was dead, the others were married and lived on the hill. Only her relationship with Jorge seemed perceptibly cool, and yet she felt more pain for him than for any of the other children. Once the authorities took Jorge away:

> We were so poor! And he'd gotten this strange idea of going out on the street and asking the rich ladies for some money, and then he'd come back and give it to me. One day he didn't come back. After I'd waited all afternoon one of his friends came and told me that he'd been picked up by a police van, so I went to the precinct and that's when they told me what had happened to him. He'd been sent to a reformatory in another state. They kept him there for five years, and I never had any money to go visit him. Then one day I looked out the door and he was back.

When Celina and I ran into Jorge one day they greeted each other with such formal cordiality it never occurred to me that he might be her son, and I thought the explanation lay in her statement, in answer to my question, that she had never written him while he was in the reformatory. But then one afternoon after our first conversation I went over my notes with her, asking her to confirm that I had transcribed her story correctly. I showed her the notebook and asked her to verify the spelling of her name. She turned her head away and mumbled something. "What?" I said. "I can't read," she repeated.

Of all the women I met on the hill, Dona Jurema the baiana led the most perfect life. A large, well-muscled woman with close-cropped gray hair and a voice to shatter bricks, she had been saved from the evident danger of her volatile temper by the structured equanimity of her days. Mid-mornings, after the day's washing and cooking were out of the way, she would drag out a little stool from her three-room brick house and set it on a spot consecrated as "Jurema's stop" in a clearing just behind the *quadra*.

This clearing leads directly off the central plaza in front of the viaduct. To the right is the area were Ping-Pong is played when the weather is good. Behind it, the passageway formed by the overhang of a two-story house, where the Ping-Pong table is moved when it rains. To the left, two soft-drink and beer stands and the crossroads through which many Mangueirenses pass on their way up the hill from the bus stop. Jurema places her stool next to the smaller of the two stands, gets herself a beer and settles in to watch the day. People go by and say *"Tudo bem?"*—"Is everything well?"—and Jurema says, *"Tudo bom, minha filha,"*—"Everything's fine, my daughter." More people go by and say, *"Oi, Dona Jurema,"* and she says, *"Tudo bem?"* When one beer is finished she gets up and buys herself another one, and when that one is gone it's probably time for lunch. Some of the nine people who live in her house will be back for lunch, maybe a couple of her nine children, maybe a grandchild or two. After lunch is over Jurema figures it's probably a good time for a beer, and with the good fortune that characterizes her life there's one waiting for her right at the little stand where she found such excellent drink a while before. Pretty soon the day is cooling off, the light is turning liquid and violet, and all sorts of people are heading up the hill back from the buses and the grime and the pain of hustling it in the city, and every one of them says, *"Tudo bem, Dona Jurema?"* and she booms out in her big voice, "Everything's fine, my dear!"

When money is really tight she plays the daily numbers game— the animal game, it's called—hoping to win enough to get her out of the squeeze. She promised to teach me how to play, but we never got around to it. She did, however, give me a recipe:

Trim the tendons off some nice second-class meat and set it
to marinate in a sauce of garlic, salt, vinegar and white pepper.

Brown the meat in oil and add as much tomato as you
can afford, some parsley and a little bit of green pepper.

Add water and your choice of potatoes, zucchini, chayote
or cabbage, and cook until done.

"It's tasty, and the advantage is that if you serve it with rice and
beans you can feed a lot of people on a little bit of meat," Dona
Jurema said. "Besides, you get variety by putting in a different vegetable every day." The best accompaniment, she added, was an ice-
cold beer.

I sat next to her with Eurides on what passes for the stoop of
Eurides' house and asked the baiana what had been the happiest
moment of her life. She thought about the question for a while and
took a sip from her glass, and eventually answered in a voice loud
enough to carry all the way to the *quadra*: "Look here, I think the
best moment of my life is the present one. How could I pick out
another? I've got nine children, and none of them died. There's always
money for rice and beans, and when there's more we buy a chicken
and have a feast. I was never one to pinch and save. I have come out
with the baianas every year for the last twenty-five years and I have
the pride of having eight children and three grandchildren in the
school. My daughter is Mangueira's youngest soloist. I've got a place
to live in that no one is going to kick me out of, and I'm in good
health. What else is there?"

4 *Baianas II*

Celina dumped the tubful of wet clothes on the ground. "You want to talk now?" she asked sharply. Her grumpy mood was a direct consequence of the turbulent weather, which, after pouring rain on Rio for five days straight, still could not make up its mind to clear up and let the sun dry out the soaked Cariocas. In the course of the rains part of the tunnel connecting Mangueira to the South Zone had crumbled. Traffic was a confused mess, buses crawled through back streets looking for ways out and missing half their passengers, ground-floor dwellings flooded, and Celina's laundry wouldn't dry.

She put a hand to a skirt she had set out in the morning and muttered under her breath. She owned only one clothesline of the tangle that crisscrossed the little Mangueira plaza, and she had run out of space, even though she'd already borrowed two lines from her neighbors. The dirty laundry had piled up during the rainy days, and other women who also took in washing for income were waiting to use the lines. She had more complaints: her back hurt, the 100 cruzados ($1.50) she got for a day's worth of work was hardly worth the trouble, neighbors were uncooperative. *"Oi, Dona Celina,"* a passerby called out. *"Tudo bem?"*

"Oi, darling," she answered dryly, barely glancing at the well-

wisher, and snapped a towel free of wrinkles before flinging it on the line.

"*Oi, Celina!*" cried a heavyset woman about Celina's age. "Are you getting your measurements taken this weekend?" Celina said over her shoulder that she was not parading, at which her neighbor raised her eyebrows and moved closer. Celina stepped back so that her voice would carry. "It's a set thing; I'm not coming out for carnival. Twenty years as a baiana and I've barely missed a parade, but I've decided. I'm not coming out. Have they told you already how much this year's costume is going to cost?" The woman nodded. "Well!" Celina exclaimed. "Maybe you can pay four thousand cruzados for a baiana costume. I can't! I'm poor. And I know I'm not the only one. Four thousand cruzados! Do you remember how much last year's cost? Not even a thousand! It was still a sacrifice, but it could be done. But this year, I am not going to take the food out of my mouth, no, I am not going to take the food out of my children's mouths just in order to come out. It hurts in my heart, but it's set: there's no way I can afford it."

She had shifted her body gradually toward Dona Neuma's house, until she was standing almost directly facing her bedroom window and within earshot of the front porch. Dona Neuma was no longer the head of the baianas, but she was still an influential member of the school directorate, and it was a good bet that she was either having an afternoon nap in her room or sitting out on the porch. "Twenty years!" Celina repeated for Neuma's benefit, and for the lunchtime stragglers at the little restaurant who were obviously paying attention. "Doesn't that count for anything? Doesn't tradition count for anything? Just who are they expecting to come out with the baianas? Rich people? Not the people from the hill! I know the costume measurements are being taken this weekend, but I won't be there, you can be sure." She picked up the clothes tub and headed for home, pausing at the water spout to borrow the hose from a man who was washing his hair. Gingerly she rinsed her feet and wiggled them into a pair of sandals. "Now we can talk," she said to me.

Although Mangueira was behind schedule because of Dória's death, by mid-October almost all the wing chiefs had received a sketch from the school designer for their costume. Every wing's would be different, designed to complement a specific float representing a "chapter" of the overall story being told. Some wing chiefs had already budgeted the cost and were well on their way to producing a sample for the directorate to approve. The fanciest wing had budgeted its costume at around $300 and most ran upward of $150. By tradition, only the *bateria* and the directorate got their costumes free, but the baianas were charged a fraction of the real cost of theirs. Celina was right: the previous year's costume had been sold for less than a fourth of the current price. Exploding inflation had more than doubled prices in Rio, but that still did not account for the 100-percent difference in the real price.

Many of the slots in the school's fifty-six wings would be filled by relatively prosperous blacks and even larger numbers of well-off whites from the South Zone or the residential northern suburbs, who made a point of buying into the most luxurious wing available. But the baianas, everyone knew, were different. They were expected to be poor and to come from the hill. Together with the *bateria* they were what gave the school its root.

In the very beginning, the women who paraded at carnival time costumed as baianas often actually came from Bahia. Men came out as baianas too, because the costume's skirts and ruffles provided an ideal hiding place for knives and other weapons. Each woman made her own costume, embroidering and embellishing it as she saw fit, sometimes helping a man in her family put his together. Gradually some of the women adopted more elaborate costumes representing princesses, turn-of-the-century demimondaines, classical muses or European sylphs. The baiana costume became the privilege of the older women, and for a long time their wing remained the only one in which the *fantasia* was not a fantasy of the white world.

"Isn't it pretty?" Celina asked, wedged in her hoop skirt amid the chest of drawers, a stool, a low table, the skeletal easy chair and another which, with a board laid over it and propped on a box, served also as a bed. She had pulled the costume from the previous carnival out of a sack suspended by a nail from the wall. "But it's really too big to wear around the house."

The wide hoops of the costume's petticoat held out a skirt at least two yards around at the hem, so heavy it had to be suspended from the shoulders by means of thick straps. Over it she had fastened a pink skirt with seven rows of lace flounces, a low-cut lace blouse with puffed lace sleeves, and a green shawl, slung below one shoulder and knotted across the chest. Above it all went the headdress, a rigid cardboard cone covered in silver glitter. The baiana costume had traveled a long way since the first carnivals on the hill, yet by the standards of 1987 the Mangueira version was rigidly traditional, almost orthodox. Other schools dressed their baianas in dresses made from newspaper clippings or costumed them as Statues of Liberty. The Mangueira baiana was, as always, pink and green, frilly and charming.

"The problem this year," Celina said, folding the costume away, "is that we're not making any money. Last year was good, last year we had a lot of outings before carnival, when people hired a group from Mangueira for a party or a show. You wear your old costume, you get a little money, and you pay for the next one. Last year by this time we were having maybe an outing a week, sometimes more. We even went to Bahia! In a plane!" She struck a pose for the imaginary photographer recording this signal event—"Celina Boards an Airplane"—and let the gesture drop. "Now there's nothing. Maybe the murder is keeping people away."

The Mangueira school directorate was doing its best to overcome the numerous consequences of Dória's murder. To avoid a power struggle it took the unusual step of postponing the election and appointing an interim president, Dória's brother Elísio. The decision was surprising not only because he was even less root than Carlos, but because his brother had been such an unpopular president.

The members of the directorate had voted Carlos Dória into the presidency in 1986 even though he had not come up through the ranks, did not enjoy a great following and was not particularly imaginative. Yet the stronger members of the directorate had felt that he would not get in the way of the reforms they were trying to promote: strengthening the school's social programs, increasing school membership from the hill, and rekindling Mangueira's sense of its own history and traditions. In fact, during his brief rule Dória proved surprisingly effective in promoting these changes: he opened the school's doors to the neighborhood children during the day and provided the rudiments of a sports program, so that for the first time the hill's children had a playground; he lobbied the city for a large vacant plot directly across the viaduct from the school, which he wanted for a sports complex and day-care center; he approved the reform wing's plans for reviving the Mangueira newsletter and the legal aid and health programs. Perhaps most important, he "turned the school around so that it faced the hill" by inviting the presidents of Mangueira's three neighborhood associations to join the directorate.

The associations were as much as most Mangueirenses ever knew of organizational or political life, and the election of their leader was the only democratic event in which many of the younger favelados had ever participated, given that those under the age of forty-five had lived their entire adult lives under one of South America's longest-running military dictatorships. The association presidents were friendly with the local drug traffickers, with the municipal authorities, with the "Christian-base communities" of the liberal faction within the Catholic Church, with the leadership of Rio's nearly four hundred other favelas and with almost anyone else who mattered in local politics except for the samba school directorate, which had long been perceived as elitist. When Dória invited them to the school, the association presidents brought with them their valuable political constituencies.

Dória's commitment to the school and the community earned him more full-hearted support from the directorate than he had received at his election. But he suffered temper tantrums, and in the course of one of these he authorized a coup against Dona Neuma, removing her from the leadership of the baiana wing; when most of the directorate protested this, he fired them. The 1987 carnival was plotted and planned in a little house rented by the directorate-in-exile down the road from the *quadra*, with a few loyal go-betweens ferrying messages and requests for money to the lonely Dória, who still controlled the funds assigned by Riotur, the Rio de Janeiro tourism board, and who signed off on all the directorate plans while refusing a reconciliation. Mangueira's electrifying 1987 carnival victory was a triumph over these harrowing conditions, and it took Dória months to accept that he needed the directorate back if Mangueira was to stand a chance in 1988. Two weeks after a tearful reconciliation between him and the exiles, he was murdered.

It now seemed to the directorate that Elísio Dória was their best bet to succeed his brother. True, Carlos had been a wing chief for many years before his jump to the presidency, while Elísio, who was a prison guard, had inherited his brother's wing and had run it for only a year before Carlos was murdered. Nevertheless, the school leadership, shocked and frightened as it was, reportedly thought that Elísio understood what was being asked of him: to manage the school while meddling as little as possible in the virtually complete design for the 1988 carnival, and to carry on in his brother's name, thus sending a message to his anonymous killers that Mangueira was not to be intimidated, even by death. As one of his first gestures, Elísio asked Dona Neuma for help: his brother had started the feud with the directorate by replacing her as head of the baianas with a prosperous white woman from the South Zone. Would Dona Neuma not contribute to the process of reconciliation by helping her successor coordinate the baiana wing? Dona Neuma swallowed her bitterness and accepted.

And it was to her that Celina and other baianas looked for help when the new wing chief announced that the 1988 costume would be made from the best available cloth and sewn in the shop of a famous couturier. Never mind that in the past much of the sewing had been farmed out to the baianas' families, and that part of the traditional delight of carnival had been the arrival of this extra income. This year's would be a costume worthy of Mangueira's status, and if it cost more, the baianas need not worry: the Association of Samba Schools had extracted a larger cut on parade ticket sales from Riotur this year, it was explained; the school's subsidy to the baianas would cover more than two-thirds of the cost of the costume; and the women would be asked to pay only 4,000 cruzados.

Dona Neuma held her tongue, an effort that must have contributed greatly to her long list of aches and pains. But privately her entire family worried and raged. "We don't need you," her daughter Guezinha commented to me. "We don't need any white person like you from the South Zone. If you want to join and pay for a fancy costume, that's fine. And if you don't, there are thousands more who want your slot. But none of you have any spirit, and with our energy and soul we have to make up for that and fire all of you up to come out on carnival day with the proper Mangueira spirit. It's not our costumes that win! Beija-Flor and Salgueiro, those are fancy schools with costumes and floats to knock you dead, but once on the avenue, the crowd goes crazy for us, because we have root and we have spirit. And the soul of that is the baianas. Mangueira is nothing without them. How can we do without Celina, without Yvette, without Daisy?"

While part of the directorate fretted about Celina and the baianas,

another power struggle was taking place, this time between some of
the reformers and the man in charge of staging the theme the school
had chosen, the *carnavalesco*, or parade designer, Julio Mattos.

The man who creates the parade's "look," supervises the costumes and designs the parade floats has become the single most
important member of every samba school. In the early days of the
modern carnival he was not needed. The parade was not a performance but a street festival, and while it was important to have floats,
and even better if they were bigger than the competition's, it was the
community's energy and the dedication its members had invested in
their homemade costumes that carried the day. But now the Rio de
Janeiro parade does not even take place on the street but on a mock
"avenue" inside a specially designed Sambadrome, where a previously nonexistent breed of carnival devotee—the spectator—can
watch the parade from boxes and bleachers. Against the Sambadrome's Wagnerian proportions, floats must be huge in order to stand
out. And for the forty million spectators who watch the parade on
their living room televisions, the design of the floats is even more
important. The television camera does not capture crowds well; large,
glittery moving objects register much better on the screen. To create
"mediagenic" floats, and to orchestrate harmony among dozens of
different costumes and ornaments that will be seen and filmed from
a great distance, the *carnavalesco* is indispensable.

The seed for his preeminence was sown in the 1950s, when the
sambistas on Salgueiro hill became the first to entrust the design of
their floats and costumes to complete outsiders. Salgueiro had always
been considered a root hill and its three samba schools among the
best, yet in almost twenty years none of them had ever won a first
prize. In 1955 the directorate of the newly unified Acadêmicos do
Salgueiro decided to look outside the hill for leadership. They approached Nelson de Andrade, a white fish merchant with a large
store just off the docks. He had a little money, he was passionately
devoted to the school, and he knew how to think big. For the 1959
parade he recruited a Brazilian museum exhibition designer and his
Swiss wife to design the school's costumes. Salgueiro did not win
first prize that year, but de Andrade noticed that one member of the
city-appointed jury had given his school top marks. The man was
Fernando Pamplona, a white, leftist, middle-class stage designer for
the municipal theater with links to carnival; he had designed the

decor for several costume balls. The day after the jury declared the parade winners de Andrade arrived unannounced at the theater and abruptly thrust a package into Pamplona's hands, a painted cloth banner from the parade. A few days later de Andrade appeared again, this time with offerings of glossy fresh fish and shrimp. Awkwardly, he came to the point: Would Pamplona care to design Salgueiro's 1960 parade?

The paradoxical relationship between black carnival and the white world was never clearer than in the 1960 Salgueiro carnival. Pamplona turned his back on the traditional parade themes of white heroes and white history and put together a sort of "Black Power" plot: a hymn to the black leader Zumbi, who in the late seventeenth century died defending the rebel slave enclave of Palmares in northeastern Brazil. Sensitive to many sambistas' complaints that dancing carnival was being crowded out by huge, showy floats, Pamplona put almost no floats in his design, returning instead to the cheaper headdresses and hand ornaments long favored in the favela. Pamplona—a leading *carnavalesco* to this day—took his assignment carefully and seriously, and he came up with imaginative, inexpensive and delightful solutions. Probably no one had worked harder or more self-consciously than he to reintegrate black culture with the carnival tradition; but he knew nothing about Salgueiro hill and very little about black carnival. School members were outraged by his Palmares designs: on their one day of glory, Salgueiro blacks were being asked to come out fantasized as blacks and, worse yet, as slaves. Many threatened to quit, but mollified by de Andrade, they stayed on to stage the Zumbi plot, and when the revolutionary parade with its tastefully designed costumes was presented, everyone recognized it for what it was: Pamplona's triumph, not Salgueiro's.

Salgueiro failed again to win a first prize, but the radical impact of a professionally designed carnival was as instantly recognized as the qualitative leap that the first samba school represented in the 1920s. This led to another paradox: without the theatricalization of the samba schools their parade would never have attracted television attention or become the focus of international tourism to Brazil. Uncorrupted and uncommercial, the samba schools would likely have disappeared in the great potter's field of folk art, as was so often and so grimly predicted by black carnival's most devoted followers in the past. Instead, even the second-division schools today hire art school graduates to design their parades. The generally white *carnavalescos* are the only paid members of a school, and they switch schools and trade themselves off like soccer coaches.

Julinho Mattos is different. He's white, but he comes from São Cristovão, the neighborhood directly behind Mangueira, and he taught himself how to design and make floats during a long apprenticeship with a respected second-division school in the neighborhood. He has no pretensions to being an artist and no ambition to stamp his signature all over the school in the fashion of Joãozinho Trinta of Beija-Flor de Nilópolis, the single most extravagant personality on the carnival scene today. Instead, Julinho likes to do what he does best: design a carnival that looks as much as possible like the preceding one, with few floats, lots of space for the wings and a plot that sticks closely to the traditional themes of Brazilian heroes and great moments in history. During his eleven parades with the school this formula has almost invariably been successful. Mangueira, loved nationwide as the embodiment of samba tradition, knows what it likes, and so does Julinho: frills, no barebreasted women, lots of princes and princesses and lots of pink and green.

But in 1988 the reformers, led by Marilia Barboza, wanted a major change in Julio's design for "One Hundred Years of Freedom: Reality or Illusion?" Unusually for Julinho, he had actually scripted the story line himself, and it had been approved by Carlos Dória before his murder. But Marilia, who had been largely responsible for the previous year's hugely successful script on a famous Brazilian poet, had objections: Where, she wanted to know, was the depiction of the current situation of blacks? She and the other reformers were willing to concede the absence of slave costumes during the historical section of the parade, but where were the costumes representing black reality in the favelas today? Where were the street cleaners and maids who bring in the income to the hills and guarantee their survival? Was Mangueira ashamed of them? Think of what the other schools were doing: 1987 was the year in which the first civilian president in twenty-one years was hurtling down the polls in the steepest decline in popularity ever seen in Brazil; José Sarney was presiding over the collapse of the Brazilian economy, a farcical constitutional convention and the highest inflation of Brazilian history—400 percent and climbing. Several schools were preparing scathing scripts with titles like "Bye Bye, Brazil" and "This Is a Joke." Was Mangueira going to ignore social reality altogether? It would be eaten alive by the critics. No one wanted to break with tradition, but why couldn't the baianas come out as washerwomen, with magnificent baskets of laundry on their heads? Wasn't that the most authentic baiana of all?

Julinho resisted. After all, if sordid reality were what attracted him, he would not be a *carnavalesco*. Who wants to look at street cleaners during a parade? There are enough of them already, a platoon of real ones trailing along after every school, clearing the way of feathers and broken shoes and paper streamers for the next contestants. Exactly! said the reformers. And Mangueira will close the parade this year, so just imagine; the audience always applauds the street cleaners anyway, and now we're going to be the final school in the parade, and just when everybody thinks it's over, here comes our last wing, dressed in gold lamé versions of the street cleaner's orange uniform, followed by the real thing! What more do you need to say about reality and illusion? But Julinho could not be persuaded to see carnival that way at all.

This is precisely the sort of argument a school president is called on to arbitrate, but Elísio Dória procrastinated, letting the reformers lobby their way around the directorate, waiting to see if there would be a shift in opinion before making his move. Meanwhile, the wing chiefs whose costumes were under discussion chafed, unable to go ahead with the budgeting and sewing of the first sample. In theory, all the sample costumes had to be exhibited and approved by the second week in November. Guezinha, whose wing was one of the three up for changes, knew she had no chance of getting her sample in before the end of that month, which would leave her little time to have the remaining forty-nine costumes ready for distribution the week before carnival. She showed me the sketch for the suggested "reality" costume. If the reformists triumphed, our wing's elegantly draped white skirt, sequined top and feather headdress would be replaced by a music-hall version of a maid's outfit, complete with ostrich-feather duster, miniskirt and miniapron. Sympathetic as I was to the reformists' argument, I began hoping they would lose the battle.

Dona Neuma lost hers. An initial decision to cut the baianas' contribution in half, to 2,000 cruzados, was reversed almost immediately. The news that she was in, then out of the parade again reached Celina quickly.

"I should have married my first man," Celina complained. "When he got me pregnant my father was still alive. I was seventeen, and my father tried to get the boy to marry me—that was the custom then. But I was embarrassed when we went to court and that man accused me of trying to force him into a wedding. I ran away I was so ashamed. But that was a great stupidity, because the woman who did marry him is living right on this hill today, and that man is prosperous, and he's happy to pay the four thousand cruzados for her baiana costume so she can come out like a queen next carnival. I was a fool!"

The only person I knew who was not fretting about the baianas was Eurides. Nearing the end of her pregnancy, she was much more worried about whether she would be able to come out herself by February, and this depended on the baby: she had no plans to leave it behind, but what if it wasn't strong enough to parade? As her term came due, her monologues gradually shifted from their usual course of humorous and knowledgeable comment on the lives of other Mangueirenses and focused inward: What would the baby look like? Girl or boy? She knew she would like it immediately, but would it like her back? Would it be healthy? Would the father, Lilico, get along with this new person? Would there be enough clothes? Would her milk be good? And would it be all right to parade?

As for Celina and the baianas . . . Eurides knew about baianas. Her mother had been one right through until she died in the hospital a couple of years back, gasping and weak and eaten alive by cancer. Baianas were a hardy lot, capable of finding a way around almost any situation. Like Dona Lina, Eurides' next-door neighbor, who died just the other day at the age of ninety-odd. Such a tough old girl, such a cantankerous old biddy, so vain, so full of life. Eurides had studied the cooling body and known just how badly Dona Lina would have wanted to look pretty even in her grave, so she stretched Dona Lina's crumpled sparrow limbs out to full length before they stiffened, and put little cotton swabs between the toes and painted the toenails red, one by one, in reparation perhaps for all the times she had made Dona Lina cross by raiding her unequaled collection of ferns for some shoots or flouncing around in front of her with her skirt too short or making disrespectful remarks about the old lady herself. But maybe, Eurides said, it was more because she already missed the indomitable old woman's strength and temper—a Mangueirense to the marrow, a baiana to the root, a woman who came out dancing no matter what. It didn't seem fair that such a gallant creature should disappear into the ground forever looking defeated, unprepared, with shabby toenails. So Eurides paid no attention when her neighbor's relatives clucked and muttered among themselves; she got out her little pedicure kit and sent Dona Lina off to the other world with bright red toenails, and very prettily done too.

Eurides paused for breath. And the baianas this year? "Oh, I wouldn't worry about the baianas, girl. Every year it's the same thing. 'Ooh, I don't have the money! Ooh, they're making me pay!' You should see the way those ladies carried on last year. 'O my Lord, what sadness!' they all went, and they put their hands to their foreheads and rolled their eyes. But right after Christmas they began popping up one by one: 'I've got two hundred!' 'I've saved four hundred!' And so on. It's just like their dancing; you saw Dona Nininha the other day? With her legs all bandaged, and limping about? One minute they're nothing but aches and pains and their back hurts and their legs hurt so bad and they can't go on, and the next minute they hear the music in the *quadra* and they're up and hopping like anything. Just wait. Dona Celina is telling everyone on the hill that she's not coming out, right? Don't believe a word of it! Wait until Christmas is past and carnival is really just around the corner. She'll be putting her pennies together and saving like anything. Nothing's going to stop her, believe me!"

A few days later the directorate spread the word that measurements for the baiana costume would be taken Sunday morning in the *quadra*. A 500-cruzado down payment was required. The sample costume, it was announced, would be on exhibit.

A pink confectioner's fantasy, richly flounced and overlaid in silvery organza, shivered in the breeze in a corner of the dance space. For a long time the women did not touch it. Leaning back on the flimsy *quadra* chairs, feet well apart for balance, muscular arms settled firmly on their comfortable bellies, they bided their time, ignoring the designer and his assistant, studying the dress while the conversation edged around it, drifting instead from the subject of granddaughters to wages (higher for beauty parlor assistants, lower for maids, never enough for anything) to the most recent episode of the current favorite television soap opera. Newcomers pulled up chairs while the early arrivals gradually shifted theirs, so that in time there were several dozen women sitting in groups that inched closer to the costume, until eventually one woman rose, took a ruffle between two fingers, examined the texture critically, head cocked, and returned to her chair. "It's nice," she said noncommittally.

"You could sit here all day and never notice the time go by, you're so caught up in the gossip!" Dona Neuma's hoarse whisper announced her arrival, and it was met with a joyful hubbub. "Neuma! What nostalgia!" "Neuma, aren't you looking fine!" Smiling, waddling painfully on her puffy feet, Neuma exchanged hugs and kisses and taunts with the baianas and plopped herself down at a desk across the dance area from the designer. She took out her spectacles and polished them, opened the huge baiana ledger book and smoothed down a fresh page, examined a ballpoint pen, cleaned it with the edge of her blouse and set it alongside the ledger. "For you, Neuma," a baiana said, producing a doll dressed in a crocheted pink-and-green baiana costume. Neuma set it carefully at the front of the table. She polished her spectacles again.

"Ready? Well, then, line up, for Christ's sake! You expect me to take all of you on at once?" The women obeyed, brisk as schoolgirls. Neuma took the first one's name, address and contact phone number and waved her off across the room, where the designer wrapped his tape measure across the woman's shoulders and belly, and from the waist down past the knee to her splayed foot. "Chest: forty-five inches!" he called out to his assistant. "Waist! forty-eight! Length, waist to floor: Forty-nine!"

"Next!" said Dona Neuma to a burly, deeply wrinkled woman. The baiana posed flirtatiously for a second, hand on hip, smile arch. "Do you want my stage name or my Christian name, Neuma?" "Oh, for fuck's sake." Neuma sighed, eyes heavenward. Then she grinned from ear to ear. "Next!"

I found Celina a while later sleeping on the floor of her shack, a grandson cradled in one arm, a cat curled at her feet. She raised her head at my approach but made no move to rise. "I missed you at the samba last night," I said. "Were you out partying somewhere else?" "No," she answered, and lifted an imaginary bottle of beer to her lips. "I stayed home and drank." Then, ignoring me, she turned over on her other side and slept.

5   *Malandros*

"I want to be in your book!" said Ademar the sambista, a man I had never seen or heard of before.

We went to a bar several blocks from Mangueira and drank beer. The after-work crowd from a nearby government office jostled us for space at the counter, and Ademar talked desultorily about samba dance form and show business—influenced bastardizations of it that had crept into the parade (cartwheels for the men, for example, and for the women, hip circles from standing to squatting positions). Then a table opened up in a quieter corner and we ordered more beer and pickled eggs and Ademar cleared his throat and told me this story:

There was a couple who lived in the favela of the Skeleton, and they had three children. One day the man was arrested and sentenced to two years in prison. Six months before his release, the woman gave birth to a child. She knew the man could not come home and find the baby there. That baby was me.

As it turned out, a couple in Mangueira had lost their newborn son the week before. They agreed to take me as his replacement. My new father was a very hardworking man who was determined to do right by his family. He was black and was just a money collector on a bus line, but he insisted that in his house everybody had to eat with a knife and fork. And nobody could sit down for a meal if he wasn't there to sit down first at the head of the table. He was a right-living man.

He died when I was five years old. Six months later my adoptive mother found a new man and had another child. Life became difficult for me. It wasn't so much that I didn't like the new man in the house as that he didn't like me. He beat me a lot. He would beat me and leave me tied to the table leg, to punish me for not doing well in school. I used to play hooky. I would go out with the other kids and fly kites or play marbles. That's why I did badly in school. But much later, someone in the family told me that wasn't the reason this man didn't like me; it was actually because my adoptive mother had confessed to him that I was not really her son.

At home we ate corn mush for breakfast, lunch and dinner. That was what we could afford. I wanted to eat something different. I knew who the numbers runners were on the hill. I knew who the drug traffickers were. One day I went to the biggest drug trafficker in Mangueira and asked her if she had any work for me. She had a house right next to where the *quadra* now is, a fine house, with four bedrooms. She had all kinds of money. She was white, and she had been married to an important military man, and one day she left her fancy apartment in Copacabana and moved here to the hill. She was a procuress, and she also ran drugs. When I first knew her, she was about sixty years old.

This lady agreed to take me on as a "plane." It was the easiest work in the world. I would take the packet of drugs and put it under the front bike fender and pedal off to deliver it. The best planes are always kids, because of course nobody suspects you. Mostly I delivered marijuana, but there was quite a lot of white powder as well. Of course in those days it wasn't sold in powder form but more like a rock—and it was very good quality too, not like the garbage they sell these days.

The entire time I worked with this lady she was very special to me. She had another boy living there who wasn't exactly a plane, but more like a godchild. She made sure both of us went to school. I studied right through junior high. She taught us the importance of working hard. She opened a savings account for me. She told me never to smoke anything, never to snort anything. There was a lot of cocaine going around the city by then, in the early seventies, but it was only for people with money. "Ademar, you're not rich enough to go snorting that stuff," she said.

I was still living at home, and when I was about fourteen my mother said someone had seen me smoking dope. It wasn't true, and I told her so. She accused me of this a second time, and a third. After that last time I went and rolled myself the biggest joint in the world, and I came back and I sat on her doorstep and I smoked it. I said, "See? This is what you're accusing me of. I've never done this before." She said, "Son, you shouldn't have done it now," and she threw me out.

The white lady got me a job at a cleaning firm, and then a better one cleaning a bank. Then I worked as a kitchen assistant, but some of my friends there were caught stealing, and I was thrown out too. I think this whole situation was making me very tense. I ended up in the hospital. I had these bad pains in my chest, and my hands trembled all the time. One of the nurses at the hospital told me the problem wasn't my heart but my nerves. She was ten years older than I: twenty-four. I had my first child with her, a little boy. The difference between us wasn't as great as it sounds. I knew a great deal about the world. I had a lot of money because of the drugs, and I dressed well. I think she was impressed.

When I got out of the hospital I continued working with the white lady, and then when I was eighteen something happened: I was returning from the airport after making a delivery. I was driving, because by then she was lending me her car. I parked right in front of the *quadra* and went into her house, and I saw her, tied to a chair and with her arm all dangling, broken. She shouted out to me, "Don't give them anything! Run away!" At that moment the two guys who were holding her turned around and saw me. One of them shot her. I ran straight back to the car and drove away, and then I disappeared from Mangueira for five years. It was the competition who killed her. They wanted her out of the hill and they wanted her money, but they never realized that I was her plane, and they never knew I kept the money. It was a lot of money, because I'd just come back from that delivery. It would be equivalent to about five thousand dollars today. But I knew I was in danger, and I stayed away from Mangueira, and I stayed away from drugs.

Organized crime began in the favelas with a lottery called the animal game. In 1889, after the end of the empire, Baron João Batista Drummond lost the subsidy for his private zoo. He was proud of the zoo, which was open to the public and occupied a large area in a park near the Emperor's Palace, on the outskirts of what is now the neighborhood of Vila Isabel, but the upkeep was expensive. As luck would have it, he made the acquaintance of a Mexican adventurer who offered to sell him the rights to a lottery he had invented, in which different flowers were assigned individual numerical values. The baron saw that by substituting the flowers on the tickets with drawings of the cobras, lions and zebras in his zoo, he could use the lottery to raise new funds for the animals. The game was a far greater success than the baron expected. For some, it was a charming form of bingo, but for many people in the favelas it dovetailed perfectly with common beliefs in numerology. The animal game's simple rules were quickly translated into paramystic codes and signs; animals were associated with gods and forces of destiny; dreams were related to numbers. The game spread effortlessly through the hills and became a favorite form of entertainment and income for the *malandros*—the favela layabouts and petty criminals whose close equivalent in U.S. iconography is the Sportin' Life character in *Porgy and Bess*.

The zoo was refurbished and then, after the baron's death, abandoned, but the animal game lived on, under the control of an emerging elite among the *malandros* who became known as "animal bankers." They controlled the bank and ran the daily lottery, whose results are never rigged. For the players, the game had the key advantage of offering good fortune a daily opportunity to strike at a very affordable price; a single bet today starts at about twenty-five cents, and a two-dollar win can get the player lunch for the whole family. For numbers runners it was the ideal small business: no startup capital, low over-head, no fixed capital requirements, and guaranteed profit from extremely diversified sources. In 1946 the government declared the animal game illegal, with absolutely no effect on its popularity or the numbers runners' prosperity; today some three hundred animal bankers are said to control the Rio game, and some forty thousand people are employed selling tickets.

Precisely because running the numbers was so easy, there was a great deal of competition, and because it was illegal, it required an underworld structure. A *malandro* who wanted to rise in the animal game needed ruthlessness, stamina and imagination. It was only nat-ural that the men—and occasionally the women—capable of con-solidating their hold on the game should soon be fencing for stolen goods, running prostitution rings, dealing in guns and trading mar-ijuana. In the favelas they were powerful authority figures, not the least because they contributed generously to the samba schools. Who else had the money to finance a winning parade?

In the 1930s Mangueira's chief rival, Portela, became the first school to be controlled completely by an animal banker. The one-armed numbers king Natal, a Portela samba school founder who paid for the six beers consumed at its first rehearsal and who went on to lead Portela to eighteen parade victories, is revered in the samba world to this day for his fierce devotion to the school, his generosity to the favela and his sheer force of personality:

> I had more than fifty streets paved. . . . I helped orphanages, churches and hospitals. I had more than two hundred shacks built. I sheltered the homeless. I paid for an average of forty funerals a month. I gave food to whoever asked me. I protected the needy. I defended the weak. I did all of this with the money I earned and I never asked anyone for a receipt. I'm dying as poor as I ever was. I could be a lazy rich man today, if I hadn't done what I did. Am I sorry? No way! I've fulfilled my obligation on earth: I can die in peace.

Natal died soon after this testament, almost as poor as he claimed; his only extravagance had been an enormous house in Madureira, the Portela neighborhood he never left. "I've visited more than fifty countries," he said, "and Madureira is better than all of them." The house is still standing, complete with an outlandish mural depicting the creatures of the animal game, the propriety of which a reporter was once foolish enough to question. "If I'd been a dentist," Natal retorted, "I'd have ordered some false teeth painted on that wall."

"He was a Man," sambistas will say thoughtfully, after recounting how he bribed rival schools' wing chiefs to set fire to their own floats on the eve of the parade, or how he guaranteed victory for his school seven years running, showing up at the vote count with a gun in his one hand. Accounts of Natal always end the same way: "He may have done wrong, but he loved Portela. That's what a school needs from its president." And: "They don't make men like him anymore."

In the way new money has of turning into Old Money, animal bankers eventually became more respectable than Natal. A few consolidated empires, invested in legal businesses and moved out of the hills. Natal was black, but the wealthiest animal bankers have always been white, and as they prospered they became socially restless, for despite their wealth they were still considered outcasts by white society. Even at carnival time, they were stuck in downtown Rio with the samba schools, while high society cavorted in Copacabana at ever more elaborate costume balls.

In 1975, a white animal banker named Aniz Abrahão David decided to buy his due share of respectability. He hired a young *carnavalesco* who had gotten his start as an assistant to Salgueiro's Fernando Pamplona, and set him to design the parade for a small, relatively new school in a working-class suburb in the flat outskirts of Rio, about an hour's drive from the center of the city. The school was called Beija-Flor, the Hummingbird of Nilópolis, and its major claim to distinction up to then had been a series of parades in honor of the military dictatorship. The new designer was Joãozinho Trinta, a flamboyant former dancer with a remarkable capacity for single-minded concentration and hard work. When Trinta's first float appeared during his debut parade in 1976 there was a gasp: the extravagant, glittery tableaux vivants were among the most luxurious Rio had ever seen; cascades of sequins and mirrors caught the morning sun and blinded the crowd. Dozens of barely clothed women smiled benevolently in their feathers. Yet this was not what made spectators murmur and point and laugh. Riding every float were huge papier-mâché lions, zebras and snakes. There were roulette wheels and card tables. And to ensure that no one missed the point, the parade's title was "If You Dream of a King, Bet on the Lion." Beija-Flor, Trinta and Aniz Abrahão David were the talk of Rio.

It could be argued that all the animal bankers profited from David's *coup de théâtre*. The rulers of Rio's animal game began granting press interviews, bought into soccer teams, opened restaurants. Yet their key to legitimacy and their claim to media attention remain the samba schools, where they continue to rule either as elected presidents or through compliant appointees. Among the few exceptions are Vila Isabel, which turned its back on one of the more notorious numbers kings in 1987 and elected a woman member of the Communist Party in his stead, and Mangueira, whose freely elected and frequently rotated presidents have only occasionally been bankers.

This is why it was so easy for a new cocaine underworld to find a foothold on the hill.

Cocaine has been a part of the favela scene since the 1920s, but as a major form of organized crime it is now in the formative stage, consolidating its hold on individual favelas by means of a bloody war between the drug runners and the animal bankers. It is a young trade, run by youths and catering to the young: children make the deliveries, near-children set up the orders. *Malandros* barely out of their teens seized control of the drug traffic on Mangueira. Ricardo Lion-Heart, Tuchinha and Beato Salu, the three cocaine merchants on the hill, were all in their mid-twenties when Mangueira was planning for the 1988 carnival. Born on the hill, fiercely devoted to it, they command respect and affection no less strong because it is mixed with fear.

I first noticed Beato Salu one late morning when he and his entourage came clanking through the little clearing between his house and the Hot Hole, the narrow paved street that is the hill's principal commercial center. The group's progress was as clangorous as a medieval army's; metal clashed on metal, chains jangled and rang. At the center of half a dozen bodyguards walked Beato, a small, skinny, light-skinned youth with his hair permed in the latest fashion—corkscrew ringlets worn shoulder length. He appeared unarmed, but his bodyguards shouldered a motley assortment of rifles and machine guns, and dangled revolvers and automatic guns casually off one finger. Beato made his way through the favela slowly, stopping now and then to smile and exchange pleasantries with an acquaintance, raising an arm in greeting to a friend farther away.

Later I asked Eurides whom I'd seen. "Who knows," she said, shrugging. She didn't like to discuss topics that in her eyes were denigrating to Mangueira or to the black race as a whole. Her sister-in-law, a young white woman from another favela, had different standards, and she talked eagerly about Beato Salu. "He's so *simpático*!" she said. "You wouldn't think much of him from his looks, but the girls really like him. He's always friendly and nice to everybody, and he has a good sense of humor."

Tuchinha was different. Tall and emaciated, he patrolled the Hot Hole with his own set of armed bodyguards, and in his case the effect was unnerving. Behind their dark glasses, Tuchinha's *malandros* looked armor-plated. True to their leader's style, they never smiled, and when Tuchinha walked through the Hot Hole with his men in tow, his gaunt face set in a skull's grimace, nobody called him over for a chat. One version had it that Tuchinha got his start as an assistant to Ricardo Lion-Heart and that his ruthlessness had set him ahead of his former patron. "Ricardo is very well brought-up," a former schoolmate of both traffickers commented. "He comes from a good family. After Dona Neuma, Ricardo's grandmother was the first person here on the hill to get a telephone. Ricardo is still someone you can talk to and crack jokes with—but you have to watch out, because he's very thin-skinned, and anything can set him off. Tuchinha comes from a respectable family too, strangely enough. In school he was always very serious, very well behaved. But he was never friendly or outgoing. They say, but I couldn't vouch for it, that the reason Tuchinha is now more powerful than Ricardo is that he's killed people. Among *malandros* that gets you respect."

I was never introduced to Ricardo, but I got to know his son rather well, and he came to represent for me the child Ademar the sambista must have been. I would see him, skinny, tense, strikingly self-sufficient, at the *quadra* rehearsing for his role as one of the majordomos in the school's children's division, always alone. Sometimes we would watch television together at a friend's house, and once, after a gruesome scene in which a man got stabbed in the genitals, I saw him flinch. But then he commented, "That's not the way to do that. If you want to kill somebody, you go for the gut." Eventually I realized that although he was eight years old, he still did not know how to read, tell time or count beyond ten. We spent a few mornings studying the clock hands and rehearsing numbers from ten to twenty, but then we both gave up in despair. Yet there was nothing wrong with his intelligence: he would know immediately when I had failed to understand a word in Portuguese, and provide a clear definition on the spot. "*Hairpin*: that long thing with two legs women use to keep curlers on their head." It was just that he lost heart so quickly.

There wasn't much incentive for Ricardo's son to learn the formal subjects people tried to teach him in the little local school. Eurides was, after all, among the most intelligent and intellectually curious of all the people I met in Mangueira. She had helped start a black studies group on the hill, joined an Afro dance group, taught herself to type. Yet the most money she ever made came when she freelanced as a manicurist, and when time came to guarantee a steady income, she did what women in Mangueira do: she hired herself out as a maid. Tuchinha, Ricardo and Beato, ambitious and intelligent, had grabbed the only opportunity for real advancement available on the hill. For this reason alone, Mangueirenses would have respected the three *malandros*. "They're not thieves, they're not vagabonds," a baiana said. "They sell something people want, and do no one any harm. Why should we condemn them for that?"

Other sambistas felt different, men from another generation who had fought for their own dignity and self-respect at backbreaking menial jobs, who held on to their wives and brought up children on salaries that virtually determined how many spoonfuls of corn gruel each one would have a right to. These men did not find the boy drug lords prankish or amusing, but the fact remained, the men would say, that the kids were not thieves—a key point of honor—and that they were so much better than what went before, during the 1970s, when the murder of Ademar's benefactor, Dona Solange, had inaugurated a decade of terror on the hill.

"The worst time came when Branco was in charge," a baiana told me. "He was a real no-good, and he brought nothing good to the hill. People didn't leave their houses at night. There were two Christmases running when we couldn't even go visit our relatives, everyone was so scared to go out. The only movement you ever saw was Branco's men carrying refrigerators and air conditioners and furniture up the hill—hot goods. And the *quadra* and the Hot Hole were empty. You know how on weekend nights you can hardly move through the Hole, it's so crowded? During that time you couldn't count six people out on the street."

The woman who told me this lived near the top of the hill, and her neighborhood was so regularly crisscrossed by fleeing gangsters and pursuing cops she eventually closed down the little restaurant that had been her main source of income. The *quadra* was deserted because no one wanted to risk being mugged by members of a gang that had decided to ruin the school as punishment for its alliance with a rival gangster. The police brought little comfort; Celina's mentally impaired son and two of her nieces were shot in the foot, the arm and the chest by an impatient cop who thought they did not get out of his way fast enough. No gangster stayed alive or out of jail long enough to consolidate his power and enforce a truce. Mangueirenses mourn the death of Dona Solange and remember the subsequent years as the most bitter in the community's life. Not surprisingly, the demoralized school did not win a single parade between 1973 and 1984.

But during these years a new underworld leadership was undergoing an education in the prisons of Rio, tutored by captured guerrillas whose romantic notion it was to raise the consciousness of the lumpenproletariat. Illuminated by visions of class struggle, power to the people and the community as the ocean in which the revolutionary fish swims, a generation of young holdup artists and drug runners founded a prison brotherhood, the Red Phalanx. By 1987 it was organized enough to pay for prison escapes, provide family support to members' widows, establish new identities and livelihoods for members wishing to leave the criminal life, organize ever more perfect bank holdups and run the network that receives cocaine from Colombia and Peru and distributes it to Rio from headquarters in a dozen or so favelas. The leader of the Red Phalanx in 1987 was Escadinha, a folk hero revered for his good looks, charitable deeds and daredevil escape attempts. A cousin by marriage of Ricardo Lion-Heart, Escadinha trained in Mangueira as a low-ranking member of a gang that temporarily held sway in the 1970s. In turn, he helped form the ethics and highly organized work habits of the rising drug lords on the hill.

Class consciousness, racial pride, loyalty to one's community were the elements the Red Phalanx contributed to the wildly successful new outlaw style, but in reality they served to mask relationships of domination and submission that in Mangueira were lived out as medieval fantasies about kings of the hill. The fact that the three *malandros* could turn their weapons against anyone in their realm— and for any reason—seemed secondary to the Mangueirenses, whose view of their local dictators was distorted by years of bitter experience with officialdom. At least the *malandros* delivered: free bricks, jobs for unemployed teenagers, quick interest-free loans for medicines were tangible benefits that ensured loyalty. Invoking the name of Robin Hood at every turn, Ricardo Lion-Heart, Tuchinha, Beato Salu and their clanking entourages led their rebel fiefdoms in a sullen confrontation with a state that managed to be criminally negligent and authoritarian in turn. When in mid-1987 the Rio police overran Mangueira hill in an attempt to capture Beato Salu, two of the hill's three neighborhood associations called on their members to descend on the viaduct, where they blocked traffic for a whole afternoon. I asked one of the association leaders if the demonstration had been against police ruthlessness or in favor of Beato Salu. He shrugged. "Both." Later, I asked Dona Nininha if the word *malandro* meant good or bad things. "Good things, of course! A *malandro* is someone who doesn't let himself get stepped on."

Power became authority. The underpaid teachers at the under-staffed primary school in the Hot Hole turned to Tuchinha—a former student—when they needed pencils for the children. The government wasn't about to provide any, and students who often did without breakfast or lunch certainly could not be expected to buy their own— though it hurt to say so, the school staff was grateful to the young gangster and spoke even more favorably of Ricardo, perhaps the most generous and community-minded of the three *malandros*. He had a reputation for fairness in his business dealings and a certain accessibility—he could sometimes be seen touring the Hot Hole with no bodyguards at all. There was no exact moment at which this became his position, but Ricardo ended up as one of Mangueira's higher legal and moral authorities. It was Ricardo who sentenced those accused of robbery, rape or child molesting. He gave his moral sanction to lynchings after "trials" in which the evidence against the accused was weighed. I met a man who had survived his own lynching after Ricardo became convinced midway through it that he had been falsely accused. The man was already covered with blood, kneeling on the ground, waiting for Ricardo to strike the last, fatal blows, when his would-be executioner had a qualm. He stopped, tried to land another blow, lost his nerve, stopped again. "If I am about to commit an injustice, may God forgive me," he said, and overwhelmed by a sense of wrongdoing, he put the club down.

The man accused of child molesting would probably not have fared much better if he had been arrested by the police. Police death squads make a point of eliminating "scum"—child molesters, gay prostitutes, petty thieves—no questions asked. Brazil's justice system is bankrupt and nearly inoperative. Its jails are so hellish that suicidal riots are commonplace. And as a result of *malandro* vigilantism, there is no crime on the hill. The treasurer of a neighborhood association once informed me gleefully that the last person caught stealing had been "taken care of." Individually, the Mangueirenses might resent or fear the drug lords' guns. Someone who had lost a son or a brother to them might even loathe the traffickers, while those with some political sophistication might understand that in the long term, *malandro* rule guaranteed the favela's continued social and economic isolation. But as a body, the Mangueirenses accepted the drug traffic on the hill as part of the given order of things. They had no experience of drug addiction to tell them that the youngest generation of Mangueirenses was about to go to waste, and they counted themselves lucky to have such benevolent lords.

Malandro—bandit, outlaw, brigand, ne'er-do-well—is a word with origins in Renaissance Italy. Fernand Braudel mentions the *malandrini* in the chapter on the rise of poverty and brigandage in *The Mediterranean*. The entire section is breathtakingly applicable to the underworld of contemporary Brazil. "Banditry was in the first place a revenge upon established states, the defenders of a political and even a social order," Braudel writes, and he quotes Stendhal on the brigands who still plagued nineteenth-century Italy:

> Naturally a population harassed by the [Italian lords] loved and respected their enemies. . . . Even in our own day, everyone dreads unquestionably an encounter with brigands; but when they are caught and punished, everyone is sorry for them. The fact is that [the Italian populace], so shrewd, so cynical, which laughs at all the publications issued under the official censure of its masters, finds its favourite reading in the little poems

which narrate with ardour the lives of the most renowned brigands.

So the favelas of Rio rose up in near-insurrection during the summer of 1987 when the leading trafficker in the favela of Jacarezinho died in a helicopter escape attempt from prison—an escape he had plotted in order to elope with the lovely young (and white) daughter of the vice-governor of Rio. In the face of censorship, one of the hit sambas of 1986 was a song written by One-Arm Beto and S. Merití begging a pardon for Escadinha, who before his capture was revered as the king of the favela on Juramento hill.

The samba's interpreter was Bezerra da Silva, virtually unknown in white Rio and esteemed in the favelas as the hippest singer around. Bezerra buys his songs directly from the hill composers, and as a body the songs are perhaps the most complete chronicle of *malandro* life ever assembled. They are typical outlaw art—self-aggrandizing, self-justifying, sentimental and cynical. There is a song about a pimp who has finally managed to beat his good-natured woman into exasperation. "Go have a talk with the commissioner, my man, because she's turned you in," Bezerra advises. Many of the songs are diatribes against the *malandro*'s natural enemies, the police and the stoolpigeons. Others denounce society at large: "If you're looking for thieves, go right back where you came from," Bezerra instructs a detective. "They're all down there in the city, disguised in their white collars and ties."

The hit of the 1987 samba season in Mangueira was a composition by Jayminho that the censors banned from the air: it was played over and over at the beer stands on the hill and during the *bateria* breaks at rehearsals, when almost everybody would get up to dance to it. It is a request for assistance sung by Bezerra to his "granny," or *candomblé* protector:

> Tell me, Granny, tell me please,
> Who put cornstarch in my coke?
> They think they can fool me,
> But I'm no dope.
>
> I'll buy you a nice silk dress,
> A corncob pipe, the kind you like,

Candles for your altar
To increase your might,
But tell me, Granny, tell me, yes,
Who were those low-lifes? Help me guess.

They think they can fool me,
That witches' coven,
But my nose is not
A baker's oven.

Thanks to a glut on the world market, cocaine in the 1980s was no longer the white man's luxury that Ademar's patron had warned him against. People loved Bezerra da Silva's catchy song, and during samba breaks a lot of them would head for the alleyways around the plaza and cluster together under the benevolent vigilance of Beato's or Ricardo's or Tuchinha's smiling troops, pressing their faces to cardboard squares covered with thick lines of cocaine.

6 *Carnival Stars*

Carnival progressed. Against and despite itself, for everywhere the season was suffering the effects of what Brazilians call a "bad configuration of stars." There were feuds, shootings and deaths. In November Fernando Pinto, perhaps the most gifted of all the *carnavalescos*, died in a car crash. Pinto, who designed for the Independent Youth of Padre Miguel samba school, had a unique capacity for imbuing the ponderous architecture of a carnival float with humor and irony, and at the time of his death he had already begun work on the floats for the 1988 celebration, whose theme, in honor of the collapsing economy and the shameful state of Brazilian politics, was "Bye Bye, Brazil." His last parade had been a daringly original depiction of what modern Brazil would look like if the Indian population had been allowed to survive and rule. There was a float representing the armed forces with a tank designed as a giant armadillo, male dancers in leopard-skin platform boots and dark glasses, and bare-breasted women in straw skirts, feather headdresses and silver lamé tennis shoes. A visiting Native American delegation might have had its hackles up at the implied racism of the parade, but Brazilians, who know that Cariocas tend to wear things like leopard-skin platform boots and silver tennis shoes anyway, simply had a good time. Although Padre Miguel lost to Mangueira, Pinto got the critical acclaim. Then the car he was driving home from the Padre Miguel *quadra* slammed into a lightpost on the loop-the-loop circuit from the North to the South Zone, and he was gone.

The bad star shone brightly. There was Dória's murder, and Pinto's death, and the crazed policeman who tried to shoot Elizabeth Nunes, president of Salgueiro, and ended up killing an elderly member of the directorate instead. And there were the events at Império Serrano on the final night of their samba harvest: the composer One-Arm Beto, who had written several hits (including the song extolling the drug trafficker Escadinha) and two winning story sambas for Império, this time placed second. According to the first statements by witnesses and by Império's president, Jamil "Aromatic" Maruf, when the winning samba was announced in the middle of the packed *quadra*, One-Arm Beto took out his gun and shot Maruf and a school vice-president, Roberto da Cunha Peixoto. A few days later da Cunha and Maruf were well on their way to recovery and One-Arm Beto, out of hiding, was engaged in serious beer drinking with his fellow composers in Mangueira. Da Cunha and Maruf declined to press charges against the composer. "I was confused," da Cunha said. "I don't know who shot me; the press said it was Beto." Império rehearsals continued, as did planning for the parade, a nostalgic tribute to old Rio. But it was several weeks before the crowds returned to the *quadra* and longer before Beto did.

Probably no school faced so many difficulties as Vila Isabel. Having overthrown the longtime president, the animal banker Aílton Guimarães, and elected a woman member of the Communist Party in his stead, the school suddenly found itself evicted from its traditional rehearsal space and deprived of a major source of funds as a result. Like all samba schools, Vila Isabel received most of its income from two sources: a percentage of television broadcast rights and parade ticket sales advanced by Riotur, the city tourism board, and receipts from tickets to its weekend rehearsals. In normal circumstances, the school's samba nights attract perhaps the most eclectic crowd of all. The neighborhood of Vila Isabel, on the other side of Maracanã Stadium from Mangueira, includes two root hills and a quiet and pleasant enclave of the traditional middle class, full of winding streets with gracious 1950s apartment buildings, first-rate Portuguese-style restaurants, bars, and several samba clubs. Despite its reputation as a white school, Vila Isabel has a real samba tradition. It was home to an excellent white sambista, Noel Rosa, who died young in 1937, and is the adopted home of Martinho da Vila (after his chosen school), one of the few sambistas with a crossover white audience. Martinho, who happens to be married to the white woman who succeeded Guimarães in the presidency of Vila Isabel, works absolutely within the classic samba mold, but his intelligent, lyrical verse, rich voice and Ethiopian good looks reach a public that extends well beyond the hills. His very presence was an additional attraction at school rehearsals. Without its *quadra*, Vila Isabel lost all its income-earning advantages: a showcase for its star, its charming neighborhood, its privileged location only a short drive from the South Zone. It would have to compete with the other schools with only the approximately $160,000 received from Riotur.

In the prevailing chaos, the suburban school of Beija-Flor was a serene island of efficiency and purposeful toil, where Joãozinho Trinta avoided all potential messiness by making every key decision himself. He chose the story samba. He committed heresy and pasted different composers' sambas together to achieve the result he needed. He selected the theme, scripted it and supervised the costume design. By late November his entire carnival machinery was in gear and a small team of in-house seamstresses were well advanced on the costumes for the "school's own": the *bateria*, the opening commission, the baianas. Like Mangueira's Julio Mattos, Trinta had chosen to commemorate the first century of Brazilian black life after the abolition of slavery, but typically for Trinta, he was doing so in a fashion that let him circumvent a carnival regulation allowing only Brazilian-inspired themes. Trinta's script was called "I Am Black, from Egypt to Freedom"—the central conceit being that the Egyptian gods were one and the same as the *candomblé* deities. For the *carnavalesco*, the script was meant to glorify the universality of black culture. In the opinion of his vociferous detractors at Mangueira, Trinta was indulging once again in his favorite pastime, turning his back on Brazil.

Indeed, Trinta's critics were legion everywhere except in his own neighborhood, where he was revered. Nilópolis is a bedroom community of shantytowns where much of the population are first-generation arrivals from the arid Brazilian Northeast. Here Trinta had managed to substitute his own forceful personality for the absent samba root, and his crusading style extended to all aspects of Beija-

Flor community life. He ran the costume factory with local employees, limited access to the school's youth division to children who
showed him good report cards, campaigned for a higher fiber content
in the local diet and even set up his own model backyard vegetable
plot to show that home farming was not only healthier but cheaper.
Trinta and his sponsor, the animal banker Aniz Abrahão David,
based their empire in Nilópolis with such success that in 1986 they
were able to move from a more than adequate *quadra* to a new
auditorium, with a real roof and polished wood floors and room for
six thousand sambistas. Just behind it, a recreational center with
special facilities for the neighborhood children was under construction. A few blocks away an armed guard stood watch at the entrance
to the school costume factory, and a formidable woman within monitored the seamstresses' contact with the press. Beija-Flor was the
school with by far the most expensive costumes. They were not
subsidized, but community members got them at cost: the school
had a program enabling members to deposit monthly installments
toward their costumes in a special bank account. Trinta scorned the
white critics who sniffed at his extravagant use of sequins and female
nudity. "Only intellectuals like misery," he said. "What poor people
go for is luxury."

In mid-November, drastically behind schedule, Elíseo Dória finally
signed off on a closing "reality" segment for Mangueira's abolition
script. It would be made up of Guezinha's all-woman wing, dressed
as maids; a wing of cooks, armed with gigantic spoons; and Nilsemar's mixed wing, dressed in gold lamé copies of the streetsweepers'
orange uniforms. Guezinha and her best friend, Elania, immediately
set out to shop for the costume ingredients, and they invited me along
on one of their excursions to the suburb of Madureira, home to the
Império Serrano and Portela schools. The northbound suburban train
rattled by a confused and colorful landscape of fin-de-siècle working-
class "villas" built by factory owners for their employees, Portuguese-
style nineteenth-century residences with ornate stucco façades,
modern office buildings. In Madureira we swam in an ocean of shop-
pers and peddlers. "Sunglasses! Look at these!" "Bikini panties!
We've got your size!" "Wedding dresses this way!" "Watches, joy-
sticks, Walkmans! The best selection, the best prices!"

We pored over a selection of pink satins and organzas in a suf-focatingly crowded store. "There isn't much to this costume," Gue-zinha explained. "So we have to make sure the material is as showy as possible. And we're going to be parading in broad daylight, at the end of the Mangueira parade and after a whole evening's worth of schools. People are going to be tired, so whatever we use has to be something that won't look pale in the sunlight and will really revive people's attention." I looked again at the designer's sketch she had brought along: the costume was undistinguished—a sleeveless bodice with a deep V-line décolletage, and a short flounced skirt topped by an apron. The only ornaments were a lace frill for the head and a pink feather duster. There was little in it to capture anyone's attention.

"No good," pronounced Elania over a bolt of pink satin. "Not bright enough for the sun." Guezinha considered an expensive bro-cade. "Doesn't drape well for the skirt," Elania declared. She was a tall, big-hipped woman with a face as smoothly curved as an almond, who dressed with flair for every occasion; stunning in a housedress and with her frizzy mane of hair caught up in a kerchief for house-cleaning, blinding in the white dress and silver bangles she had chosen for this morning's outing. She supplemented her clerical income by selling clothes to her friends, and Guezinha deferred to her on all questions of style.

Guezinha had been running her wing for only three years, after more than fifteen years' absence from carnival. "I had the two girls to bring up, and my husband didn't like me to parade," she said. "But once both girls were in school, and after so many years, I couldn't resist. I used to come out with the baianas, but when I returned I saw how expensive all the wings had gotten. My older daughter wanted to parade too, and she couldn't afford any of the costumes, so I decided to found a wing in which all the members could sew their own. But in Mangueira if a wing survives for three years it's incorporated into the school structure and has to conform to the standard. This is the first year this has happened, the first year of standardization, where the costumes have to be made by a single seamstress and meet the norm. But my intention is still to run an affordable wing, so my friends can stay in carnival."

We threaded our way through the crowds and the vendors' carts on the street to the next cloth shop and the next. There was nothing anywhere. A bolt of shimmery organza was not the right shade of bright pure pink, another covered entirely in sequins "wasn't right for a maid." I gasped at the prices: $20 to $40 a yard for anything worth considering. "That's not an issue this time around," Guezinha explained. "There's hardly a yard's worth of material in each costume, so we can afford to spend more. We have to spend whatever it takes to make sure the costume looks right." We had been inspecting materials for nearly three hours. "I don't know what we're going to do, though. There's no selection at all this year."

"Downtown," Elania decided. "There's nothing here; let's go to the City." The train took us to a crumbling old station near the Old City, and we scoured the narrow streets for shiny pink, but there was nothing there either. Guezinha was exhausted and glum. Elania remained practical. "Let's get the shoes ordered this week, and the jewelry, and then we can really concentrate on the material later." Guezinha winced; that would leave only eleven more weeks till carnival.

If it hadn't been for Seu Tinguinha, Guezinha might never have had to deal with the problem of a standardized costume for her wing members. Thirty years before, the old *bateria* director had gone on strike to bring uniform parade outfits into Mangueira.

I went to visit Seu Tinguinha in his storybook house in an alley behind the school; there was a bell at the front gate and a parrot gossiping to himself on the porch, flowers in the tiny yard and antimacassars everywhere in the neat living room. Seu Tinguinha lived there with his wife on a modest retirement pension. Many other pedestrian-sounding things could be said about his life: he had held on to the same factory job for twenty-five years; he played cards every Saturday and bingo on Sundays; he had been married to the same woman since his early youth and still treated her with hovering tenderness; all his sons had jobs. In Mangueira these were such outstanding achievements that he was always addressed with the respectful *Seu*, or "Sir," attached to his name. Seu Tinguinha showed me into the living room, called out his wife, made the proper introductions and guided her to a sofa. Her enormous green eyes were nearly sightless, the result of diabetes, and blindness had made her quiet and sad, but Seu Tinguinha said softly that in her day she had been quite a baiana.

He brought out a box of old photographs and newspaper cuttings and selected an old sepia tint of a smiling girl in braids wearing a sequin-embroidered costume that was charming and not glamorous at all: a milkmaid's outfit, with a long wide skirt and a bodice topped by puffy sleeves. I asked if the dress his wife was wearing in the photograph was the standard baiana dress or if it had just been the costume for one particular year. "There didn't use to be standard costumes," Seu Tinguinha said. "My wife made this one to suit herself. Everyone did." So when did costumes get standardized? Seu Tinguinha smiled. "It began in 1958," he said:

In those days, I was the director of the *bateria*. The way things worked then was that on the day of the parade we'd take the train down to Central Station, and line up in formation there so we would march all together to Rio Branco Avenue, which is where the parade had moved after [the plaza in Little Africa] was torn down. By the time you were lined up at the station, you had a pretty good idea of how Mangueira would place. All the schools used the same train line, and while you waited for the rest of the school on the platform, you checked out the competition as they arrived.

So! We're in the 1958 carnival, and I get to Central Station with my men, feeling pretty good, when all of a sudden I turn around and see the Portela *bateria* go by. I felt my skin crawl. Every single one of those Portelenses was wearing a suit in the Portela colors. The same suit, every one of them! A fine-looking outfit too. Elegant. The trousers were white and the jacket was blue. Cut just right.

I felt so sick I broke out in a sweat. I looked around at my group and saw what we looked like: tattered, grungy, all dressed any old way . . . we were a mess! Some had embroidery and decorations on their shirts, some didn't have a thing. Some of us had painted our tennis shoes pink or green, some others just came out in their plain old sandals. I thought I was going to throw up, I felt so ill, and I could hardly wait for the parade to be over. Afterward I went right up to the school president and I told him I was never going to come out again. Ever. "You can't do that!" he said. And I said, "Not until we get a decent outfit, I swear it." In 1959 they sent a school delegation over here to talk to me just before carnival, but I wasn't about to be humiliated like that again. I didn't parade.

We didn't win. The day after carnival, on Ash Wednesday, I was sitting with the other *bateria* members, having a beer, feeling down, and I said, "This can't go on! Let's set up a real *bateria* wing!" "You're on!" everybody said. But where were we going to get the money? In those days I was still in the military, working at the munitions factory, and all the others had a job too, or a little hustle of some sort, but that wasn't the kind of money we needed for this size project.

As it happened, 1960 was the year Carlos Lacerda was running for governor of [the state of] Rio de Janeiro. One day our school president came up to me with a message: "What if Lacerda promised you 150,000 reis [about $350] for your wing? All he wants in exchange is for the *bateria* to perform at one of his campaign rallies." "Just that for 150,000 reis?" I said. "It's a deal!" That was a fortune! "Well then, just go over to his office and pick up the check."

Actually, I felt a little strange going over to his office all by myself, so I asked a colleague of mine from the *bateria* who was white to come along. It was very simple; the check was ready and we picked it up. But we were so ignorant in those days we didn't know what to do with a check. We cashed it the very next day and put the money in the safe-deposit box of the ceramics factory down the hill, where the Mangueira president was the general manager. We thought that was the only way to keep money safe! We bought the material and took it over to a tailor in the old favela of the Skeleton.

I remember carnival morning that year! We had all the finished costumes ready here at the house, and when the first guy came over to pick his up he put it on right away and we all stood around and stared at him. And then we all got dressed up and just stared at each other. It was unbelievable the way we looked, it was really something else! The jackets were pink-and-green-striped satin, and the trousers were satin too. Glory, that's what it was. Pure glory.

Nineteen sixty-two was the most chaotic year in the history of the carnival jury. The Império Serrano parade was initially supposed to glorify the War of the Triple Alliance in 1865–70, a conflict in which Brazil, Argentina and Uruguay eliminated virtually the entire male population of Paraguay. After strenuous protests from the Paraguayan ambassador and under intense pressure from both the Brazilian foreign ministry and Riotur, Império radically revised its script at the last minute. The story samba was rewritten, floats were redecorated, all references to the Paraguayan dictator Francisco Solano López were eliminated, and the parade was rebaptized "The Brotherhood Between Brazil and Paraguay." Naturally Império, which had been heavily favored to win early in the carnival season, lost, but so did Salgueiro, with whom Fernando Pamplona was making his debut with the revolutionary script about the independent republic of rebel slaves. Mangueira lost as well, despite the striped-satin splendor of the *bateria*. Portela, led by the gun-brandishing Natal, was declared victorious once again, and the general agreement was that this time the jury had gone too far. There was a riot on the downtown street corner where the prizes were announced. The police stepped in and kicked whatever bodies were handy, the president of Mangueira protested the extravagant display of brutality, all the injured samba schools declared that they would not parade again, and finally, after a week of tumult, Natal declared that his school would divide its first prize with all the other top-ranking schools.

"So Mangueira had to share," Seu Tinguinha concluded. "But we got our own first prize the following year, and I'll tell you, the secret was all in the costumes."

A muscular, handsome man with a firm handshake and military bearing, he saw me to the front gate, "I'll see you in the parade," I said. He shook his head. "I don't know how to parade except with the *bateria*, and I'm too old for that."

Seu Tinguinha was sixty-nine years old. Delegado, the stilt-legged master sambista, was sixty-six, but there were secrets to dance that he was just beginning to explore. For years he had been the school's principal *mestre-sala*—a term that translates as "majordomo" but was probably chosen as the name for the flag-bearer's partner for its much more impressive literal meaning: "master of the salon." Although he had retired from the post some ten years before, he was still a school soloist; this year he was getting fitted for the most extravagant costume of his life, a bejeweled pink frock coat and trousers he would wear to escort Nininha in a special float created to honor them. Nininha, who had left the position of flag-bearer nearly forty years before, had never worn anything remotely similar, in terms of weight and volume, to the white sequined ball dress studded with pink and green rhinestones now being prepared for her. "All that? Just for me?" she said when she saw the drawing. But Delegado said, "They are making a costume worthy of me."

He lived on the opposite side of the *quadra* from the Hot Hole, in the jurisdiction of Beato Salu, on the alley known as Olaria. Mornings, he liked to sit in a clearing across from where Beato Salu's new day-care center for the community was going up and take his ease watching the bricklayers perform. I found him there late one morning, shirtless but not without his hat, sitting folded up in sections like a slide rule, on a couple of planks that had been left on the ground. "He won't be friendly to you," people had warned, and he wasn't, but eventually he motioned that I could crouch alongside him on the planks. "Nobody taught me how to dance," he was saying. "I learned in my own head. I used to run home from school, throw everything down and start to rehearse. Nobody taught me, but I've taught many; a lot of majordomos from this and other schools learned what they know from me."

Delegado had done two things all his life, work as a price inspector for the city markets and samba. On his fame as the best carnival dancer ever, he had traveled to Mexico, Europe and Japan. On his salary, he had gradually built a five-room home bordering on the *quadra*, and he was just now converting two rooms from adobe to brick. He still worked, and he still danced. "Every year I come out with a new step," he said. I mentioned that in his new role this year as an allegorical figure on a float, he would be prevented from dancing by the weight of his costume and the car's movement. "That's an ignorant thing to say!" he snarled. "I'm going to be on a float, all dressed up, with my only authentic flag-bearer, Dona Nininha Xoxoba. She was one of the greatest flag-bearers of all time. I made my name with her and she became famous with me. We are going to be on the prettiest float of all because Mangueira wants to render us homage, but that doesn't mean I won't dance. The step I'm rehearsing for this year is unbelievably difficult, and it's going to leave everybody with their mouths hanging open. I can't reveal it to you now, but you'll see when the time comes: it's done balancing on one leg while the other does a complete dance on its own. This step is going to create astonishment—what do you mean I won't be able to dance!"

We walked over to his house, stepping around a pile of bricks at the entrance and into a room where a number of identical narrow-brimmed straw hats were perched on hooks. Delegado described his work as a member of the harmony department. "We're in charge of supervising the school's progress down the parade grounds," he said. "Mangueira's harmony department is intelligent, because we actually teach people how to move in time to the samba; that's why we're one of the few schools left that can still carry out a carnival on the ground, where it's not all left to the showiness of the floats and the costumes of the allegorical figures. The problem lately is keeping those huge numbers of people under control; Mangueira is too important a school to come out with just a couple of thousand people, even though from the point of view of the harmony department that's the ideal number. So there's four, five thousand people, and for us the work comes in making the flow look natural."

With something approaching a smile, Delegado showed me his back room. It lacked a back wall: the narrow brick ledge that replaced it gave out on a commanding view of the *quadra*—the *inside* of the *quadra*. Delegado had built his house to abut directly on the side wall of the Samba Palace, and we were standing in the gap between the top of the *quadra* wall and the suspended tin roof overhead, looking out on the dance area and within easy shouting distance of the singers' tower. "You see?" he said. "This way, even if for some reason I were ever too tired to go to the samba, I can sit here comfortably and still be in touch with what's going on."

We stared out at the empty dance space. "No, I don't get tired of the school." He shook his head. "Ever. Fridays, Saturdays, Sundays . . . I'm always there. I've been dancing with it since I was thirteen years old. I've been a *bateria* member, a *bateria* director, president of the composers' wing, watchman for the *quadra*. I was there this morning until five. I got up early, got my clothes ready for this evening, and started thinking about what areas we have to concentrate on during the rehearsal. I'm not tired. There'll be plenty of time to rest after carnival."

HOW TO SAMBA (MEN'S VERSION)

Find yourself a street corner and pretend it is the edge of the *quadra*. Practice just standing there. You should feel loose, but pleasantly expectant. Check how much time elapses before you feel the need to look at your watch. When you can complete a two-to-three-hour stint without having to know the time, you are ready to start practice.

1. The first thing is attitude. You should look and feel relaxed, yet vigilant, playful and ready to pounce. A slouching posture is easiest, but some crack sambistas manage a straight-backed nonchalance that is highly prized. Practice both and decide which suits you.

2. Put the music on. Listen to the beat. It is the road you will walk on, but whatever flow develops in your movements will come from the little plinking guitar or banjo pegging away just behind the singer. Your task is to follow the drums with your feet and spell out their rhythm by flinging your legs as far away as possible from your torso on every beat. Master this, then practice the same movement with your torso casually thrown back at a forty-five-degree tilt.

3. As your legs cut circles in the air with your torso planed back away from them, it is critical that your head remain level, as if you were dancing wedged under a shelf. Hopping up and down is tasteless. Also, don't fall down.

4. If you have mastered cakewalking in place, swinging your legs under and over each other as if you were climbing an invisible spiral staircase, and pulling up to a sharp halt after sliding sideways very fast with your feet, you are ready to time your performances. Timing is the difference between dancing to devastating effect and looking like a fool.

5. Remain in your street-corner mode until a woman approaches. Let her walk by. Let a few more women pass. Remember, you're not desperate.

6. Wait until a woman you really like comes along, and let her go just past the point where she can see you out of the corner of her eye. Break into samba. If your energy is strong, she will perceive your movement with her back and turn around. Stop. Smile. (Not at *her*!) Tug your clothes sharply into place. Wait for another woman. Repeat many times. With luck, a woman will eventually walk by who turns your spinal column to jelly and sets your ears on fire. She will stop and look at you and smile and avert her eyes and look at you

again and start to walk away and turn and grin and throw
caution to the wind and break into samba and you'll move
right up and dance a couple of circles around her and shrug
up behind her real slow and catch her by the hips and circle
her down to the floor and spatter a starstorm of steps around
her feet and grab her and carry her home and ride her and
catch her screams in your ears and lie back and breathe easy
and watch her wash up and sing and cook and ask you for
a cigarette and give you the eye.

If none of this happens, you can always form a circle with
the other men and really dance.

7 *Eurides' Baby, Celina's Visitor*

Eurides' baby was born, undersize and exhausted, after hours of labor that ended in an emergency cesarean. She named him Anderson, but after studying the tiny thing for a few days ("Is that all?" she asked the doctor who showed her son to her) she took to calling him He-Man. "Just to encourage him," she told her friends when she exhibited the baby proudly back in Mangueira. But then someone mentioned that He-Man was associated with evil forces in some branches of *umbanda*, and she dropped the nickname instantly.

For the first few days after her return from the public hospital Eurides spoke little and moved about less. Her skin looked chalky and she had lost too much weight. She spent most of her time with friends—Imaculada and her mother, Dona Nadir—leaving Anderson's father on his own while she recovered under Dona Nadir's vigilant care. Dona Nadir and her husband, Seu Arnaldo, were sharecroppers in rural Minas Gerais before they became favelados, yet in its design and relative comfort their home seemed one of Mangueira's most thoroughly urban corners. The private spaces in this two-story wedge of concrete, built by Seu Arnaldo, were as crowded as any in the favela—at least five people slept in the cubbyholes that passed for rooms—and the daytime area was cramped as well, but its blue walls were spotless, the tile floors cool and polished, the bloom of the plastic roses unpolluted by dust. The couple was fortunate to have two sons with clerical jobs living at home, and the luxuries their income added to the household included a sound system and a large television comfortably placed on a bookcase directly across from a puffy sofa. The minuscule kitchen was well stocked, and because Dona Nadir was a prodigious and generous cook, the house filled on Sundays and even on weekday evenings with friends and neighbors and relatives, who watched television over a plate piled with roast chicken and manioc meal, black beans and salad, fried fish and macaroni or, at the very least, with a bowl of sweet rice pudding set on their laps.

Eurides, who lived with Lilico in a single room whose most imposing piece of furniture was a crib, had no television, so she was a regular at prime time even before she came hobbling back from the hospital with her cesarean wound still fresh and Dona Nadir and Imaculata told her sternly that she was in no shape to take care of Anderson on her own while Lilico was at work.

Her friends washed diapers and cooked and prepared bottles of thin cornstarch gruel to supplement Eurides' milk, and she watched television, one eye on her sleeping son and whatever visitor had come by to dandle him and wish her well. "That is one black baby!" said Dona Nadir's pregnant daughter-in-law when she dropped by. Eurides grinned in agreement. "What else would he be with the parents he's got? But you better stop feeling so smug just because you've got yourself a white man with big blue eyes. Mark my words: That baby's going to be born black like coffee, with hair like peppercorns and lips so thick he won't be able to whistle!" Her friend smiled a secret smile of pleasure. She and Eurides both knew there was no chance of that; Dona Nadir's family was of pure Portuguese extraction, so pale they sunburned easily. Her baby would be fair.

"He is tiny, isn't he?" the pregnant woman murmured, holding Anderson lightly in one arm. "Doesn't he ever wake up?"

He hardly ever did. Anderson had undergone two radical transitions in less than a week, from womb to the white silence of a hospital, and from there to this jumbled universe where from dawn into the night a television competed with several neighboring radios over a cacophony of loudly shouted conversations, and where creatures of different shapes, sizes and smells hovered constantly over him, prodding and lifting and jiggling him experimentally, pressing their eyeballs to his when he was awake, sniffing around his neck and waving him in the air when he wasn't. He slept through diaper changes and barely woke for bathings, and a few minutes after his mother put him to her breast he was asleep again. When she nudged him to stay awake for more milk, he mewled and squeezed his eyes shut tighter.

Yet he was the constant topic of the conversations he slept through. His fluttering, paper-thin ribs and recurrent hiccups were discussed. The day-care arrangements that could be made for him when Eurides found a job. The resemblance to Lilico, a quiet man with finely drawn features and somber eyes. The serious education his parents were determined to give him. His carnival future.

"I can't parade," Eurides decided one evening, interrupting a climactic moment on the screen. "I won't parade without Anderson, and someone told me that it's a sin to introduce a baby to a pagan ceremony before he's been baptized."

"What's pagan about it?" Imaculada wanted to know. She liked samba and was a frequent visitor to the *quadra*, but she was not a school member and had no knowledge of carnival culture. Eurides had to explain to her that costumes are inherently pagan, and then she had to explain to me that Anderson's christening wouldn't take place until long after carnival because children should not be baptized before they "set."

"What's 'set'?" I asked. " 'Set' is when the baby's firm," one of the brothers explained patiently. "You know, like 'ripe,' like 'ready.' " To be set, I gathered, means that a child has survived long enough to be judged hardy, justifying the expense and effort of a baptism, which usually takes place between the first and second years of life.

"Before that, I can't put him in a pagan costume," Eurides concluded.

"But not all costumes are pagan," Dona Nadir protested. "You can make a little Indian outfit for him, and I'm sure that won't be sinful at all." She was speaking with unexpected authority, given that she was generally shy in public and neither a carnival devotee nor deeply religious. "What's in an Indian outfit? Just a little headband with a feather and some face paint. . . . You wouldn't even have to use face paint. If you make the headband and some little sandals you can hardly call that a costume at all, so it can't count as pagan." The others were doubtful. After all, what could be more pagan than an Indian, even if there weren't much to the costume? Besides, who knew if any of the school's wings were going to come out as Indians this year? On the other hand, think how wonderful it would be for Anderson to know that he had paraded for the first time when he was barely three months old. His mother stroked him thoughtfully, and promised to think it over.

As soon as she was strong enough to walk easily again, Eurides took Anderson to Celina for a blessing.

Celina imparted blessings regularly, as I discovered the first time I chanced on her praying over a child just inside the doorway of her house. She blessed for general good luck and for emotional distress, but because her patron was the god Omolu, who assigns diseases among humankind, her blessings for health were particularly important. "She prays for lower-back problems very well," her son Sidney declared, but in the community, where there was no clinic or health post, and where infant mortality hovered around 120 deaths per 1,000 live births, it was her blessings for newborns that were most often requested.

She was an ordained daughter-of-a-saint. Nearly thirty years before, a father-of-a-saint had supervised her monthlong fasting, praying, ritual head-shaving, body-painting and the slow preparation for the trance state that would allow Omolu, who had chosen her, to claim and enter her body and speak through her voice. Had she lived in the neighborhood of a proper temple with an established *candomblé* father- or mother-of-a-saint, she could have aspired to perfect her knowledge and eventually become a "little mother" or even a full mother-of-a-saint. But for reasons that were never clear to me there was no *candomblé* temple in Mangueira, although ordinarily a favela of its size and prestige would have had at least one. Celina was the highest-ranking *candomblé* authority on the hill still in active practice. When doctors failed, or simply in order to buttress medical craft, people came to her and asked that she invoke Omolu's help against their child's colic, or diarrhea, or general jumpiness.

By all accounts, he is a frightening god. Known also as Obaluaê, he inspires such terror his name is rarely mentioned. Addressed as

"He Who Slays and Eats" he is hardly less awesome. The straw domino he hides under conceals pustules, which cover his body. When he appears in a ceremony his dance is hobbling and twitchy. With one hand he makes the gesture of killing and eating. With the other, he sweeps the world before him. One legend says that he was born a leper and that his mother threw him into the water to drown. Saved by Yemanjá, mother goddess of the ocean, he retained the power given him by his diseases to distribute illnesses among humankind. By the same token, he is a healer, and he is identified with the Catholic saints Roch and Lazarus.

Omolu likes to eat corn with *dendê* palm oil. His colors are black and white. He speaks on Mondays and rewards those who make him offerings of goat or pork meat, but his blessing to Eurides' son on a normal weekday afternoon was simply given and demanded nothing in return. Celina said sharply, "Turn that television off!" but it was the only interruption in the household's usual chaos while she sat Eurides on a chair with the baby in her lap, broke off a sprig of fresh greenery from one of the tin-can planters outside the doorway, lit a candle and held the leaves and a glass of water over Anderson, praying quietly. "Don't stand between the chair and the doorway, or you'll get in the way of the force flow," one of Celina's sons warned me, and we continued our conversation.

The blessing was ready in less than two minutes. Celina swished the glass of water that had absorbed the negative forces and tossed the water and the sprig of greenery out the doorway. Anderson, who had remained wide awake and silent throughout, fell asleep. Sidney and Marcelo, Celina's youngest son, went out, and Bebeth, the youngest daughter, wandered in and turned the radio up.

The house was always crowded. There were the five children who lived at home, Celina and Gregory, the grandson she was bringing up for a son who had not yet found lodgings for himself and his wife. A curtain along one side of the room hid an old four-poster and a chest of drawers. Whoever didn't fit on the bed slept in the public area, on the floor or on the easy chair with the board set across it. Since no one in the family was employed, they were always about, coming in to change clothes, serve themselves a plate of stew from the dented pot on the stove, iron a shirt, watch television. The two oldest daughters each lived with their husbands in neighboring alleys, and they were frequent callers as well. There were also the visitors, people who came in to chat or consult or borrow things or, like Eurides, now sitting happily with the blessed Anderson, to ask for some magic.

"Blessings are a very delicate thing," Celina said, steadying the tongs she had just put on the fire for a girl who had come in for a hair straightening. "You have to know when they're needed. A lot of times you need to bless to break someone else's evil. Like Gregory, for example," she said, pointing to the chubby grandson who was just learning to walk. "People give him the big eye all the time, because he's so pretty and light-skinned it makes them envious. I have to keep protecting him. Strange, isn't it, that people's good points are what put them in danger?"

"I would never be envious," Eurides said. "I don't understand people who want to have more then they've got. My mother always said to me, 'You're not extraordinary-looking, but you're just fine the way you are. Nobody has everything.' Like in your case." She was addressing the girl who was having her hair done. "You've got nice light skin, but I've got better legs, that's my best point. Maybe yours aren't so great, but your face is very pretty. It's always like that." She traced Anderson's profile with her finger. "You know what I've heard? I've heard that some white people actually like black skin."

Bebeth, who rarely spoke, and who was very aware of the impact her own extreme good looks had on the hill, cut into the conversation eagerly. "It's true, it's true! White men like *mulatas*!" "No girl, I don't mean *mulatas*, I mean *black*, like you or me. They think black skin is pretty, just as good as white. Like fashion models; they use colored ones now, and you'd think they'd choose the light ones, but no, they go for the blackest skin; they actually prefer them that way, they say."

"Do you think that?" she demanded, turning to face me. "Do you think black skin is as pretty as white?"

Mangueira was asked to send a delegation to a free concert sponsored by the city in honor of the black hero Zumbi on the anniversary of his death. In Rio, when state or local officials want to show appreciation for black culture, they visit a samba school, and when they want to exhibit solidarity with black suffering, they stage a ceremony in honor of Zumbi. It was not always so. Until the Salgueiro *carnavalesco* Fernando Pamplona decided to script a parade around his life, Zumbi was an obscure figure, unknown to most blacks and unsung by official historians. By rights his rediscovery by Pamplona should be considered one of the most significant events in the cultural history of Brazilian blacks, for Zumbi, who led the last defense of the federation of runaway villages known as the Republic of Palmares, is now the lone black hero in the official history of Brazil.

The Palmares federation was a highly functional guerrilla state based in a series of palisaded enclaves in northeastern Brazil. Its farthest outreaches were 100 kilometers apart, and at the peak of its near-century-long existence its population was estimated at sixty thousand rebels. They fought and grew crops, traded clandestinely with nearby towns, staged raids, defended their territory and, within the authoritarian strictures common to guerrilla societies, enjoyed considerable freedom. Zumbi, the last ruler of this rebel federation, was killed in a final determined onslaught by Portuguese royal forces in 1695.

Until the recent discovery in Portugal of a cache of letters and eyewitness descriptions of Palmares, the only information generally available about it came from a 1947 biography of Zumbi by the ethnologist Edison Carneiro, who pieced together an account that by necessity included much hand-me-down hearsay and fantasy. It was this version that Pamplona adopted and embellished further for the Salgueiro parade. Carneiro believed that Zumbi was a native African prince who refused to accept his Brazilian enslavement, which fit well with carnival culture and Brazilian love of royalty. But he was actually a native Brazilian, born in Palmares, captured as a child in one of the many Portuguese assaults on the enclave and brought up, fluent in Latin and versed in European culture, by a priest. As an adolescent he fled back to Palmares, shed his Christian name (António) and quickly developed into the runaways' acknowledged military chief. In Carneiro's day Zumbi was believed to have committed suicide by throwing himself off a rampart rather than surrender to the Portuguese. In fact, he died fighting in an ambush. The myth persists nonetheless, and at risk of making too much of it, one might speculate that it is because Brazilians like black heroes who prefer self-annihilation to a fighting death.

The Mangueira school could hardly be absent from the anniversary concert, not only because Zumbi was featured prominently in the lyrics of its story samba, but also because the star attraction was Alcione, a famous woman sambista who was a devoted follower of Mangueira. This year she was almost singlehandedly financing its children's samba school, and in past years she had paid for a number of costumes for the poorer baianas—in the end, it had been Alcione who solved Celina's costume problem as well. A member of the directorate, desperate at the possibility that Celina would be cut out of carnival, had come up with the idea of asking the drug lords Beato Salu and Tuchinha to split the cost of her baiana costume. Beato Salu agreed readily, but before the second emissary could be sent out to Tuchinha's headquarters in the Hot Hole, Alcione stepped in with subsidies for twenty baianas. Celina had appeared triumphantly at the previous weekend's measurement session, dressed for the occasion in a flowing white outfit provided by her employer and sometime spiritual disciple at the downtown store Celina cleaned once a week. (The dress was one of the several "gifts" Celina had received in exchange for her counsel and praying. "You don't pay for prayer," Eurides had told me sternly when I asked how much Anderson's blessing had cost. But gifts, whose cost depended on the giver's means and gratitude, were standard practice, and to judge by the stylishness of the shirred cotton skirt and tunic, Celina's employer was grateful indeed to her floor scrubber.) Reincorporated into carnival, Celina volunteered for the unpaid Zumbi outing and joined the other sambistas on a bus waiting to take them downtown.

The big municipal bus had idled through the sunset, gathering the Mangueirenses. The children were first: the mosquito brigade of skinny dancers, none older than ten, who sing in sharp tuneless voices and gyrate at hyperspeed, and the boy drummers, banging on their instruments inside the bus until the noise level became unspeakably painful. Eventually Guezinha's older daughter and another teenager joined them, fiddling with the elastic on the minimal outfits worn by the *passistas*, or samba soloists—six ounces of sequins attached to a waistband and two shoulder straps. A few more baianas climbed aboard, carrying their voluminous costumes in neat bundles. Finally, Delegado arrived, in a pink suit and green shirt, and Dona Zica, the widow of the legendary samba composer Cartola.

She was an intriguing figure. Dona Zica looked far younger than her seventy-eight years, more middle-class than her impoverished background, more conservative than her heroic past. When in 1952 Cartola—widowed, alcoholic, alienated from the school and suffering the effects of a bad romance that had kept him away from Mangueira for almost seven years—seemed lost to even his closest friends, it was Zica, then a good-looking widow, who sought him out and brought him back. He was bitter, burned out, in ruined health, with a monstrous growth on his nose that made it difficult to look at him, unable to work even at the odd jobs that once had kept him in pocket money—bricklaying, making deliveries, selling homemade popsicles from a small cooler he carried on his chest. "They say that I'm disfigured, / Oh my heart," Cartola sang, and he seemed broken.

Zica set up housekeeping with him back on the hill and searched out old acquaintances with the influence to find him a job. Government officials who in the past had come to Mangueira begging for votes tried to get Cartola into the bureaucracy as a messenger or a watchman, but he couldn't pass the physical exams. Zica then found someone who got the composer a night position as a car washer in Ipanema, but the effort was too much for his health. Searching again, she convinced the Association of Samba Schools to make Cartola the watchman at its headquarters in the Old City. During the day, while Cartola slept, she cooked for the sambistas who hung out at the Association, and then she stayed up late cooking meals to sell the following day from a pushcart to workers in the nearby business district.

The speed with which the food sold out gave her the idea of starting a restaurant. Cartola's drinking had stabilized, he was composing and singing again, and the couple's quarters in the Association building were becoming a gathering place for both black sambistas and young white intellectuals looking for authenticity. Zica found partners among the journalists of the samba world and opened a restaurant, the Zicartola, in one of the Portuguese-style two-story buildings in the Old City. It was 1963, a few months before the coup that submerged Brazil in a twenty-one-year-long military dictatorship, at a time when Brazilian popular culture was in a state of unprecedented innovation and effervescence. White journalists, filmmakers, artists and intellectuals (many of whom would soon be branded as subversives) sought out Zica's food and Cartola's singing and the opportunity to be in a black establishment that felt root and yet shared easily with whites. The most important names in traditional black samba and the white bossa nova, or "new beat," gathered there to perform and listen to each other and talk. Then after two years the restaurant went broke and Zica and Cartola were homeless again. Only in 1974, when Zica had lobbied the municipality for a plot of land on which the legendary sambista could settle, and after sales from his first record provided Cartola with his first real income, did the couple's life become easier. In his light, clear voice, remarkably similar to Fred Astaire's, Cartola, the bitter poet of samba, wrote his gentlest verses: "As day was breaking I found what I wished for in the blackest night. / . . . All the sadness has gone with the song that arrived." And he recorded his friend Nelson Cavaquinho's song: "When a poet dies / Mangueira weeps. / I live peacefully in Mangueira; / I know that when I die, there will be tears."

Cartola died a celebrity in 1980, and Dona Zica, then in her early seventies, became the living symbol that posthumously reunited Cartola with the samba school he had effectively abandoned years before. Now she was on the bus on her way to the Zumbi outing in her capacity as one of the school's two living monuments—the other being Dona Neuma, her next-door neighbor. Zica had none of Neuma's expansiveness or style, and she was an uneasy conversationalist, but there was a quiet orderliness about her, and a sense of invincibility that people in the samba world and beyond found appealing. Dressed as she was today, in bright pink Bermuda shorts and matching shirt, grandmotherly in her glasses and neat fluff of silver hair, she made samba look reassuringly respectable. But she did not mix well with the bamba crowd on the bus. Celina, climbing aboard, nodded at Zica briefly before choosing a seat on the other side of the aisle.

The concert site was a short ride away, in a large plaza at the heart of the commercial and banking district in the Old City. Rio whites with money make most of it here, but the district's tight grid of narrow streets, colonial churches and nineteenth-century shops with stuccoed cake-frosting façades is not fashionable. At dusk the old warehouses and new skyscrapers empty out, as white managers and secretaries head for the square marble-fronted high-rises of the South Zone while black office workers and cleaners stream toward the suburbs; but on this evening the blacks stayed, blanketing a gently sloping hillside at one end of the plaza in the shadow of the church and convent of St. Anthony.

Zumbi went unmentioned by the performers and announcers

throughout the concert: the star of the evening was really Alcione, a lively middle-aged woman with a rich sweet voice, then at the top of the charts with a song about a boy teaching her to love. Around her performance the organizers had sprinkled brief gigs by a handful of root sambistas and the *batucadas* of the samba schools. The night was hot and cloudless; the planet Venus shone blue and unnaturally large above St. Anthony's seventeenth-century bell tower. On the open-air stage the eighty-four-year-old Aniceto, star of the Império Serrano school, was in splendid form, improvising effortlessly in a querulous voice in the *jongo* style Nininha's mother had been famous for.

Backstage, the baby flag-bearers and majordomos were stupefied with tedium. Unable to play for fear of dirtying their costumes, they got harassed by street kids standing outside the police barriers, who taunted them and threatened to throw mud on their silver lamé. The older sambistas passed the time restlessly, wandering up toward the stage and back again, and looking for a place to sit. Delegado and Dona Zica perched together silently and uncomfortably on a tube surrounding a lamppost. Celina danced. She danced alone, couple style, her arm around an imaginary partner's shoulder, her feet tracing easy circles and figure eights on the ground. She danced with unruffled grace and lightness and a playful sense of rhythm, fitting a hip switch or a sudden stop into the music's nooks and edges, shifting directions against the flow and then shifting again for a slow turn. A rakishly good-looking young sambista dressed in the blue and white of Vila Isabel watched with pleasure, and then with smiling admiration. Celina danced, humming to herself, until the sambista could restrain himself no longer and burst in on her pleasurable monologue with a bow and a smile and a "May I?" before gathering her delicately into his arms. They were a perfect match, and they floated together happily, circling and weaving against each other in complete harmony, until it was time for him to go onstage.

On Mondays, Celina's body was often on loan to a scoundrel by the name of Seu Malandrino, who wore her chunky, comfortable flesh with a menacing swagger, spit obscene words out of the corner of his mouth, straddled her only chair horseback style, and kept his face wreathed in a halo of cigarette smoke.

The first time I saw him, while poking my head in Celina's door and running directly into the stare from his dirty yellow eyes, I found him very frightening indeed. It took a couple of seconds before I recognized a face under the white boater hat with red trim and babbled an apology for the intrusion. "I'm sorry, Celina," I began, and was cut short. "Celina isn't here. My name is Seu Malandrino." The voice was gravelly and sinuous. I felt unequal to a conversation, but Seu Malandrino's yellow gaze flickered as I was backing out the door. "Let the gringa come in!" he said to a frightened young couple sitting on the sofa, and to me: "Sit in that corner and shut up!" He cackled at the originality of the situation—a black man ordering a meek white woman about, or, you could say, a barefoot black woman addressing an upper-class white insolently. The lips twitched with mirth: "I'll bet she's never seen anything like this."

He stubbed out one cigarette and lit another. Celina never smoked, but then neither did she speak with grand assurance or heal the sick. "You're going to forget everything I'm telling you; write it down," Seu Malandrino snapped at the young woman on the sofa— long-legged, honey-colored, face taut with worry—and she scribbled on a strip of paper torn off a supermarket bag while the snake voice repeated the instructions: "One rooster is for you to use on your bodies. The other is for The Man. Candles. *Cachaça*. Beer. And two hundred seventy-seven cruzados." The young man on the sofa listened half absently, his dark skin ashen gray. His companion tucked away the list of magic ingredients and asked timidly if Seu Malandrino might perhaps like another beer. "Of course," came the snarled reply. "Can't you see this one's almost finished?"

Celina—or someone—had set the stage for Seu Malandrino with a few small props. A glass of water, a candle and a sprig of something green on a corner altar tell the saints and spirits they are welcome in nearly every house in Mangueira. This time, however, the altar had been set before Seu Malandrino himself, on a rickety table—a backless chair, really—dressed with a white towel and set in front of the guest. Celina's body had received the most preparation of all: the string of white beads with small black and red notches she wore around her neck tied her to her patron god, Omolu, and was supposed to help her enter the trance state that would allow the otherworldly visitor access. The most impressive stage props—a white shirt and matching trousers and the red-trimmed hat—were what she had been able to approximate of the classic *malandro* outfit: a white zoot suit and fedora. The beer was simply to keep Seu Malandrino happy.

We waited silently for the sick man's girlfriend to return with the beer. The man was slight and very young—barely twenty, it seemed—and dressed in the favelado's shorts and flip-flops. He had seemed merely tense, but then he grimaced and his back arched and he shot straight up off the sofa, moaning and clenching his hands. For a moment, Celina's apprehensive look fluttered across Seu Malandrino's face. "It doesn't stop?" he asked. The man gasped and shook his head. Seu Malandrino placed his hat on the table, stood and, grasping the sick man's hand, whipped into a crouch. He cocked his head from one side to the other with his eyes closed, listening intently.

A slow exploding hiss crept out of him, his face contorted, and he let out a deep-pitched yowl, a scream that, receding, ebbed into a low rumble. He opened his eyes. The sick man collapsed back on the sofa, shaking, his thin belly distended. His girlfriend, who had been watching from the doorway, wept softly.

"It's that other woman," Seu Malandrino told her matter-of-factly, making little chewing movements between each phrase. "She may have found a new man all right, but she's still trying to hurt the two of you." He smoked and drank and spit on the floor.

We waited. The pain that racked the man's body appeared to shoot from a region around the right kidney to a spot below his rib cage, where it caught fire. When the pain burst it sent the victim stretching upright away from it. When it subsided he sat down. Presently, he informed Seu Malandrino that with all due respect, he could no longer bear to sit, even in his presence. "Lie down, then," Celina's voice said, and when I looked under the felt hat I saw she had returned and was worried. She stood up, muttered an incantation, snapped her fingers and left the room. "The saint's gone," she announced at the doorway. "But he'll be back, and so will I."

While she was gone I asked the sick man if he had thought of seeing a doctor. He nodded. "We went to the clinic," the woman said, "but the doctor said there was nothing wrong with him. He gave him a shot of penicillin and told us to go away." I touched the man's neck; he had a scalding fever. It seemed sensible to try to reach a real doctor, and as I headed for Dona Neuma's house and her phone, I ran into the returning Celina and explained what I was doing. "I hope you find one," she said with her worried look. "I only help people when I'm sure it's not a medical affair. They told me they'd been to the clinic and there was nothing wrong with him a doctor could cure, but I think he's very sick."

"Girl, you look like you've seen a ghost," Dona Neuma said, just up from a nap. "What's wrong with you?" I tried my doctor's numbers, but he was out of reach. "Don't worry, Celina will take care of it," Guezinha reassured me. "You shouldn't let Seu Malandrino scare you. He won't do you any harm. But it's true, we should have warned you about him. Normally, he's only around on Mondays, like today, because that's Celina's saint's day. But sometimes he steps in to defend her even if it's not his day. You should have seen when he appeared one afternoon! Just imagine: Celina and Dona Jurema and her son-in-law were drinking beer right at the little stand here and Celina was insisting that the others should pay for her beer, and Dona Jurema's son-in-law—this big, heavy guy—kept saying no. They'd all had a few too many, so with one thing and another, pretty soon they were yelling at each other and Dona Jurema's son-in-law said I don't know what about Celina's mother and all of a sudden, *wham*! Seu Malandrino appears and lets fly with an uppercut and sends Dona Jurema's son-in-law right to the floor.

"Darling, he fell so hard he set the dust flying. You know how small Celina is? Well, believe me, Seu Malandrino had this huge guy flat out on the floor. And then he stood over him, waving his fist, and he shouted, 'Nobody insults this woman's mother!' We were watching from my mother's bedroom window and I tell you, I thought I'd kill myself laughing."

I stopped dialing phone numbers. "Child, I don't know what's the matter with you today," Guezinha said. "I can't even make you laugh. I'll tell you what: If you really think that boy's in trouble, and you want to help, get a taxi and take him over to Pedro Ernesto Hospital. That's right near here. You're white and they'll be certain to pay attention to you. Get a doctor to check him out."

Seu Malandrino was back, brooking no interruptions, when I returned to Celina's. The sick man's girlfriend had been sent to buy raw kidney, and Celina's daughter Janice had tied a ceremonial lace apron over her shorts and was frying the meat in *dendê* palm oil. Seu Malandrino prayed and chanted and rubbed the half-raw kidney over the gasping man's abdomen and chanted again. Janice left the room, came back and stood in the doorway, moaning and shivering, and left again. "See that?" Seu Malandrino told the man. "She's taking your pain away with her." But the pain did not go away at all.

It was a very long afternoon. When I could stand the sick man's groans no longer I gave him my phone number and told him and Seu Malandrino to call me the moment they needed to.

A few days later I asked Celina what had happened to Seu Malandrino's patient. "Who knows," she said, half cross, half sheepish. "I'd never seen that couple before, but I took the trouble to find out that they live way up the hill, and I sent someone up there to ask how he was doing. Apparently he got well again a couple of days ago. And they didn't even bother to send a word of thanks. Imagine!" For once, she was reticent in her answers to my questions: No, Seu Malandrino was not a god. Yes, the owner of her head was bubo-covered Omolu, and yes, Omolu was a god. Seu Malandrino was an *egun*, the spirit of someone who had died. He had the ability to flit between the divine and the human worlds. Omolu was lord of the cemeteries, and he facilitated these connections. She changed the subject and I let her. Seu Malandrino's nasty little eyes had scared me, and I did not want to provoke his return.

8   Rituals and Celebrations

Guezinha and Elania, on a wave of inspiration, had decided to overlay
sheer silvered organza decorated with pink and silver roses on a pink
satin lining. Working through an adrenaline rush, they had put the
rest of the costume together, and when I went to get my measurements
taken in December the sample outfit was ready, approved by the
directorate costume commission and available for viewing in Guezinha's second-story suite of rooms at Dona Neuma's. Two women
who had just put down their 2,000-cruzado ($25) deposit to sign up
for the wing were coming down the stairs, giddy with excitement
and pleasure, when I arrived. "Oh, Guezinha, that is so pretty!" they
exclaimed as they left. "Thank you!"

Elania displayed the costume for me, pulling the different parts
one by one out of a plastic bag: the gauzy pink dress with its deep-
cut V neck and hip-length skirt; the frilly apron, bordered in ruffles
and decorated at the center with an extra rose; the huge pink bow
for the back of the skirt, stuffed with foam rubber to remain lively
throughout the parade; and the ornaments: a ruffle of glittery silver
for the head, mint-green platform heels with ankle straps, a magenta-
pink feather duster, and a set of earrings, necklace and bracelet that

looked to have been made in the Emerald City. There were two more women waiting to sign up when I left, bewitched by the irresistible costume.

Dona Neuma's house, always crowded, now also had a definite commercial bustle. In addition to the costume selling, carnival plotting, accounting and cooking, there were the related activities carried out by household friends like Carlinhos, who sold crinkly white nylon polo shirts with the Mangueira logo pressed on in green felt letters. Chininha and Guezinha fried empanadas and stuffed little balls of dough with chicken that would be sold at the *quadra* rehearsals. Dona Neuma received visits from disgruntled baianas and requests for help from second- and third-division samba schools. She was in charge of the costumes for the children's division of the Mangueira school as well, and she spent the days relaying orders and requests and donations in a befuddling number of directions. But all these activities—and the routine tasks of buying and preparing food, cleaning house and washing clothes—were secondary to the task of costume production. Two sewing machines on the upstairs balcony started humming late in the afternoon, after Ceci got home from work and was joined by a neighbor from down the hill, T-shirt Carlos' wife, Iracema. Ceci was in charge of the all-male African warriors' wing that would open the parade. Iracema was doing the costumes for Guezinha's wing, for a wing of nineteenth-century soubrettes for Dona Neuma's youngest daughter, Chininha, and for several wings from the children's division. A third machine downstairs was rotated between Dulce, Iracema's assistant, and Fia, a stunning woman with an equally beautiful child who had grown up with the Neuma household and was one of Guezinha's best friends. And there was Elania herself, Guezinha's co–wing chief, who would usually sit down for a couple of riffs of stitching whenever she came over.

As carnival took hold of the household, intensifying the work rhythm and narrowing the range of everyday concerns, it also spread for the first time beyond the hills, sneaking into the South Zone on the radio waves and taking command of the North. For the first time in the course of the season, the *quadra* was as full of outsiders as locals on rehearsal night, many of them whites who in their residential neighborhoods sensed carnival's return and one evening, without quite knowing why, said, "Time for rehearsal!" and set out from Copacabana or from the northern suburbs for the samba world, dressed in their best starched whites and with flowers stuck in their hair.

Ipanema on a soft, hot night. The white girls smile under the almond trees, strolling, swinging their manes and their heavy jewelry. The men smile back, perfect in their linen trousers, silk shirts, nubbly cotton jackets. We pass them as we drive, gaze longingly at the warmth of their tanned skin, their cantilevered buttocks, the relaxed grace with which a group of them just now is easing into the rosy light and *faux-marbre* setting of a chic postmodern Italian restaurant. There is time for one last glance at the narrow street with its canopy of trees and the shoulder-to-shoulder apartment buildings looming above, and the black doormen in their khaki uniforms below, their transistor radios held to one ear. The white waiters are setting out beers on the restaurant terraces, and the gorgeous couples stroll and smile, smile and flirt through the steeplechase arrangement of the cars parked on the sidewalk beyond, dodging the cars and the street urchins without seeming to notice that they were ever in the way, the night being too soft, and too hot, and too pleasurable.

And now the stoplight changes and we are swinging into the great loop-the-loop sequence that will carry us from south to north, onto the drive that circles Rodrigo de Freitas Lagoon, so flat and glossy at this promising premidnight hour. Past the most elegant apartment buildings of all, solid cubes of marble on our right backed into the rock of the bulky, abrupt hills only recently cleansed of a last, stubborn favela. On our left, in the manicured park that rings the lagoon, we see the illuminated tennis courts, and a quartet of late-night players lobbing a tiny moon over the net. Our taxi speeds the tennis dancers out of sight and loops once more, bringing the wall of Corcovado into view, the tallest hill of all, topped by the great awful cast-concrete Christ, whose outspread illuminated arms we crane to see before our car is gulped into the tunnel and we vanish into the mountain's gullet, our ears filled with a rush of roaring for long minutes until the tunnel expels us again and with a gasp of relief we emerge from the mountain's gut into the viaducts and overpasses of the North Zone and see the dockyards in the distance, and in the foreground, the first favela slaloming down Kerosene Hill.

A party here. In an abandoned lot beneath our overpass we see the dancers first, a few dozen, and then the drummers lined up against the hill wall. Their music does not reach us, and we stare at the revelry like children with eyes pressed to a peepshow. Our taxi zooms down a long incline past Estácio and São Carlos hill, the great mother favela of the samba schools, then swoops again, over and up the overpass floating us above the string of light bulbs that announces the Estácio samba school and down to the traffic clover of Cidade Nova, the New City that was rising up among the marshes two hundred years ago, where now we can just guess the rigid outlines of the Sambadrome against the vast expanse of President Vargas Avenue as we reach ground level and swoop around the clover past a crowd we are familiar with, the residents of the bushes, whom we like to watch in daytime bathing and washing their clothes in the reflecting pool's stagnant waters, now gathered on this samba night for a small party. There is a bonfire, and a *batucada* with a real tambourine and a drum improvised from an empty box, and an old man we have seen before naked and howling imprecations at the passing traffic, covered in soap lather, now dancing in the center of the samba circle, whipping his legs under and over each other, smiling ecstatically while his friends sing.

The light ends here. With another swoop our taxi has chosen the dark road that leads to the park surrounding the Emperor's Palace, and here we can look for the whores: the one we like, who strolls in the shadows carrying a parasol and wearing a long Empire dress above whose wide décolletage two breasts pop out, and the one who scares us, who appears suddenly from among the trees and turns to display two enormous, perfect buttocks through a hole cut into her spandex pants.

They are not here tonight. We pass a couple of women in shorts and halter tops before the car swings free of the park and into the final curve around the base of Mangueira hill. The car is speeding now, whistling through the empty night with no other traffic to obstruct its path, and no distractions on a road whose only alternative is the long progress past the soldiers' barracks and the gas station and then the gathering favela as we emerge on the viaduct parallel to the railroad tracks and the world is lit again, illuminated from above by a procession of lampposts and at ground level by the thickening cluster of light bulbs above beer stands, pool halls and general stores. The taxi loses speed, the sound of laughter and chatter and singing and shouted greetings fills the car, the clusters of revelers in their glitter and spandex and pomaded hair churn into a single hopped-up crowd that fills the entire width of the viaduct and slows our progress to a crawl until, resignedly, the driver stops honking and joins the procession now heading toward the pink-and-green splendor of Mangueira.

The flow of outsiders altered the dancing. There were the slummers, like the five drunken white men who egged on a baby sambista into performing her bumps and grinds for them, a pacifier stuck in her mouth; or like the couples who tried unsuccessfully to imitate a black couple dancing an unusually explicit samba—the woman opening her legs wide so her partner could bend and hop between them, rubbing the nape of his neck against her crotch; or the fat white man dressed in Bermudas, black socks and shoes, dancing with a smiling light-skinned black woman—a *mulata*—who reverently removed his shirt to fan his dripping armpits dry.

But there were also the white wing members, easily distinguishable from the slummers; enthusiastic, disciplined followers of school ritual, they were the first to show up for rehearsal in their official T-shirts. Early in December a wing that commuted to rehearsals every weekend from the town of Petrópolis showed up in black shirts with pink and green stripes. The "Nobody Messes with Me" wing, mostly white, appeared shortly thereafter in T-shirts with the wing name printed in pink letters above a display of green leaves stamped on white. The wings from the hill were far less disciplined; Guezinha, who had entrusted production of her wing's T-shirts to Carlinhos, told us that it would be a few days yet before we would receive them, and Carlinhos, bustling around the *quadra* in his Prince Valiant hairdo, suit jacket and Bermuda shorts, peddling hideous polo shirts and T-shirts with the parade theme's logo, apologized profusely and swore our T-shirts would be ready next Tuesday, next Monday, tomorrow for sure.

The wing Elíseo Dória inherited from his brother Carlos wore dark green shirts with its name, "Only Those Who Can," lettered in pink. It didn't act like a wing; its members didn't arrive early and sit around in the little plaza taking the evening breeze and chatting with the locals, nor did they push together several tables inside the *quadra* and cover them with beer bottles and stand around this altar, arms over each other's shoulders, singing the samba loudly and swaying to the beat. Instead, the men who made up Dória's wing stood singly around the *quadra* walls, arms folded across their barrel chests, glinting meanly at everyone, scrutinizing men's waistbands for signs of a gun, never dancing, moving or smiling. The old pink "Mangueira Security" T-shirts, worn by kids from the hill who knew almost everyone in the *quadra* and could predict exactly what kind of trouble he or she was likely to cause, were gone: their dark green replacements were worn by professionals—the Dória brothers' colleagues from the police world.

There were other T-shirts: Ricardo Lion-Heart's followers wore shirts with a heart composed of hundreds of tiny lion faces stamped on the chest and the slogan "Bamba Night" on the back. One of Tuchinha's men showed up one night in a white shirt that said "Be an Outcast; Be a Hero." A woman wore a printed one that said, in English, "The Cat He Is Crazy in the Love." Delegado sported a bright pink T-shirt just long enough to skim his waist, with the words "Universidade do Samba" stamped on the back. He and Alberto Pontes continued with their rehearsal chores, ignoring the tourists and the fools and the rowdy drunks who threatened to pull guns when they were yanked out of the women-only dance space. Pontes blew on his whistles and Delegado brandished his baton, yelling at the women to sing "for God's sake, what do you think you're here for," and made them practice short-stopping and rushing forward behind the flag-bearer and the majordomo. Outside the *quadra* the white arrivals followed the scruffy Mangueira kids to a parking space, and then perhaps to the spot where another child was waiting with little newspaper-wrapped packets of cocaine, and then to the steaming shish kebab grills where at two, three, four in the morning you could get a bite to eat. Fortified, they took a deep breath and clattered through the turnstiles into the noise.

"Come on," said Eurides, tugging me into the circle. "Let's dance!" She wasn't supposed to be there. "It's okay," she shouted over the music. "Anderson's asleep, Lilico's with him. I couldn't stand it anymore. Come on!" She was transformed. Blue eye shadow. Smooth hair. Black skin glowing in a white shirt crossed and tied around the waist and very short shorts. It seemed that after all the women had been ordered into the dance area there was hardly enough room to smile, but she let go every which way with feet, elbows, head, clearing a space for both of us and charging into the samba full-tilt, singing so loudly Pontes actually smiled in approval. She bounced up and down when the words were "Black men dance" and raised her arms wonderingly when the song went "Can it be, is freedom really here?" When the song started a second time I realized the space, which had seemed crowded when we began, was only just beginning to fill up. We moved forward in a packed wall of bodies, a third, a fourth, a fifth time through the song, jumping and shouting, Eurides far ahead of me now, bounding twice as high as her neighbors, while I felt in a surge of panic that all the oxygen had been sucked out of the air, leaving only empty heat. I pushed my way through the jelly of sweat-drenched women to the sidelines and gasped for air, watching Eurides come around again, a seventh time through the song, legs and arms spinning, and saw her friends on the outside of the circle point and laugh at the nursing pads that centrifugal force sent flying straight out of her blouse. "Come on!" she yelled, pulling me into the circle again.

The song played for forty minutes, and at the end she looked a little shaky, and very pleased with herself. She headed back home to Anderson and I pushed my way to a table. The *quadra* was filled to the very edges, frothing over with dancers, fizzy with a kind of reckless excitement I would not see again. It was the last rehearsal before the Christmas holidays, and when we next convened, carnival would be ahead of us, its prospects shaping the samba night into something more intense and purposeful.

On Christmas Eve, Dona Zica set out a feast in her front yard, with juicy, meaty codfish swimming in olive oil, and enough side dishes to cover the enormous table. Dona Neuma also served codfish, as well as roast leg of pork and Chininha's famous *farofa*: manioc meal stirred slowly into bacon fat, olives and scrambled eggs. Celina spread a checkered cloth on the rickety wooden table in her one room and set out a plate of "Russian salad"—vegetables with plenty of mayonnaise—a cold meat dish with potatoes, codfish croquettes and, for dessert, French toast. Her family mingled with friends who came from up the hill or a half-hour's ride away to toast each other with cheap Brazilian wine mixed with Coca-Cola and wish each other

"Merry Christmas and everything good." The television played brightly throughout the midnight meal, tuned not to the Christmas mass being broadcast live from the cathedral but to a Joan Crawford movie.

I headed back to Ipanema, where the tall buildings were also sparkling with parties, curtains pulled back at every window to reveal the glowing feasts within. All around Rodrigo de Freitas Lagoon the lights twinkled and welcomed. Men in tuxedos leaned against a balcony balustrade. A knot of tipsy adolescents giggled and screamed on a terrace. For once, the streets in Rio were empty.

On December 27, the women in Dona Neuma's house had a party. The hundred-degree heat had just broken, the sun was descending spectacularly, and two teenagers were beating a lazy rhythm on conga drums in Dona Neuma's front yard when the household women drifted into a circle, chanting, telling dirty jokes, whooping, urging each other into the dance. The newest trend in music from Bahia was songs rich in intricate backup rhythms and lyrics full of double entendres. Guezinha, Neuci, Ceci, Elania, Inez, Iracema and Fia stripped the music of its complications and chanted the refrain, *jongo* style: "Open your little circle, open it just a little bit." Ceci gurgled with laughter while Inez leapt into the center of the ring and shook her buttocks, then leapt out again and shoved Guezinha forward. Eyes half closed, grinning, Guezinha sat back on her heels, rotating her hips, then shaking them, then rotating again and shaking her shoulders as she leaned farther and farther backward until her shoulders touched the floor, her thighs tilted to heaven and her smile by now outrageous. The other women hooted, pointing at her, "Girl, you have absolutely no shame whatsoever!" but Guezinha was laughing too hard to answer.

The hilarity was somehow inseparable from the rhythmic chanting, as if the mood were a spirit convoked there by the drums, a presence that would vanish as soon as the noise stopped, leaving everyone empty and listless. The drums fed the spirit, whose name is not joy or happiness or delight but gaiety, and kept it alive, transferring it to the women who in its possession abandoned their individual traits—Guezinha her insecurities, Neuci her laziness, Ceci her sharp temper—to sing the visitor's song. Gaily they clapped their hands—African, straight-fingered style. Gaily they took their turn in the circle, the teenaged Neuci dancing now, dreamily spinning around, switching her hips easily back and forth as if they were on tracks, while her feet carried her smoothly around the ring in a tiptoe shuffle. Neuci, daughter of Ceci, mother of Carolina, had lost the father of her child a year before, when he was killed on the steps of this very yard by the drug gang he had decided to leave. Neuci was eighteen years old and a widow, but that was irrelevant now. The bad tempers and fits of depression that afflicted her belonged to someone else at the moment. Night was falling, she was dancing, a tall dark girl with a face that looked carved and polished, and voluminous buttocks that rode high on her hips. She shimmied and spun and eventually slid up to Guezinha, who linked up to Ceci, who latched on to Inez, who picked up the chant, "Open your little circle, just a little bit wider," leading the conga line, until it was interrupted by Dona Neuma, who appeared in the doorway waving one of her Christmas presents, a carefully detailed, optimistically life-size wooden dildo.

"Where are all the men?" Dona Neuma asked querulously after the laughter had subsided. She turned to Guezinha. "Where's your husband?" Eyes a little out of focus, smile still blurred, Guezinha called back across the yard: "He's around the corner, playing cards. Do you want me to call him?" Before Dona Neuma had time to answer, Guezinha leaned forward and spoke more sharply: "Think about it. Because when the men arrive the fun will end. Which do you want: the fun or the men?"

It was New Year's Eve. I was going to go to the beach at midnight, like most of the residents of Copacabana and Ipanema, who, dressed in white, congregate to light a candle in the sand and throw a white flower into the ocean with a prayer for the goddess Yemanjá. I asked Dona Jurema how I should pray.

"I would say something like this," she began. "Yemanjá, Our Mother, please make 1988 a better year than 1987. Not that 1987 was a bad year, don't get me wrong: I received many benefits, many good things happened to me, and I'm not complaining. But now, thinking over everything that's happened, I would like to ask you for something from the bottom of my heart: please bring me twice the amount of good things, and take away half the number of bad."

Part Two

CARNIVAL TIME

9 *Early January*

In the new year. Anyone who entered Dona Neuma's house glowed perceptibly on departure. Sparkling dust from warriors' shields, maids' aprons, baby baianas' skirts covered the furniture and the floor and adhered to the visitor. In the afternoons, when Dona Neuma or Guezinha or Fia made fresh coffee and sent out for a couple of loaves of bread, the margarine-covered slices they passed around winked with specks of iridescent green. "Carnival glitter?" asked the man at the photography store in Ipanema early one morning. I was dropping off some film, coming in straight from rehearsal, and wondered why the camera was jamming. He blew into the winding mechanism and choked on the cloud of pink dust that floated out. I found myself sparkling in supermarkets, extending a glowing hand for a coffee-vanilla at the ice cream parlor. Increasingly out of place in the real world, I moved to Mangueira.

Baiano, who ran a freight and moving service from the back of an ancient flatbed truck in a plaza in Ipanema, loaded a cot, a folding chair, an electric fan and a reading lamp onto the truck and introduced his wife. "Did the lady say she wanted to move to Mangueira?" she asked, using the respectful Portuguese third person. "Does she not perhaps mean Laranjeiras?" Laranjeiras is a residential neighborhood; I repeated that I wanted disreputable Mangueira. Eva squinted and studied me against the backdrop of the elegant building I was moving out of. "Are you a cook?" she asked, now using the extremely familiar *tu*. I didn't understand the question. "Are you a cook like me?" she repeated.

Baiano, jump-starting the truck, apologized for his wife. He knew more about the world, he said expansively. He knew important people because he often drove a truck for one of the most successful show business impresarios in Rio. It was clear that I was a foreigner, and obviously not a cook. A governess, yes? People who wrote, as I said I did, often got jobs in that field. It was easy to see that I was going through a difficult moment, no need to try to hide it—anyone can lose his job, find himself on the street overnight. All would be well; he was sure he could use his connections to help me find employment.

The truck coughed its way down the road at under twenty miles an hour. My situation absorbed Baiano entirely until the motor rasped to a halt on the overpass beyond the South/North tunnel. Revived after some tinkering, the truck swerved drunkenly into the retaining wall farther on, either because Baiano's hand was unsteady on curves or because the steering was shot. We ran out of gas on the approach to the Emperor's Palace. Eva patted my hand. "He'll find a gas station, don't worry. He always finds the solution to problems." She was small and trim and looked much younger than her fifty-odd years, her brown skin pressed smoothly over admirable cheekbones. She had gotten back together with Baiano the previous week, after a year's separation that had nearly killed her. Now she felt that she had never been happier. "So many men are disrespectful when they have sex with you," she explained. This was intriguing but she said no more, for Baiano was shuffling back with a bucket full of gas, perspiring like a faucet and bright red under the scorching afternoon sun. "Baiano, don't you think the three of us could look for a place to share somewhere more peaceful than Mangueira?" she asked as he heaved himself back into the truck. They could use a little more room, she reasoned, and I could probably use some help with the rent. They shook their heads at my insistence on living in Mangueira. Everything they had heard about it made them wary of so much as parking there.

On Dona Neuma's porch, Eva decided that she rather liked the hill. She saw a famous actor walk out the door, emerging from a costume try-on for his two children. Stepping over the mounds of tulle and feathers blocking the way, she approached the table where Fia, Iracema and Dulce stitched and drank beer. She watched Elania arrive, moving in for the season with her cot and electric fan, and a sewing machine. "Good-bye!" called Eva. "I'll be back for carnival!" "Good-bye!" Baiano called. "Remember, I know important people. And if you ever need to move again, look for me in the plaza, and never mind about the money." He coaxed the flatbed onto the viaduct, and it did not break down or halt as long as it remained in view.

Guezinha recruited the local drunk, and together with one of Celina's sons we hiked my belongings to the top of the hill. Below us the Saturday bustle along the viaduct grew dim, then inaudible. Only the roar of a train occasionally reached us. A dozen kites floated in the sky, bobbing and dipping in conversation with the kites on the opposite hill. Just below the point where Mangueira crested there was a last stretch of shacks and a cluster of relatively solid brick houses, some with second stories pitched on the original roof. I unpacked here, in a prosperous home with a tile kitchen and bathroom and running water, and four bedrooms on the upper story. After nightfall I attempted a downhill shortcut to the Hot Hole and fell down twice trying to follow Delegado's sister, a spare, tall old woman with a harsh profile who scampered down the gullies in the dark with arms full of fresh laundry for her brother. She was in a hurry; the season's first street rehearsal was about to start.

The viaduct had been closed to traffic for the evening, and the stretch leading up to the police barricade was packed with cars. The Hot Hole was jammed with strollers. Two *batucadas* were in progress, and many more card games. Small crowds gathered in front of every beer stand, drinking and laughing over the sound of Tropical Radio, now broadcasting the major schools' story sambas almost exclusively. Every once in a while a murderous rush of noise made everyone skip off the center of the street; Tuchinha, with no bodyguards in sight, was racing his brand-new Honda down the Hole to his last safe border, the viaduct, pedaling back uphill to the dead end, roaring down again. He wore the lost, ecstatic countenance of the blessed and talked to no one.

In the little plaza, the Dancing Days restaurant had set out tables where wing members chattered and compared T-shirts. The wing chiefs strutted back and forth between the sound truck and the little plaza, counting their members and trying to look busy, though there was very little for them to do. The real work was, as usual, in the hands of the *bateria* and the platoon of harmony directors, more irritable tonight than ever. The rehearsal was an endurance exercise designed to keep the school moving forward at full energy level for the eighty minutes the actual parade would last, and the harmony directors didn't have much to work with. The sound system was sputtering. The rehearsal director, Percy Pires, could not get his microphone to work. The wing chiefs could not be made to understand where they were supposed to place themselves. Children were pressed into service, standing disconsolately with numbered placards where the wings were supposed to go, getting bored, wandering off and getting yanked into place again by Delegado. With a megaphone, Percy repeated the marching order over and over again, to no effect: "Sector One, Wings for Our African Roots: Only Those Who Can, Moana, Sambrasa, Hippies and Renewal. Sector Two . . ." More restless than the children, the wing members converged now and then in the designated areas, complained about the heat and the wait, and wandered back to the plaza or to the restaurant beyond the *quadra* in search of more beer. Percy yelled into the megaphone.

Two women appeared at the spot where our wing was supposed to form and remained taciturn and uncomfortable until they were reassured by the sight of Guezinha, barreling down the road an hour late with her full complement of friends, daughters and other female relatives. We were, I pointed out grimly, almost the only wing not wearing our T-shirts. "So what?" said Guezinha, flipping her hair. "Don't we samba better than anybody else?" And what about the other wing members? How come there were only ten of us? And what were we supposed to do? Weren't we supposed to have any steps? Guezinha laughed: "Stop worrying so."

In their own good time, a few baianas strolled to their assigned positions. The drummers slowly formed in rows, taking up their instruments with sullen procrastination. Eventually, the *bateria* director signaled that his men were ready. A samba puller, or parade singer, tested a verse of the story samba on the sound-truck microphone. A mandolin set up its urgent, plinking Morse code. Like fragments of a kaleidoscope reassembling, the wings were briefly agitated, then coalesced into smooth rows. The samba puller began the song. I tugged at Guezinha's elbow: What's happening here? What are we supposed to do? How do we know when to start? Orders were what I wanted, but there were none, because the *bateria* director threw the switch and we lit out, jerked straight up into the air by the beat, the drums slamming into our diaphragms, forcing the song out of our lungs. The sound truck moved and in its pursuit we charged down the viaduct, obsessed and blind, roaring, arms pumping, hearts on fire, dimly aware that on the overpass, in the plaza and along the *quadra* balcony the nonparading Mangue-irenses were screaming at us, to us, for us, in an agony of pride and desire.

Buses stopped on the overpass to watch our stampede. Cars honked in solidarity. We ran and danced and jumped, drunk with space and oxygen after so many weeks in the overstuffed *quadra*. We sang:

> "*Black men dance, sing* jongo, *play* capoeira,
>   *They are the kings, pink and green, of all Mangueira!*"

The crowd on the overpass grew thick. We sang some more:

> " '*Who painted this landscape?*'
>   *We ask the Lord above:*
>   '*So free of slave barracks,*
>   *So full of misery.*' "

We ran to catch up with another wing; stopped when a harmony director performed frantic traffic signals at us; stood in place for little free-form improvisations when time allowed. We executed hairpin turns and doubled the caravan back from the viaduct toward the *quadra* and from the *quadra* to the underpass. With the others, I shouted the song as if only its energy could keep me this side of death, but my legs were shaking. The *bateria* maneuvered its eighth U turn down the block and led the school up the steps into the *quadra* to continue the samba night. In Guezinha's wing, Inez and Elania seemed to have enjoyed the warm-up and were now ready to party. They followed the drummers, but I headed up the hill to sleep, drip-ping wet, shaking with chill in the seventy-degree night. Dona

Neuma, who had been watching from the porch, smiled as she saw me limp by. "Nice, wasn't it?" she said.

The house I had moved into belonged to Dona Esmeralda, a former baiana whom heartbreak and religion had separated from the Mangueira school. At the end of five years during which her husband refused to touch her or admit there was anything wrong with the marriage, he announced he was leaving her for the younger woman he'd been seeing all the while. Her devastation was so great that she lost her faith, and although she was, together with Celina, one of the few properly ordained daughters-of-a-saint on the hill, she renounced *candomblé* and joined a born-again Christian sect in the neighborhood. Under strong pressure from her fundamentalist minister she agreed to give up carnival, although it meant the end of a quarter of a century as a baiana. As it turned out, the withdrawal pangs proved too great to bear: less than a week before the 1987 parade she had appeared on Dona Neuma's doorstep and begged her to find her a costume, any costume—if she didn't parade she would certainly die. That was the year Mangueira won its second championship in a row. But nothing, she swore this year, would make her come out again, not even the possibility of a triple championship. She was not parading, but the pain of the sacrifice was such that she could announce it only by raising her right palm high and shouting "Praise the Lord!" to give her strength.

She was making her way up the hill, returning home after visiting a daughter in the Hot Hole, when I caught up with her. The moon showered light on us, on the garbage piled under a cliff drop where a late-night pig was still rooting, on the teenagers in their corkscrew hairdos and Bermudas flattened against the wall of a shack farther up, waiting for customers with a supermarket bag full of packets of cocaine wrapped in newspaper. "A blessing, Aunt," they asked respectfully as Dona Esmeralda passed.

The blessing was requested of her in her old capacity as a daughter-of-a-saint, but she cheerfully dispensed it regardless, with hardly a break in our conversation. "If I were you I would never have left the rehearsal so early," she was saying. She puffed and put both hands on one knee to push it straight and get herself up on a steep rock. The smooth dirt path sloped up gentle inclines, followed by straight rows of concrete steps bordered by shacks, and in between, untouched stretches of gulches and mudslides on this, the easy way to the top of the hill. "In the old days, I never missed a rehearsal, and I hardly ever left before it was over. I could drink anybody under the table, and when finally everyone was too drunk to stand up but me, I would come home." We had paused for breath on one of the cement steps, in front of two women sharing a drink by a beer stand that was closed for the night. "There was a time when the shortcut up through the back of the Hot Hole was dangerous. But since the boys have been in charge it's safe everywhere, so I would take that path because even though it's steeper, it was easier for me. It's narrow, and there are houses almost all the way to the top. So I'd lean on one house and push myself across to the next one, and then the next one, and I'd think, 'I'm drunk as a skunk!' but I'd keep going. And then when I got to the clearing where there was nothing more to lean on I'd think, 'I'm drunk as a skunk; I'll never make it to the top!' But I'd put my head down, and get a running start, and I always made it to the front door without falling down." The women laughed with us, a little boozily. Dona Esmeralda's speech changed gears. "But God took pity on me, and gave me the strength to give up sin and live a healthy life, and now I'm free of alcohol and evil, praise the Lord!" Her right hand flew up to bear witness.

"Praise the Lord!" the women agreed.

There was no possibility of sleep in the narrow room Dona Esmeralda's family had vacated for me. The walls were burning. The fan, churning full-speed, could not make the air move. Eventually I joined my hosts on the cooler rooftop, dozing uneasily to the train-track rattle of the drums below, soon woken by a swollen red sky that announced yet another day in flames. It was carnival weather.

The Mangueira world of reality and illusion grew secretly in a gigantic tin-roofed hangar halfway between the Old City and the Samba-drome. Early in December the metal skeletons of a dozen carnival floats had been ripped apart, soldered back together and covered with pink-smeared plywood, so that it had eventually become possible to distinguish, amid the jungle-gym confusion of bars and ladders and pink platforms, the differentiated shapes of several lumbering beasts. One skeleton was fleshed out into a stage, another into a ship. Here there were three towers, there a monumental staircase. The floats-to-be loomed alone day after day, ponderous and awkward, while two or three workmen soldered a rung or a column into place and pounded a plywood skin over the top.

One day in mid-January they were finished. A transistor radio shattered the silence. Julinho Mattos, the school *carnavalesco*, moved in with his crew of artisans, and the hammering took on the obsessive rhythm of the *bateria*.

Elíseo Dória arrived with Percy, the rehearsal director, to coordinate the wing chiefs and the directorate, whose members constantly came in with questions about materials, schedules, parade orders, money. Seu Sixteen, a sweet man in his fifties who was in charge of the kitchen, passed around a tray with miniature cups of coffee and glasses of ice water for the carnival plotters. He also slept at the hangar to protect the floats. "Last year they came by in a car and sprayed the entrance with machine-gun fire," he volunteered. Who were "they"? He shrugged. He had a cherubic smile and baby pink skin to match the floats.

While Mangueira worked in privacy and relative comfort in the spacious hangar a few blocks from the Sambadrome, most of the first-division schools had to make do with rented space in the São Cristovão trade pavilion, a few blocks away from the Emperor's Palace and the access road to Mangueira. The crumbling modernist building was the ruin of what had been a 1960s project to revitalize the North Zone by attracting commercial activity on weekends, when the dusty park surrounding the trade center was overrun by impoverished migrants from the barren backlands of Bahia state, gathering there to eat home-style food and sing the keening, desperate music of northern Mexico they have mysteriously adopted as their own. Late on Sunday afternoon the migrants would depart, leaving behind a carpet of beer-bottle caps and gnawed chicken bones, and the grounds would remain silent for the rest of the week.

But during carnival season the pavilion itself filled up every day with welders, carpenters, Styrofoam sculptors. Their work gradually became visible above the plywood fences separating the individual schools' carnival factories. An elephant peeked out over one fence; an Egyptian temple, lovingly detailed in trompe-l'oeil marble, rose over another. In the Vila Isabel compound a gigantic African mask stood guard. Nearby, a clown spraddled on a mountain of yellow and green sheets of paper, intended to represent the new Constitution and the inept Congress charged with drafting it. The carnival workers seemed sullen, but many of them were simply trying to fight heat prostration: the designers of the trade pavilion had neglected to provide air circulation for the crowds they had hoped to attract, and underneath the convex roof heat concentrated as under a magnifying glass, often climbing above 100 degrees. Workers escaped as often as possible to the zinc bars in the busy plaza outside, and the parade took shape slowly.

I went to visit the pavilion for the same reason I had begun to spend a great deal of time at the hangar, in order to escape Mangueira. Less than three days after moving to the hill I got on a bus without looking at the destination, willing to go anywhere that offered a newspaper. After only a week I was overwhelmed by deprivation and a parallel need to spend money. I needed to spend in order to prove that I could still do it, that I would never again have to slice an onion with a chipped knife blade with no handle, or sleep on a single folded-over sheet made out of flour sacking with my ankles sticking out at the end, or eat stringy chicken three days in a row because that was all that was offered on the dusty hilltop—a half-hour's trek from the nearest bus to somewhere. I wanted choices, privacy, freedom and comfort, I craved magazines and fluffy towels. I wanted air-conditioning if I was hot, a hammock if I was listless, a movie when I was bored, and if the coffee container tipped over I did not want to sweep the dirty grounds up off the floor and back into a leaky coffeepot. The near-hysterical longing not to be poor drove me onto a bus and into the hangar neighborhood every afternoon.

I got into the habit of taking myself to lunch in the Old City at one of the outdoor cafés in front of the ornate municipal theater. Provisioned with a stack of newspapers and magazines, I would drink the gamut of available fruit juices and read about Brazil. Intense death-squad activity in the North Zone slums. Indian protests in the Amazons. Jocasta and Oedipus: will they kiss? (This from front-page stories about the leading TV soap opera, a modern-day rendition of the Oedipus legend that was monopolizing the ratings.) The constitutional convention gives sixteen-year-olds the vote. Inflation likely to top 400 percent. War between animal bankers and cocaine lords continues in South Zone favelas. The one-piece bathing suit is back.

There was this story one day in the *Jornal do Brasil* about child neglect and abuse in the flatland slums of the North Zone:

Between January 1987 and July [1988], 306 minors died violent deaths in the municipalities of Nova Iguaçu and Caxias. Many of the children lacked birth certificates, and could be buried only with special authorization from a judge.

And this one, about the preparations made for a visit by President José Sarney to the church where the daughter of one of his political cronies was to get married:

The smell of disinfectants invaded São Francisco Plaza yesterday afternoon, substituting the bad smells left by beggars who have made the plaza their home for many years. The city's sanitation department and the state social services office worked efficiently to make the plaza presentable for President José Sarney.

The food at the downtown cafés was greasy and overabundant, but at least I enjoyed a solitude of sorts, uninterrupted except for the steady stream of beggars, here in this plaza a few blocks away from São Francisco Church, where Sarney's hygiene patrol had not ventured. They were cheerful even as they waved their stumps at you, uncomplaining if you shooed them away. "Ten cruzados?" a little girl suggested. I offered her my pizza instead. "No, thank you, I don't care for pizza, no." At other times a beggar would hurry off to find a plastic bag and empty my plate of leftover steak, french fries, cucumber slices. "The bread too?" The bread too. The waiters didn't like this, but the beggars often came back and said thank you after they'd finished their meal.

After lunch I would progress slowly, so as not to provoke the heat, through Rio's narrow nineteenth-century streets crowded with shops now offering carnival costumes at discount prices; a ballerina outfit for 800 cruzados, a Pierrot, Superman, a tiny bikini with panther spots. I loved the downtown streets because they were several steps removed from the end-of-the-line poverty of Mangueira and yet offered everything wealthy Ipanema lacked: mystery, chaos, weirdness. There was, for one thing, the difficulty of guessing what might go on behind the ornate stucco façades. The tall, once-sumptuous rooms might contain a wicker-chair factory. A contemporary office building sandwiched in between the birthday-cake Portuguese *hôtels de ville* could lead off into an eighteenth-century mews with shoe-repair shops and lunch counters wedged among skinny houses painted in bright pastels. Inside the eyeless windows of a colonial ruin a family might be living, crouched away from the street's glare, with an electric hotplate burning on the wood plank floor and a clothesline stretching from wall to wall. And in front of all that unknown life playing itself out on hidden stages were the churches and record stores and pastry shops and the constant bright bustle of the street.

The downtown area ended at a shady park where agoutis, strange large rodents, nibbled peacefully on the grass and watched out for tidbits from the noontime crowd. Beyond the park there was no relief from the sun in a succession of warehouse-lined streets that led northward to the Sambadrome. The silence was unsettling, imploding as it did so close to the deafening blasts of traffic on the other side of the park. In the most scorched, treeless street of all, a pink garage door announced Mangueira.

Human figures had begun to take form in the hangar's shadows. One afternoon a giant fist, taller than a man, appeared lying on its side between two of the floats. The next day two men sanded down a plaster woman wearing a simple shift, one leg poised in the air, an arm drifting out in a dancing posture. The blue-eyed woman in a face mask, Anastácia, loomed large in a corner. There was a child, a sprite with a red cap and a pipe in one hand whose hips tapered down into a single leg. On the floor behind another float lay a black man, his knees bent in a sitting position, his arms up to support a load. With three other black column-bearers he would be placed on a platform at the head of a palatial staircase, supporting a giant cupola which was now getting a coat of gold paint. This was to be the luxurious backdrop for Princess Isabel, who signed the decree abolishing slavery. Julinho supervised its decoration carefully, trying out different shades of gold until he found a variation with a burnished coppery tint.

Julinho had a drooping white moustache, and he liked to wear a cap on top of an early Beatles haircut. Other than that, he dressed in the favelado uniform: rubber flip-flops and shorts. He exuded the relaxed bonhomie cultivated by white Brazilian men, but questions about his craft invariably made him shifty: it was difficult to maintain his sense of himself as a craftsman when the media focused increasingly on *carnavalescos* with fine-arts studies who aspired to genius. When I asked him how he, a white man, had come up with the idea of a black parade theme, he squirmed. "I have a black dentist, I have a black accountant. We all make money off blacks, so I figured, what the hell, don't they deserve it?"

He gave me his card, which had a picture of a church and a calendar printed on the other side: "JuMats. Everything for carnival. New and used floats. Sculptures in general," with an address out in the suburbs. He had a gigantic warehouse there, where he stored each year's leftover papier-mâché sculptures. In the course of the year he sold them to small provincial schools for their carnivals. He also offered a package, which included a scripted parade theme, float designs, costume sketches for the whole school and a taped story samba written by one of his in-house composers. "That's how I make my money," he said. "Last year, aside from the first prize with Mangueira I got sixteen other first prizes in schools around the country. You should check out the carnival in Acre. Best one in Brazil. I designed the parade for several of their schools." It seemed strange that this frontier state only recently stripped of its Amazonic jungle covering should excel at a festivity heavily dependent on tradition. "Doesn't matter," said Julinho. "They're into it. But every idea I come up with."

Princess Isabel walked into the hangar in the person of a tall blonde named Marlene Arruda. On parade morning she would stand in front of the four black plaster-cast column-bearers, clothed from neck to toe in some twenty kilos of sequins and satin, and smile, and she was preparing meticulously for the moment. She had come to confirm a suspicion that hit her at the costume try-on; the train of her dress was larger than the platform she was supposed to stand on, and the hem would drape over the edge. Julinho knew better than to suggest that she shorten the dress. Arruda, the wife of a supermarket chain owner, had been occupying the star position on Mangueira floats for more than a decade, paying for costumes that were said to cost upward of $1,000, and she was not about to diminish her impact by cutting back on a hem, particularly because she would later exhibit the dress at one of the fancy costume balls that are the chief carnival activity for a peculiar sector of the Brazilian moneyed class.

Julinho said he would do something about extending the front of the platform and Marlene climbed down off the float. She wore elaborate jewelry and makeup uncorrupted by sweat even in the concentrated heat of the hangar, and her manner was society cool, but she said that in her day she had been a nonstop sambista, back in the early 1960s, when together with another young white woman, Regina Esberard, she became the first nonpoor white to parade with a samba school.

The media called them debutantes but in fact they were nice middle-class girls from Julinho's neighborhood, São Cristovão, pretty and blonde and well behaved and as mystifying to the Mangueirenses, one would imagine, as the school must have seemed to them when they first arrived at a rehearsal back in the old *quadra*, a plain adobe house in the Hot Hole lacking even an outdoor latrine. Looking back, Marlene couldn't really explain what got into the two of them to start hanging out at the funky Mangueira dances. At least on her part it wasn't daring, she said, because she was excruciatingly shy at the time. Regina, who became famous as "Gigi of Mangueira," actually invented steps that were more explicit than the black sambistas'. Marlene, more restrained, remained in the background, terrified of dancing in public until she found herself in the old staging ground for the parade, on Rio Branco Avenue, at the start of her first carnival, "and the *empolgação*, the fervor, hit me: I went nuts! I danced, I screamed, I don't know what I did!" Her careful smile relaxed for a moment into a grin. "Never before or since have I experienced anything that carried me away so completely. It was the most fulfilling experience of my life."

She has paraded ever since, and for years she made a point of coming out "on the ground" at carnival time. This is an expression of authenticity among sambistas, meaning that the parader is not seeking individual glory or a position of privilege. On the ground with the wings is where the collective experience of joy takes place, distinct and superior to the emotionally and physically restrained participation of the "standouts," or lavishly costumed protagonists on the floats. Samba schools negotiate to have television stars and famous singers appear as standouts every year, and the television cameras focus on these stars at parade time. But when celebrities wish to express their "heart" allegiance to a given school, they come out on the ground.

Marlene was a standout not as a celebrity but because she was one of the select few Brazilians with the patience and the money to invest every year in a lavish costume. Female celebrity standouts often wear as little clothing as possible. Costume standouts aim for the exact opposite, wearing as much weight as they can physically carry, and even adding to the surface area of the costume by means of a waist strap into which a voluminous "halo" is inserted. Marlene said it was the question of coverage that got her off the ground and onto the floats in the first place. "The ground costumes started getting really skimpy. You can afford to wear something like that when you're young, but after a point it didn't look good on me anymore." Which was convenient for Mangueira, since a trusted school member who was willing to pay for her own extravagant display of rhinestones was a valuable asset. Marlene was a true Mangueirense and a very professional standout. For her it wasn't just a question of standing there in her glitter; she swayed atop the float, sang, smiled and waved at the audience. "If you don't, you get catcalls. There's training involved, no doubt about it! My secret is, I go to the rehearsals every Saturday to get in shape for the season, and I tuck a caramel in the back of my mouth so I can keep singing for an hour and a half." As a reward for her commitment she always got the plum parts, like the role of Princess Isabel in the current script.

Whether Princess Isabel had really been the star of the abolition drama is a subject of often vicious debate among traditional and revisionist historians and the black movement, a debate in which Julinho sided with the traditionalists. He had learned the official history in school: Blacks had been enslaved, which was a bad thing; after some debate, the Crown sided with the forces of enlightenment and signed the "Golden Law" abolishing slavery, and that was a good thing. Even better, for carnival purposes, the decree had been signed by a princess.

Yet for his fellow white, the composer Helinho Turco, the figure of Princess Isabel and indeed the abolition decree itself were in need of revision. Helinho—gray-haired, wiry and bespectacled—liked the hangar, and he could spend whole afternoons there hunched on a narrow wooden bench, sipping Seu Sixteen's coffee and exchanging gossip with the rest of the carnival crew. Like most Mangueira whites, he was slightly more prosperous than the favela's black majority; he didn't need a job because he owned a small hardware store that essentially ran itself, and in his youth his family's relative privilege had ensured him access to a better education. He spoke with authority about Brazilian history, and when he explained how he and his two composing teammates had crafted the winning story samba that year he was quick to point out his disagreement with the whole idea of a golden Princess Isabel float. "It was a great act of cowardice, the abolition decree," he said sternly. "Just think: Before, the owner of a plantation had to feed and clothe and house the slave and his entire family; then one day the decree was signed, and all the blacks were out on the street. It was the plantation owner who became free, free to pay the black man half of what he used to pay him before, in real terms, while the former slave was left to fend for himself."

So the revisionist historians insist, arguing that in decreeing abolition the Crown was simply bowing to historic inevitability, given both international pressure and the mechanization of the sugar industry. The 1888 abolition decree had been preceded by an 1871 "Law of the Free Womb" that granted freedom to all the offspring of slaves, and an 1885 law granting freedom to those lucky enough to survive in slavery past the age of sixty. Together with the well-established practice of granting loyal slaves their freedom on their masters' death-bed, and the relative ease with which slaves could purchase their freedom from Brazil's impoverished gentry, a significant percentage of blacks—probably around half—were already free by the time Princess Isabel followed her father's instructions in 1888 and signed. Even if she hadn't, the 1871 law ensured that the entire black population would have been free in another generation at most. What the abolition decree did accomplish, as Helinho pointed out, was the preemption of any demand for reparations by the former owners.

Helinho's story samba (described in the media as "militant") asked, "Is liberty really here or was it just an illusion?" But neither Mangueira nor Julinho was willing to challenge the status quo further. Vila Isabel, on the other hand, whose script ostensibly covered the same ground, ignored Princess Isabel (even though she was the school's, and its neighborhood's, namesake) and the abolition law altogether. The school leaders had concluded that there was not much to celebrate about the centennial anniversary of the end of slavery, and opted instead for a plot entitled "Kizomba: A Feast for the Black Race," an exaltation of black culture and history in Brazil proposed by Martinho da Vila, the composer whose wife was now president of the school. Vila Isabel's celebration of Brazilian blackness relied heavily on traditional African tribal culture, but there was also the usual small roster of Brazilian characters used many times before and being used this year as well by Mangueira.

Foremost was Zumbi. "Hail Zumbi, it was not in vain!" is how Vila Isabel's story samba opened. And Mangueira sang, "I dreamt of Zumbi of Palmares' return." But his story was translatable into carnival floats only if some of its more essential facts were glossed over.

Zumbi was one of a long chain of rebel leaders at Palmares who used guerrilla warfare to defy white authority with extraordinary success, but he was ultimately defeated. With his death, and the end of the Palmares federation, the political history of Brazilian blacks almost appeared to come to a halt, and to mention him in the context of abolition was hardly to provoke rejoicing: while there had been other, isolated, black rebellions following the destruction of Palmares, they did not build on one another or constitute in themselves a serious challenge to the established order. The most spectacular and best-documented nineteenth-century slave uprising—again, unknown to most blacks—took place in Bahia in 1835 and lasted just over three hours; when the abolition debate monopolized public discourse half a century later, the issue was Brazil's standing among the industrial nations and not the threat posed by the slaves. This was hardly material for a triumphant parade, but could one then look to the historical figure of Zumbi himself for inspiration? He left no writings, and oral tradition preserved nothing of his speeches, deeds or personality; he had survived—and only barely—in this century's memory endowed with a few historical facts but as impersonal as an archangel. One could ask if his spirit lived on after the end of slavery in the acts of other black leaders; if there had been founders of black unions or education funds, political parties or voting-rights movements who could claim the warrior slave's mantle. But at least according to both the official and the carnival versions of history, there were none. For parade purposes, he was useful as an archetype: the Hero in all his phases, rebel, warrior, king, martyr. And ultimately, it was at this deepest level, where the facts and the dates didn't matter, that he was so powerfully resonant to blacks. Whether he had died fighting or thrown himself off a cliff, whether he was defeated or, as Vila Isabel's story samba prudently put it, he had "influenced abolition," hardly seems relevant to those who, ever since the place and circumstances of his death became known, travel to the hillside where he last fought, and weep.

Having resurfaced in carnival memory thanks to Fernando Pamplona, the Hero gradually was incorporated into official history, and the public figure of Zumbi increasingly became the product of both. In 1986, during the administration of the populist Leonel Brizola, governor of the state of Rio de Janeiro, a bust of the warrior was finally placed in the middle of President Vargas Avenue, on the spot once called Little Africa, the plaza where black carnival first began under the leadership of so many famous bambas and baianas. But the plaza no longer exists, and the bust atop its pedestal is removed from pedestrians and is almost unnoticeable in the rush of traffic. Zumbi, Brazil's major black political figure, presides invisibly over a stretch of pavement directly in front of the Sambadrome, a hero only of carnival culture. (And typically, the bust has its facts wrong: in all likelihood Zumbi was of Angolan descent, a Bantu, but the statue represents the head of a Nigerian.)

At Humberto de Campos Elementary School in Mangueira—where all the teachers are white and all the pupils are black—I asked the principal if the hero of Palmares was part of the children's curriculum. "Only because the teachers here make a point of it," she said. "But he's still not in the textbooks." The teacher of a second-grade class asked the children if they remembered what they had been taught about Zumbi. Indeed they did, they yelled out. He had been their favorite subject. Questions about Zumbi received prompt, enthusiastic answers. "He was a hero!" "He fought so blacks would be free!" And what had they liked best about him? "The fact that he worked so hard," a little boy volunteered. "And that he didn't give up," added a girl. "The part I liked best," said a shy little girl with a big smile, "is when Zumbi got to marry Princess Isabel."

The floats grew, the costumes took shape, the heat magnified. I slept on the roof again, a muddy slumber stirred thickly with images of the *quadra*, frantic dancing, the smell of the glue with which I'd been pasting sequin drops on Ceci's African costumes, the soughing, shifting noises of the family around me. Someone came in late from rehearsal and hauled a mattress up to the roof. One of the children paced restlessly, called to the *quadra* by the persistent roar of the drums. He lay down in a far corner and sighed, got up again and danced, lay down, got up. "Quit that!" someone yelled sharply. We slept.

10 *Mid-January*

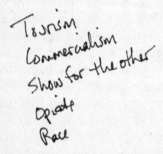

Tourism.
Commercialism
Show for the other
Opiate
Race

In the middle of January, Brazil's gigantic television network, TV Globo, won a round in its ongoing fight with the much smaller TV Manchete and obtained exclusive broadcast rights for the samba schools' parade. Ever since the 1960s the nightlong parades have been broadcast live in their entirety, beginning on carnival Saturday, when the second-division schools take over the Sambadrome, and ending mid-morning on carnival Tuesday, when the final first-division school's parade closes the carnival season. By tradition, broadcast rights had belonged to the state tourism agency, Riotur, which used to offer them to both Globo and its four-year-old competitor at a fixed price.

Just as traditionally, the Association of Samba Schools had had little say in the negotiations, and the schools received only a small percentage of the broadcast money. But that was changing fast. Whereas a decade earlier the samba schools had been scruffy organizations whose directors felt uncomfortable in the presence of a check, the influence of the animal bankers had made them all financially knowledgeable. Then Beija-Flor's Aniz Abrahão David led most of the major samba schools in a break from the sclerotic Association of Samba Schools and formed the League of Samba Schools, headed by financially adroit animal bankers like Aniz and Vila Isabel's Captain Guimarães. The cause of the split was something the animal bankers knew and Rio's official carnival establishment had long been happy to ignore: there might be carnival balls and beach concerts and neighborhood parades and a carnival queen, but the biggest tourist draw and only profit generator for carnival was the samba school parade, which made money for everyone but the schools.

It was sufficient for the League to state this uncomfortable truth and threaten to move its parade to the North Zone suburbs, for Riotur to agree to a drastic revision of its traditional carnival arrangements; for the 1988 parade the schools were guaranteed a forty-percent cut on Sambadrome ticket sales. The League also broke the long-standing arrangement between the story-samba composers and the Top-Tape record company and set up its own recording company, which now puts out a record with the first-division story sambas every December and which increased the composers' advance on royalties almost a hundredfold in the first years of the arrangement. And whereas in 1984, when the League was first formed, TV Globo's contract with Riotur awarded the schools a total equal to $80,000 for broadcast rights, a new arrangement imposed by the League in 1988 extracted a million-dollar contract, of which Riotur was grateful to receive ten percent. But the agency was still refusing to grant the League's most radical demand: that Riotur rent the Sambadrome out to the League for the carnival season for a fixed rate and let the schools keep the profits. Riotur regularly made such an arrangement with other performers, but only the samba schools had the audience to fill the Sambadrome to eighty-thousand capacity for three nights running, at prices that went as high as $16,000 for a private box: the agency was understandably reluctant to give up this single major source of income.

To compensate for what it had already lost, the incoming president of Riotur, Alfredo Laufer, announced that it was his mandate to turn carnival into a "profit-making enterprise," and decreed a 700-percent increase in ticket prices for the Sambadrome. This meant that the cheapest ticket would sell for the equivalent of about $40 —equal to one month's minimum wage—and that no one below the upper middle class would have access to Rio's most traditional form of popular entertainment. When the media relayed the citywide howl of outrage, Laufer pointed out that there was a provision for free tickets for favelados, which Celina just as quickly took advantage of. "Do you know any foreigners who want to buy cheap tickets to the parade?" she asked me one day. "A friend of mine got some free ones, and she'll split the profit with me if I can sell them." As for her own family, rather than spend the equivalent of a month's minimum wage on one night, no matter how special, they would watch the parade, as always, on television.

The estimated television audience for the two first-division school parade nights was about forty million or nearly twenty-five percent of the Brazilian population, an audience that did not necessarily peak at the beginning of the broadcast; regulations specified that the two parade nights would open with the previous year's two lowest-ranking schools and that the rest of the parade order would be determined by a lottery draw. This year Mangueira was supposed to close the second night—or morning, in fact, since its parade was scheduled for 5:30 a.m. There was no question that it would draw one of the largest audiences.

Advertisers were bidding frantically for all the time slots, and already, while TV Manchete took TV Globo and Riotur to court in a desperate effort to rescind Globo's exclusive broadcast rights, both stations were flooded with carnival ads. A supermarket chain used one of the traditional instruments in the *bateria*—a frying pan beat with a fork or stick—to play a little samba riff. Others advertised a "carnival of prices." Tennis shoes were shown dancing a samba beat. And those unable to buy advertising time—or unsatisfied with so little—tried other ways of catching the camera's eye. Kodak set up a gigantic blimp with its logo at the foot of the Sambadrome, where it could hardly be missed in long shots. Soft-drink companies fought for hot-dog–stand franchises. And there were frenzied negotiations with the schools and Riotur to persuade the only noncostumed members of the parade, the float pullers, to wear T-shirts with commercial logos. The debate on whether schools should accept commercial sponsorship was taken up again on television among the school presidents, and the answer was not an unqualified no, but only, "Not this year."

While doubts remained about commercial sponsorship, the schools sought funding wherever possible. Cardboard fans printed with the story-samba lyrics, distributed at rehearsals, always had a sponsor whose pitch appeared on the reverse side. "Congressman Rubem Medina, City Council Member Tulio Simões and Casa Queiroz (Shoes and Bags for Men, Women and Children) Wish You a Happy Carnival" said the fan from Vila Isabel.

To advertise the coming all-night broadcasts, TV Globo brought out story-samba music videos, which played during station breaks and featured the schools in last year's costumes singing this year's song. And Globo instructed its writers to promote carnival by writing allusions to it into the soap operas. Thus, after the fateful televised kiss and under heavy pressure from government censors, Globo moved Jocasta away from Oedipus toward other, more mature relationships, and introduced her to an animal banker, who took the heroine to visit his samba school while her son sulked at home. TV Manchete, which as the underdog was the favorite in the favelas, did not pump its programming full of carnival spots. Instead, it devoted ten minutes at the end of the local news to carnival reporting, with folksy interviews with old-timers, reverent interviews with the *carnavalescos* and, here and there, in the background, as an octogenarian quavered through an old samba or a majordomo showed off his steps, a glimpse of a favela. "They showed our house!" shrieked my hosts' children when I arrived one night, irritable and gummy with sweat. "The helicopter filmed it and it was on television!" Samba stars. Kings for a day.

There were, in truth, a few ways the Mangueirenses could fish in the river of money carnival generated. I found Celina in a dreamy mood on a sweltering afternoon that had driven everyone else on the hill to extremes of bad humor. She was sitting alone in her dark room, unaccompanied even by the television set, which had burned its tube and was now turned on only in the evenings so the family could follow at least the dialogue of the Oedipus soap. Celina had been worried lately, about money as usual, and about a godson who had gotten drunk and insulted her over New Year's and then made her truly unhappy when he appeared dead in a garbage dump in the North Zone, and she had also been suffering from a mysterious illness that blew her legs up until they burst into sores and had her groaning from the pain in her stomach. But she had cured herself with leaves picked from a tree outside Dona Neuma's house and recovered enough to go on an outing to a cruise ship that docked the previous evening in Rio harbor. It had been a wonderful evening, Celina said, leaning back on the sofa and gently paddling the air with her legs as if she were sitting on the edge of the ship's sparkling pool. "The ship was like a palace. So beautiful! Lit up and glowing all over on the outside, full of mirrors inside. And we had our own dressing room, with all the cold soft drinks we wanted, and sandwiches. Quality sandwiches. Tasty.

"Then they took us upstairs for the show and we danced and at the end we each had a rose in our hand, which we had to give to a foreigner. That was nice. They loved it! Some of them stood up to samba with us. Well, not to samba, really, but just to sort of jump about. Anyway, they enjoyed it, and that was the important thing. I don't know where they were from. Tall. Blond. All of them with blue or green eyes. They certainly didn't speak Portuguese, and since they knew we didn't understand them, they didn't speak much to us at all. They just gave funny little whoops. 'Ooy!' 'Oopsie!' 'Aw!' they went. And they smiled at us as wide as they could. It was a very good outing." And, she added, she got paid 400 cruzados (about $4.50) for the evening, plus the food.

If Celina saw it as her duty to pick up whatever money became available during the season, a great deal of the official carnival effort in 1988 was geared to making sure that no coins fell out of the government's coffers. Laufer announced a crackdown on the traditional system of extending patronage by handing out press credentials, and he let the League of Samba Schools know that each school would have to announce the total number of members in the parade in advance, and that inflexible controls would be exercised to make sure no unauthorized school hangers-on made their way onto the parade grounds.

Seu Tinguinha's son, Rato, in charge of the harmony department, held a meeting one evening at the hangar to explain the new rules to his sector captains, the twelve men in charge of supervising Mangueira's fifty-six wing chiefs. Rato was very much Seu Tinguinha's son, tall and straight-backed and inordinately courteous. But he was also a man of the modern world, a moderately prosperous car dealer concerned with things like balanced budgets and clockwork schedules. He started the meeting on time even though some of the captains were late, and began by explaining the tight new rules that would govern access to the Sambadrome on parade morning, which, Rato said, would work very much in the directorate's favor. As everyone knew, the school had gotten too large, and shortly before his death Carlos Dória had taken the drastic step of closing down six wings, bringing the total number of paraders down from last year's six thousand to this year's programmed fifty-three hundred. It was essential now, Rato stressed, to keep interlopers away: "Unauthorized paraders directly affect the school's performance," he repeated. "We plan and rehearse the timing for five thousand paraders and suddenly we're in the Sambadrome and there's six thousand people taking up space and time and spoiling our rhythm. We can lose critical points for that."

Rato's main problem was controlling the wing chiefs, who liked to sell many more costumes than the authorized total and keep the profits. This year, he warned, nobody was going to get away with that: "On the night before the parade all of you will get decals for each of your sectors. There's only going to be fifty-three hundred of them, and whoever isn't wearing one won't be allowed into the Sambadrome on parade morning. Is that clear?"

At the previous meeting he had asked the sector captains to prepare a signed statement certifying that each of the wings in their charge was producing the right amount of costumes and that they met quality standards. Of course there was nothing to prevent a sector captain from lying in collusion with his wing chiefs, and Rato knew that, but the signed certification was intended to provide a measure of accountability—a fact that was understood either too clearly or not at all by one of the captains, a Mangueirense who had arrived too late to catch the first part of the speech and now knew only that he was being asked to sign something.

He was a bamba's bamba. He had been a part of the carnival world since before Rato was born, and he understood the importance of things Rato preferred to ignore: not leaning on people too hard, making allowances for a wing chief trying to make a little money out of all that hard work, handing out a free costume here and there to keep spirits up. This bamba was a master in the art of hanging out. I had seen him spend whole afternoons, whole evenings, whole days, moving from a doorstep to a card table to a beer stand and back to a doorstep in the Hot Hole, chatting companionably with whoever cared to stop and trade a few words, beating gently on a tambourine until the samba ring was formed, nursing a beer, slowing time down. His circumlocutory, under-the-breath way of speaking left much unstated and much in doubt, and this was his preference: if things are left vague they can always be redefined later more advantageously. Nothing went more deeply against his grain than a definite commitment that locked a situation into rigidity, deprived it of flow. So when Rato asked him for the letter he first feigned surprise:

"What letter? I thought this was a meeting!" Rato explained the letter. "You don't need a letter from me, my man; take my word for it, everything's under control. . . ." Then say so on paper, Rato requested. "Wait a minute, wait a minute! What good will a letter do if there are any problems? Where will that get us?" "But you just said there were no problems." "Did I say that? Did anybody hear me say that? Of course there are a few little problems here and there. . . . When has there ever been a carnival with no problems? What good would a carnival be without a few little snags, those little hitches that make it . . . but you know what I'm talking about! Trust me: by carnival week everything will be ready. I will deliver, I promise you. You know me! Have I ever let you down?"

Rato was patient. He spoke quietly: "You're talking like the old days, brother. We can't do things like that anymore. Carnival is practically on top of us and we need to know where all of you stand, and the carnival commission needs to know where Mangueira stands, and we need to have firm control of our numbers. At this point I don't really care if every single one of your costumes isn't ready. I want you to sign the letter so we know where to assign responsibility if something goes wrong with one of your wings."

This last item was really too much for the bamba, who had insinuated himself into the middle of the circle and was now standing directly in front of Rato, using shrugs and head bobs and sweeping waves of the arm to appeal to all the sector captains as he told his story, and the story of the bus strike and of the seamstress's arthritis and of the little old lady who wept because she couldn't pay for her costume and was preventing one of his chiefs from completing his group. Would Rato prefer to evict the old lady? Was he, a bamba to the marrow, to be blamed for his soft heart? Was his wing chief to be punished for showing kindness? It went unsaid, but you could read the implied question in the air, the appeal to all those present: My friends, this is carnival? This red tape and heartlessness are what we stand for?

The other sector captains' sympathies might have been with him, but the official carnival structure was making very specific demands on Rato. If he conceded the bamba's points, the school was lost, and so the discussion continued almost for form's sake, letting the bamba talk himself around into eventual compliance with the rules.

In the meantime I toured the floats Julinho was tending. Unmindful of the argument as he was of the wheeling and dealing and pleading that went on around the clock among Percy, Elíseo Dória and the various carnival notables and suppliants, Julinho and his half-dozen assistants painted and hammered at a steady pace. Except for the slave ship, which Julinho was saving for last, most of the floats were now laminated, painted and equipped with allegorical statues, and the white plaster-cast figures were in the process of acquiring skins of paint. Two women in simple shifts with baskets of laundry on their heads were turning glowing brown, joining a fellow baiana who was already black and who dominated the center of this "reality" float with her ruffled white costume, tray of sweets and beckoning smile. Elsewhere there were African masks, a giant woman's head in a baiana turban and gold hoop earrings, and a pair of outstretched hands which were now getting positioned below the two clenched fists on one of the larger floats. I thought the float had political significance, but Julinho explained that it was supposed to represent agriculture, that the fists would be holding sugar cane and the hands would carry seeds. He lit another cigarette and staple-gunned a few plastic orchids around the base of the float for Slave Anastácia. Nearby, his voice fraying, Rato continued to explain the rules of modern carnival to the bamba.

I made my way through the empty downtown streets to President Vargas Avenue. Two bus strikes in a row had turned the brief trip back to the hill into a suffocating odyssey—a desperate fight to hang on to the edge of a rare bus while crowds tried to get out and hordes tried to get on. There had been public workers' strikes, bank strikes and hospital strikes, and teachers had gone on strike so often for an improvement in their sixty-seven-dollar monthly wages that the children in Mangueira's Humberto de Campos Elementary School would probably not be able to fulfill their semester requirements. Now a strike was threatening on the samba line—the train that carried workers to the city from the northern suburbs on normal days and transported the costumed sambistas to the Sambadrome for carnival. The crowds waiting for a bus in front of Central Station seemed just fractions away from hysteria. There was a roll of thunder, and lightning sliced through the gathering night.

For days the clouds had been convening, rolling in just to the edges of the city, drifting above the highest hills, merging into larger, darker banks. They sank lower and lower under their own weight until Rio felt their oppression, a thick cloud cover stoppering the heat wave beneath. Restless, the clouds rumbled, but nothing broke. In Mangueira, the children scampered with their kites down the ravines, and in the afternoons, when the wind blew and brought more clouds, the kites skipped just under their surface, bright lozenges of china blue and scarlet bouncing off the dark cloud bellies and dipping down again. I followed their trail up the hill to Dona Esmeralda's, where the family dog was flattened against the tiles under the kitchen table, whimpering from the heat. The metal folding chair I'd brought burned my legs, the sheets on the mattress were scorching. I showered and changed clothes and headed for the bottom of the hill, where it was hotter.

A strong wind rose and cooled the little plaza. Eurides shouted me down and caught up with me at a trot, breathless with excitement and the effort of carrying the changeling Anderson, now a chubby, cooing little boy fairly bursting out of his glowing skin. "Look!" she said, holding up a bag of almost fresh shrimp. "I got these free from the fish truck!"

11 *Late January*

Toward the end of the month, we made a tour of the schools, following their path along the railroad's samba line, hunting down their lights, slipping into pockets of frenzy and noise. In the unfamiliar *quadras* we felt disembodied, unreal, and looked for the secrets we needed to turn ourselves to flesh; sensing our own strangeness and silence within them, we would leave them behind and move on.

São Carlos hill is where we started, where the first of all the samba schools was founded. Its descendant is Estácio de Sá; small, unfashionable, rough. No middle-class whites here at the foot of São Carlos hill, so close to the Old City. No cars snuffling at the curb for parking spaces in front of the small, unadorned *quadra*, no cloud of smoke from hot-dog vendors' grills, no crowds. No rehearsal as such. Only men dancing in couples and women dancing in groups on a pitted concrete floor where once I saw two gays perform an exquisite partnered samba, the woman's role taken by a tall light-skinned boy in a Little Richard pouf and tiny shorts, and the man's by a tough, wiry *malandro* who circled his partner in sharp-edged steps, oblivious to the occasional audience that gathered to watch, to the change in music and to an altercation that sent half the other dancers fanning out away from a spot where someone had pulled a gun. A few doors away from the white-and-red Estácio *quadra*, prostitutes paraded in front of their brightly painted shacks, in an alleyway that held the last remnants of the dense network of brothels this part of Rio was once famous for. The alley was as intensely lit as a stage, with red and orange light bulbs, a time transplant from some other age, some other movie. Beyond it and the *quadra*'s string of light bulbs, nothing stopped the eye in the desolate expanse of President Vargas Avenue.

Midway between Estácio and Mangueira we found the sidewalk in front of the Maxwell Club deserted. The Vila Isabel school had finally found rehearsal space in this old dance hall on a dark street, near the heart of its home neighborhood's strip of restaurants and clubs, but a heavy air of depression and defeat covered the entrance like a shield. We heard a *batucada* coming faint and smothered through the empty lobby, and fled.

At the Salgueiro turnstile a woman patted me down for weapons and waved me into a *quadra* of unimagined opulence and distinction. Facing the *bateria* and above tiers of boxes, four Styrofoam horsemen wearing Austrian Empire helmets greeted us on white Styrofoam stallions. Several dozen hopped-up drummers stood on a tower edged in mirror and blinking with neon. In the tiers of boxes around three of the four walls, beautiful white women and bejeweled men in fancy shirts drank from rows of champagne and whiskey bottles at their tables. I thought of Mangueira's scruffy drummers on their concrete platform, the six mezzanine balconies that were almost always empty, and felt sad. In the bars and buses of Rio that month, the general conclusion was that Salgueiro looked like a championship school for the first time since its last victory in 1975. Its theme—Brazil's successive squandering of its natural riches, from gold to coffee to oil— was suggestive, and wild rumors were out as to how the school was handling it: that one of the floats would be a realistic representation of the open-pit gold mines of the Amazons; that the school's most famous standout, a man who always appeared as the school's patron deity, Xangô, would this time represent the god of fire and lightning covered in real gold dust; that thanks to the generosity of several animal bankers the production budget was many times the official Riotur grant of nearly $160,000. Everywhere on the Salgueiro floor, throngs of dancers were dedicated to their task like miners, extracting rhythm and sweat out of the night, searching for victory. They jostled for space between tables, near the turnstiles, next to the toilets. Intoxicated by their own numbers, the dancers sang, "My costume is worth its weight in gold, / My treasures fill the avenue!" The whole scene conveyed a wretched certainty that whatever chance Mangueira still had of making its third championship in a row was being torched at Salgueiro.

We traveled north toward the other major cluster of samba schools, following the train tracks to Oswaldo Cruz and Madureira. Each suburb we passed was a web of silence with sparkling activity at the hub: restaurants, samba clubs, *candomblé* and *umbanda* temples, and then more darkness until the next train station generated commerce and light. On a side street in Oswaldo Cruz the blue-and-white Portela *quadra* was dark. The school had moved its rehearsals to a nightclub in the South Zone, in search of well-heeled customers.

Império Serrano—the Empire of the Hills school—had the best *quadra*. Old, tatty and root, it boasted a mural of the warrior god Ogun in his guise as St. George along one wall and a bust of one of its founders at the entrance. The shooting of its president, Aromatic Maruf, four months before, on the final harvest night, had kept sambistas away for weeks, but now we had to struggle to get in: security guards barely held back the mob.

On the mezzanine balcony an ancient member of the *bateria* started to clap his cymbals together and midway into the gesture flung his arms out and bent double over the railing. An alert drummer behind pulled him back and saved him from throwing up directly on the dancers, while the rest of the *bateria*, never losing a beat, closed ranks over the spot where the old drunk had stood.

On the worn wood dance floor, the sambistas displayed a style more elaborate and less frenzied than Mangueira's. The crowd was mostly black, bamba, relaxed and happy, but they had none of Salgueiro's carnival momentum: the feverish joy that turns a carnival song into a hymn, its theme into a cause. The school's samba was hardly sung outside the neighborhood; the theme—the beauty of old Rio—had not captured the city's imagination, and the school was not wealthy this year. Several shepherds put a long line of school members through their paces behind the school's green-and-white flag, but despite the hardworking dancers and the men in the *bateria* who drummed like lightning, the real energy was concentrated in the periphery and outside the *quadra*, in a galaxy of street parties taking place among the stands of an improvised open-air market. We bought roast corn and cubes of greasy, chewy grilled meat on sticks and moved on.

On a hillocky empty lot not far from Portela we wandered among the followers of its rival, Tradição. Tradition was the first entirely new school in Rio in more than two decades, and in only four years it had consolidated itself as a split from the grand old Portela school, making the leap from the fourth division, whose schools parade on the streets of the North Zone on the Friday before carnival, to first place in the second division, which comes out on carnival Saturday in the Sambadrome. The school was now rehearsing for its debut first-division parade in this empty lot with no sound system and no dance floor. Attendance here was mostly a demonstration of loyalty, and Tradição commanded a lot of it. Among the clusters of followers trying to dance to the unamplified drums we heard them boast of the school's heart, and energy and root, and of Portela's fear. As at the Empire school, the larger party was taking place on the other side of the fence, where hundreds of people toured the sidewalk stalls. Vendors offered bottles of *cachaça*—sugar-cane alcohol—steeped with passion fruit, pineapple, ground peanuts or basil. Established *pagodes*, or samba revival groups, set up parties near the *cachaça* stands with drums, a *cuíca* and a guitar. People approached to listen and stayed to sing and clap out rhythms, and couples danced gently on the fringes of the samba circles to old melancholy sambas and call-and-response chants.

Floating through the North Zone's night we had learned some secrets and felt almost vivid enough to sweat as one with the mysterious crowds. But we knew we lacked more, and we returned to Mangueira via Vila Isabel, where the samba clubs were just closing up. At Mangueira, where the rehearsal was peaking, crowded and loud, we knew the words, the rituals and the codes needed to dance and shout with joy. It was hard to understand how anywhere on that same night a world without samba nights could have existed.

Celina, who rarely went to the *quadra*, was where she preferred to be, out in the clearing next to Dona Neuma's bedroom window, leading the singing at the Dancing Days restaurant's *pagode*. The *pagode* sambas were unlike any played on the radio or in the *quadra*; mournful and nostalgic songs about love lost and unrequited, weeping and a bitter life. A pretty young white woman who had not joined in the singing came over to talk, effusive and affectionate. "I'm not from Mangueira either," she said. "I'm just here with my friend, who's come to pick up some stuff." She pulled me by the hand toward the opposite end of the samba ring. "Come and meet him!" Her friend was tall and very black, with a belly like a tomcat's and a crinkly beard, and he spoke in a soft growl. We were standing next to his consignment of cocaine packets, exchanging banalities, when I saw Celina coming purposefully at us. "Can I be introduced to your friends?" she demanded, hands on hips.

On the way back to the proper side of the ring I protested that she would never have interfered with my right to speak to the local traffickers. "That's not the point," she said primly. "He's not from this hill."

Dona Neuma sat in her bathrobe in the front room, disheveled and unhappy, listening to the pounding drums beneath her window. "The next time, I'm calling the police, I swear," she muttered. "These people think carnival is nothing but party time, but we have work to do. They have the whole hill to play their drums, they can go any goddamn where they please, and the only spot they can think of is right outside my window!" Two rows of sleepers lay on the floor next to her chair. They had worked long past midnight on the costumes and were too exhausted to pay attention to the noise, much less her monologue. "That is a no-account bunch of people out there," Neuma continued in her lonely rage. "*Malandros* of the worst species. I'm calling the police, really I am." But she didn't. The sun was well over the horizon, the first wave of heat was gathering strength. I went home.

Two weeks till parade day. At Dona Neuma's house the only obsession was getting the costumes out on time. Extra help had been taken on for the final stretch, bringing the total crew to nearly a dozen, including two baianas in their mid-seventies and two friends of Dona Neuma's second daughter, Ceci.

In Ceci's upstairs suite, there was no longer any place to sit, every available surface being taken by finished warriors' costumes, half-ready capes, costume ingredients spread out in the order in which they were to be assembled, boxes of glitter tape, boxes of mirror strip, boxes of pom-poms, piles of foam-rubber cutouts to be used for stuffing.

The newest recruits, Ceci's friends Jorginho and Ana, stood at an assembly-line table on the upstairs balcony and glued the finished decorations onto the warriors' capes while Dulce and Iracema, tireless seamstresses, manned the sewing machines downstairs. Elania and the beautiful Fia sewed, cooked, did sums or took measurements as needed. With Guezinha, Elania also handled orders and shipments of materials, and took charge of the steady trickle of visitors who arrived for a costume fitting or carnival instructions, or to ask if by any chance there was an empty slot left in any of the four adult wings under the household's control. The two baianas embroidered, cooked and cleaned, sipping beer with Dulce and Iracema throughout the day and night and working at the same steady pace for eight or nine hours before breaking for dinner. They took up their stitching again the moment they finished their meal, one eye on the Jocasta-Oedipus saga, where the heroine now faced a choice between the suitors she had been encouraging in order to keep the pouting Oedipus at bay. I rooted for the physically commanding but socially maladroit animal banker, but the household took that for the flightiness of someone lacking the bitter firsthand knowledge of the grief such rakes can bring; the consensus was that Jocasta should marry a respectable, bald and rather boring doctor whose very stolidity made him desirable.

Almost everyone in the household was going to parade: Ceci's teenage daughter Neuci came out as the youngest member of the baianas; Elania paraded with Guezinha; Dona Neuma marched with the directorate; Chininha's son and Neuci's daugher, both toddlers, were mascots for the baby school; Iracema worked on the costumes she, Ceci and Chininha would wear in Chininha's wing.

Chininha, a large, placid woman who vied with Dona Zica for the title of best cook on the hill, had been running her wing for so long it was virtually self-propelling, and her solid sense of how the school membership had evolved often ran counter to my preconceptions. To begin with, there weren't many Mangueirenses in it. An optimistic estimate would have less than ten percent of the school's fifty-three hundred members living on the hill, she believed, and several members of the directorate later corroborated her figures. I thought that this was shockingly low, given that the total population of Mangueira was variously estimated at anywhere from twenty to forty-five thousand people, but Chininha wasn't bothered. A lot of the current membership had once lived on the hill, or had family here, and in any event, the size of the Mangueira core had always been about the same.

Like Guezinha's, Chininha's wing was for women only, and it was her impression that about seventy percent of the school's members were women, even taking into account the three hundred and some *bateria* men and the predominantly male directorate. Again, there was nothing new in this, and the reason seemed fairly obvious to her: women's costumes are inherently more attractive than men's. Chininha also didn't believe that the so-called South Zone invasion of the samba schools—which media experts often cited to explain why carnival was no longer "authentic"—had ever taken place. Though there were many more whites in Mangueira in the 1980s than in the 1950s, Chininha believed that most of them came from the North Zone's unpretentious middle-class neighborhoods and working-class suburbs, where samba and carnival were not looked down on as they were in the South. I remembered a performance by the Nigerian guitarist King Sunny Adé during the 1987 edition of the trendy Rio Jazz Festival, in the course of which fully three-fourths of the audience had walked out. Earlier they had cheered Spyro Gira and Chet Atkins, but when Sunny Adé came onstage in his stylized tribal robes, and his costumed band went into their rehearsed bobs, hip weaves and spins, the desertions began. The hot, insistent music drew hisses that escalated into progressively louder boos and catcalls, the most insulting of which was "Mangueira!" I agreed with Chininha that to the degree that the South Zone white elite prized detachment over intensity they did not seem to have the right spirit for samba.

At any rate, Chininha said, most of the members of her wing were maids, and most maids were black. Not that whites didn't participate; she had a white doctor, a white secretary, a white teacher. But wherever the whites were, they had not arrived as an invasion. Most of her wing members were repeats, with the six or so yearly dropouts quickly replaced by other women on the waiting list, both white and black. More than an invasion, it sounded like a gradual bleaching process: whereas in the 1960s middle-class whites had been a rarity at rehearsals, by the 1970s they were accepted members of many samba schools, and in Mangueira in 1988 there were all-white wings with white chiefs, white chiefs of wings with majority black membership, and black chiefs of the most expensive wings that principally attracted whites.

Despite the gradual white takeover of the school, no one seemed to take particular notice of their presence, partly because so many of the newcomers were fervent in their loyalty to the school, and largely because it seemed enormously important to the Mangueirenses to deny that they were "racist," although the distrust blacks felt for South Zone white society (and the distrust whites felt toward them) constantly surfaced. "Why are rich people so different from poor people?" Guezinha asked me. "Is it just because they're white and we're black?" Celina's sons told me about want-ads: "When they say they're looking for 'a young man of good appearance,' you know they're not talking about us." And yet Eurides would constantly warn me: "Stay away from so-and-so, he's one of those black militants who believe whites oppress blacks. Don't talk to him."

But then Elania, the only middle-class black in the Neuma household, after confiding to me in one conversation that she was worn out by the clutter and noise, heavy food and undisciplined emotions on the hill, burst out, "You don't like the South Zone? Me neither. I hate it. I hate those South Zone people: they think they're such a big deal, so superior, and all they are is heartless and boring." The only professional I met in my time in Mangueira was a wing chief, a dentist who had emigrated from the hill after graduation and now had his own home and car and a profitable practice. His voice curdled with venom when we watched the television broadcasts of a new government "Be Kind to the Tourist" campaign: " 'Be kind to tourists,' " he sneered. "Do you know what that means? It means, 'Can I polish your boots, pretty please?' " Yet now, when I asked Dona Neuma if anyone in Mangueira had objected when whites started to become a significant presence in the school, she quickly replied, "Nobody did. Nobody. We're not racist."

Many of the last-minute arrivals at Dona Neuma's were white: school outsiders who had decided on impulse to parade for the first time and were now making their first, uneasy expedition into a slum. And while they were received with no hostility, the lower orders of the household could not always keep from smiling into their sewing at the visitors' discomfiture. "Working hard?" a marvelously tanned woman would say cheerily to someone who had spent the last three hours gluing five sequins each on a boxful of pom-poms. Another white woman who popped her head in the door one evening looking for Ceci was invited to wait. "I just love to sit on the floor," she said, sprawling gracefully next to one of the baianas. "At home I always sit like this, don't you?"

The crew replied amiably to the woman's banter about the heat and the rain and the terrible difficulties involved in finding one's way out to Mangueira, but the moment she left, the conversation got serious again. We had been talking about carnival. "You know the best carnival I ever had?" said Jorginho.

The best carnival Jorginho ever had was in 1984, when Mangueira won first prize during the Sambadrome's inaugural parade. Mangueira was honoring the composer Braguinha, author of the "Yes! We Have No Bananas!" carnival classic. The theme fitted perfectly with Mangueira's tradition of naivete and high spirits, and the word was out on the samba circuit that the school had a winner. Jorginho, who had seen the costumes, agreed, but he had not been able to afford one. "The school was looking so beautiful that year!" he said.

Lovesick, he decided he could not bear to watch the parade on television, and on carnival night he made his way to the enclosed area where the schools wait their turn for the parade, just beyond the entrance to the Sambadrome. "I had on my pink and green crocheted T-shirt and my pink felt hat, so I got past the gates. And there was this gringo who was waiting to parade, and he'd brought along a bottle of whiskey. Real whiskey, mind you. We got pretty friendly, and with every drink I got more convinced that I had to parade. By the time we'd almost killed the whiskey I had an idea, and I got myself in line with the crew in charge of pushing one of the floats. That was pretty good, but then a harmony director recognized me and chased me away. The front gates were opening, the parade was about to begin, and I felt Mangueira slipping away from me." At that precise moment inspiration and daring quivered through him: swiftly, he lifted up the skirt of the nearest float and slipped under, folding himself into a pretzel in order to make the fit. As the float started to move, he scuttled along underneath, his knees banging against his chin. "The float moved, I moved; it stopped, I stopped. I can't tell you how hot it was down there. Eighty minutes of that carnival heat, in a two-foot-high space under a float. All I could see was the float pullers' ankles, and all I could breathe was dust. But I paraded!"

That was the epochal carnival during which Mangueira whipped the audience into such frenzied joy that at the end the Sambadrome bleachers emptied and hordes descended on the parade strip, fighting for a place behind the floats. Triumphant, the school performed a U turn at the end of the strip and repeated the entire parade in the opposite direction, the crowd laughing and leaping behind. It was a no-contest win.

We received Jorginho's story with a round of respectful, envious silence, and since nobody had a better story to tell, I went downstairs. But it wasn't as much fun there. Iracema and Dulce had been working too many hours for too many days, and at times Iracema, particularly, seemed on the verge of snapping. She had promised that mine would be the first finished costume in Guezinha's wing, but she no longer smiled when I stopped by her sewing machine to ask just when I could try it on. "Soon," she had taken to saying, without even looking up, because I was by no means her most formidable harasser. She had finished most of the children's outfits, but there were still Gue-zinha's and Chininha's wings to take care of, and while Guezinha's maid costumes were simple, they were not easy to sew, what with the fitted bodice, the bias-cut skirt and the ruffles all around. Iracema was a handsome, well-kempt woman in her forties, but gradually she was becoming disheveled. For Dulce it was easier. She was not in charge, and she lacked Iracema's stubborn perfectionism. She cooked happily in the brew of heat and beer, especially delighted when someone brought out a plateful of salted fried shrimp, and stitched away.

Drained by a nervous cough that grew more insistent as carnival week approached, Dona Neuma grew moody and acknowledged that something was missing. "If I had been in charge of the baianas this year," she said one day, "you would have seen something different. I used to round up several of the women from the hill, and on weekends I would go out and buy a whole bunch of food at the supermarket and then we would have a sewing party here. Everybody worked happily because the extra money they got during the season made a big difference. For some it meant a new blender or the down payment for a sewing machine. For others it meant getting out of debt. So everybody put their best into it. They sang and gossiped and had a good time."

I had heard the same thing from Vovó Lucióla, the matriarch of Mangueira, a tiny eighty-seven-year-old who presided over an African compound of shacks and houses down the alley. I had tried to rent one of them when I decided to move to Mangueira and she had explained that she couldn't let it out, even though it was empty. The house was reserved for the last weeks of the carnival season, she said, when the women among her fourteen children and forty-four grand-children put in a stove, stocked up on beer and *cachaça*, and settled in for the final marathon of embroidery and sewing, stitching or-naments on the costumes for several different wings. Vovó Lucióla never paraded, but no bamba was crustier or more hip. She got a gleam in her eye when she described the coming frenzy. "Make sure you drop by, girl," she said. "These women here, they party!" But the house remained empty while the women waited. On the direc-torate's recommendation, almost all the wings were having their costumes sewn by professionals. Outside of Dona Neuma's and Dona Zica's, virtually no carnival work was done in Mangueira.

Two of Celina's daughters signed on for a few weeks' worth of stitching with a North Zone seamstress who had been commissioned to prepare a wing. This was welcome money for Bebeth, who was unemployed—hardly anyone in the family had the knack of holding down a job—and had just found out she was expecting a child. She was happy because she had desperately wanted to get pregnant by her boyfriend, Chimbico. It seemed impolite to ask if they planned to find a place to live, and how they were going to pay for it, or whether Chimbico's job prospects had improved since last carnival, when, moments before the parade started, he lost his position as director of the *bateria*.

Chimbico had been trained since childhood for the job by Master Candino, remembered as Mangueira's best *bateria* director. He was considered brilliant but temperamental, and there were different ver-sions of what had happened on the parade grounds at dawn during the 1987 carnival: everyone agreed that Chimbico had exploded when a powerful member of the directorate, Totoca, tried to meddle with his arrangement for the drummers. Some said that he had broken his baton in half, then flung the pieces down and stormed out, while others insisted that he had been surrounded by Totoca's goons, who had shown him a gun and told him to get out fast. Through his show business contacts, Chimbico found a nightclub job in Israel and did not come back to Brazil for six months. Totoca, a drug dealer and a close friend of Carlos Dória, had better and more powerful enemies than the scruffy *bateria* director: a few months after carnival his body appeared in a garbage dump out in the suburban wastelands.

Chimbico had still not been restored to his position at the head of the *bateria*, but he had little to say about his situation. I found him as undecipherable as so many of the Mangueira men I tried to talk to: withdrawn where the women were loquacious, suspicious where they were unreasonably trusting, defeated where the women seemed unequipped with the ability to give up. But Chimbico also seemed afraid. Surly as always, he agreed to talk only where he could not be seen, and then he said only that he had absolutely no comment at all about the entire situation. He was waiting.

I stopped by Celina's to see if she could tell me more, but it was a Monday, and she was not around. "Come in!" Seu Malandrino said genially, as if we were old friends. I backed out of the alley as fast as I could, but the ghost sent one of Celina's sons chasing after me. "Come back!" João insisted. "He's very happy to see you."

"Sit down!" Seu Malandrino instructed. "And I will let you hear wondrous things you can tell people about back in your country. I am Seu Malandrino, come from Bahia, the city of the north, to help this girl"—there he pointed not to himself but close enough to indicate that he was talking about Celina—"and to repair the evil I did." He glared at a smiling, rapt woman I'd not noticed in the corner: "Now tell the foreigner how powerful I am!"

The woman did, eagerly, and whenever she reached some especially significant detail, Seu Malandrino cut in and made her repeat it for my benefit. The woman had a son, she explained, who did reasonably well as a street vendor and got paid regularly by his boss, and yet she saw none of this money, and was insulted and humiliated by her son, who demanded three square meals a day but never gave her a cent for household expenses. Although the woman was a regular worshipper at an important *candomblé* temple, she hadn't gotten the help she needed there. ("Did you hear that?" Seu Malandrino interrupted, eyes gleaming. "Tell that to the foreigner again!") Someone recommended Seu Malandrino to her, "and three days hadn't gone by after I started doing what he told me, when I began to see the change; my son was nice to me, he gave me some money, and then on top of that he brought groceries for me to cook. I've still got fish and chicken in the refrigerator, but by Friday he'd already come to me and said, 'Mother, Monday is a holiday so I'm not going shopping, but on Tuesday I'll bring more supplies for the week.'"

The ghost snorted. "Foreign girl, you go tell that to those born-again Christian people, see what they make of *that*!" He belched a little smoke. "You've seen it for yourself. The list of benefits I have worked for those who approached me is very, very long. I have made marriages, built people houses, cured children. And yet there are fools who say I don't exist!" Another snort. He hummed a little ditty, and his petitioner laughed. "I was going to ask you for that song, Seu Malandrino!"

> "*I was born a* malandro,
> *And I was born to enjoy life.*
> *I was born a* malandro,
> *And if I ever work I'll die,*"

the ghost sang obligingly, and then he improvised a few verses about carrying a basket covered with a napkin through the open-air market of Mauá Plaza, and how the *malandro*'s magic makes everything he wants disappear from the stalls into his basket, which, given that his petitioner's son was a street vendor, amused her particularly. Laughter gurgled and hissed out of the ghost's windpipe as well, and then he grew autobiographical.

"I am Seu Malandrino, from Bahia," he repeated. "You see me now in this condition"—he gestured to his impoverished surroundings—"but I once had a lot of money, a great deal of money indeed, because I was the son of a rich family. Shoemakers, you know? I had everything I needed, I could have led a peaceful life, been wealthy and comfortable too. But I liked women, samba and drink. And"—he wheezed ecstatically—"I really liked my little reefer!" He cackled and slapped his thigh, choking with laughter and sneaking a sly glance at me. "That is the truth! I did love smoking that good grass!" He turned somber. "And then I was killed, you see, in a knife fight, and because I caused my parents to die of grief, I was sent back to this world to repair the harm I'd done."

Bit by bit, he told me the things he'd found out about me in the underworld. Sad and dreadful things that had his petitioner and Celina's family staring in pity and fascination. Seu Malandrino's yellow eyes glinted as he enumerated paternal abandonment, a mother's death, an inheritance swindled away, years of poverty, heartbreak and thoughts of suicide. He asked me if he was lying and I affirmed that he was not. "You see that?" He turned triumphantly to his audience. "Those born-again Christian people don't know what they're talking about! I know these things because I am Seu Malandrino and I have been sent to do good, and even though some people are ungrateful, and make me a present of only a packet of candles after all I've done to help, I keep on doing good because that is my mission on this earth. This year, though, I'm tired of helping people like that, and I'm going to help only this girl here." He pointed again in Celina's direction. "She's going to get a real roof for this room, and the rain won't come in ever again, and she'll build a second story on top of the first, even if it means covering up the neighbors' window, and for all the times they threw their dirty water down on this house and said, 'Fuck the ones below,' this girl is going to be able to say, 'Fuck the ones above!' You'll see."

"As for you . . ." Seu Malandrino turned to me again, hands planted on thighs, chest thrown out as he prophesied. "As for you, I have good news. I have been authorized to tell you that the bad part is over; you've left it behind for good. You are going to samba beautifully, and you are going to have a wonderful, wonderful carnival and it's going to allow you to put the sadness of your life behind you, and when you go back to your own country you will write your book and receive your true inheritance and no one will ever harm you again. Seu Malandrino guarantees it."

12 *Early February*

Soon the rains came and, with them, relief from the heat. For a few grateful hours, Rio stretched out, breathed deeply, marveled at the equanimity that comes after a cool night. The rain continued; great slashing sheets of water flung themselves against the hills and crashed below, day after day. From dawn to dark we never saw the sun: the city remained wrapped in a penumbral light that flickered like half-dead neon. On February 8 we heard that more than a hundred people were dead, buried in mudslides in the former imperial summer home of Petrópolis, the lovely city pitched high on the ridge of the Organ Mountains. In Rio, the deaths began around that time in the flatland slums of the northern Baixada, where a dozen people drowned in mud. In Mangueira, four members of a family died when an avalanche of mud and refuse collapsed their home, but the favela was too caught up in the urgency of carnival to take much notice.

I walked into Dona Neuma's one afternoon to find the downstairs area spotless, cleared of snippets of tulle, balled-up ends of thread, odds and ends of bias tape, dust, pins. The sewing machines were closed up, the smell of baking cake perfumed the kitchen. Iracema looked fresh and neatly combed. Next to her was a shimmering mass of pattern pieces entirely embroidered with magenta-colored sequins.

A subcontractor had just brought them in and now they were to be made into the costumes for Chininha's wing, to which Iracema belonged. Her only task in the six days remaining till carnival was to stitch the pieces into fifty puffy-sleeved bodices and below-the-knee skirts. The costumes for Guezinha's wing were finally ready for delivery. "Your costume is upstairs," Iracema said with a smile. I left her humming as she basted the bodice of her own costume together, and went to claim mine.

When I came downstairs again she was slumped in front of the sewing machine. Perched on the edge of her circle of doom Ceci, Dona Neuma, Dulce and Fia did not dare risk a word or gesture. Only Guezinha cooed hesitant questions: Perhaps the sizes could be switched? No? Iracema: And if we tried inserting gussets? Also no? Then let out the darts? She fell into silence. Ceci, fiddling with her bodice, declared redundantly that it was also too small. The subcontractor, who had been edging toward the door, fled.

The muslin underpinning for the bodices had been cut to the right size, but every row of stitched sequins imperceptibly puckered the material, so that each pattern piece, stitched solidly with sequins, had shrunk a total of two to three inches in width on every costume. As they had already been cut for a skintight fit, the shrunken bodices were now unwearable. After two weeks of sixteen-hour days, Iracema and the crew would have to work against the clock from here to carnival toward some makeshift solution they had not yet discovered. Distraught with the thought of the days ahead, Dulce wandered disconsolately through the kitchen. Chininha, arriving late on the crisis, froze in the doorway, caught in the glare of her mother's fury. "Turn that goddamn television off!" Guezinha yelled at one of the household helpers. I headed for the porch.

Through the window, I monitored brief episodes of rage followed by prolonged muttering. There was the sound of breaking glass, then sobbing. Dona Neuma's hoarse insults spared no one. Sluts, all of them. Where was Chininha while the disaster was in the making? Scratching her belly? Had she supervised the embroidery? Had she fretted and harassed as she knew she must? Had she been at all concerned with the honor of her own name, of her mother's name, of Mangueira's? And what about the quality of Guezinha's outfits? Was that slovenly workmanship something to be proud of? Had they inherited no sense of shame from her? Had she managed to bring up three worthless daughters?

As soon as silence fell I returned indoors, driven by the rain. Iracema and the beautiful Fia were at the sewing machines, stitching, Guezinha was upstairs in her bedroom, looking ravaged, Ceci was locked in her pink bathroom, and Chininha was wedged into a kitchen corner, eyes glued to the floor. Dona Neuma wandered through the house as if she were trying to lose the dry, nervous cough that would not let go of her throat. Finally she dragged a blanket out on the porch and made her bed under the cutting table. "The lady should not lie out here on the cold floor with a cough like this," I told her respectfully. "It will do her harm." "I need some air," she croaked, and coughing, squirmed into the blanket until it formed itself into a nest around her body.

Accidents and stress afflictions now plagued the school at higher rates than the slum average. Julinho Mattos fell off a scaffolding in the hangar and twisted his ankle. His sidekick, Melão, developed shooting pains in his elbow and showed up for work with his arm in a sling. Delegado's dyspepsia soured his temper further. Dona Zica, involved in a vicious quarrel with her neighbor Dona Neuma, was taken away in an ambulance one night. She had recently seen her granddaughter, Nilsemar, demoted from her position as wing chief at the instigation of the Neuma household, and now the two neighbors were not on speaking terms. Dona Zica's family was considered aloof by the people on the hill, who resented their quiet, orderly three-story house, where Mangueirenses were not invited to enter and sprawl about at will; but the media liked Dona Zica's grandmotherly looks and mild ways; and there was a national outpouring of sympathy and great media concern that her heart condition would prevent her from coming out at carnival. The directorate she had been considering resigning from now gave Julinho orders to design a chair at the front of one of the floats so that she could parade sitting down. Shaky but vindicated, she returned home from the hospital.

A severe case of bronchitis forced me to spend a few days away from Mangueira as well. When I was back on the hill, friends and complete strangers took turns offering remedies for the cough I had brought back:

Hot milk.
Hot milk with burnt brown sugar.
Hot milk with burnt brown sugar and a raw egg.

Orange and carrot juice.

Carrot juice with no orange.

Boiled garlic.

Boiled garlic and pomegranate leaves.

Capybara oil, offered by a man whose father had hunted and killed and boiled down the fat of this particular capybara twenty years before: "Just think; all this time it's been gathering strength!"

Eurides wouldn't say what she had prepared for me, but she assured me it would start working soon. (I never touched or saw the remedy.)

A prescription provided by Dulce after she carefully measured my collarbone. "I knew it!" she had exclaimed. "It's collapsed." What I had to do, she instructed, every morning on awakening, was hang three times from the door frame of my room, or any door frame, but "before you've touched food or said a word to anyone. And while you're hanging, you have to recite . . . how does it go?" She looked to the other women for help, but they turned away to hide their smiles. "Come on now, help me: how does it go?" Silence. "Oh, what the hell," she said finally. "You'll think it's foolishness but it does really work. Here's what you say: 'Dear God, you give. Dear God, you replace. Make my poor collarbone go back to its place.' Three times now."

This was the only remedy I couldn't try, as my room had no door frame and no door, and it was impossible to keep silent the moment I crossed the threshold and indeed long before: children posted themselves at the foot of the bed to watch me get up and then in front of my chair to observe the act of writing. Dona Esmeralda's daughters came in at three or four in the morning to use the mirror on their way out to the *quadra*. And I was always happy to chat with my hostess, who, with the orderliness and calm that characterized her new Christian life, often came in from early church service just as I was pouring myself coffee. We usually talked about her life and about carnival, and about *candomblé*, which she now saw as nothing but superstition and snake oil. One day she came back elated from church: "Do you know," she said, "I've had this really disagreeable back pain for so long, but the minister said he would pray it away for me, and it's definitely improved!"

While I was still coughing, and because of the recurrent public transport strikes, I took a taxi one afternoon out of Mangueira, and thanked the driver for his suggestion that I cut a lemon in half, cover it with salt and pour a drop of the lemon juice down the back of my throat every few minutes. "You're skeptical," he noted. "Have you been to a doctor?" I said I had. "And did he help?" He hadn't. "But if you went in there and paid him five thousand cruzados and instead of prescribing fancy medicine that doesn't work he prescribed a half a lemon, you'd feel cheated, wouldn't you? Besides," he added, "people like us who use these remedies can't afford fancy doctors."

(My cough was finally cured by one of the members of Ceci's sewing team, who suggested one evening as we were gluing glitter patterns on cardboard that it might be allergic in origin, and produced a bottle of syrup with antihistamine that worked.)

Celina didn't offer a remedy, but I suspected that, like Eurides, she had taken measures of her own. Her own health had improved after the New Year's illness, and life in general seemed to be going well for her, as Seu Malandrino had promised. But the rain had worked its usual change in her mood when I stopped by one wet afternoon and found her preoccupied again with laundry, the rain and her swelling legs. After asking about my cough she gave me a plate of okra stew and left me to be entertained by Sidney, who was at home even on the rare occasions when Celina was not.

As far as I knew, Sidney, who was twenty-eight, had never had a job, not even during the carnival season, when there was loose change to be picked up parking cars on rehearsal nights. He did not seem to need much money, spending his time at home as he did, reading old newspapers he found here and there and watching television. He was unemployed, I suspected, partly out of natural laziness and mostly out of morbid sensitivity to the ways in which menial jobs could accentuate his sense of personal waste. He was bright and intellectually curious and given to despair, and it was easy to imagine how damaging that combination would be at an $80-a-month job cleaning streets, which is how a great many of the men in Mangueira with jobs earned their living. But it was also possible that a street-cleaning job would have remained forever out of his reach: the day a few vacancies were announced in the paper thousands of applicants mobbed the municipal services office.

His best pleasure was conversation, and he was consistently well informed. He would often greet me with the latest news about a pollution crisis in Mexico City, or a question about the 1985 earthquake. Soccer was his life's passion, but he was also a careful chronicler of carnival events. While I ate, he told me that a school's chances for victory depended greatly on the story samba and that the winning school's song was usually popular long before the parade weekend. "What's your favorite?" he asked, and scoffed when I confessed that actually, although Mangueira's samba was lovely, I preferred Vila Isabel's. "That's just because it talks about priests," he jibed. "Mexicans go crazy over that religious stuff." He was right. The lines

> The priest raises the grail
> To call the masses together;
> People of every race,
> Gathered in a single emotion

were among my favorites, and the epic, almost mystical undertone of the whole song thrilled me.

However, neither his favorite nor mine was at the top of the radio charts. Mangueira's story samba was a great success in the media, but Helinho Turco's song was too lyrical and convoluted to be really popular, while no one seemed to be paying much attention to Vila Isabel's samba, complicated and difficult to memorize and sing as it was. The big hits were Salgueiro's "In Search of Gold," which remained at the top of the samba hit parade, and Independent Youth of Padre Miguel's insolent samba about how we could kiss the old Brazil good-bye ("Ciao, inflation, no nostalgia for that old debt-ridden nation").

"And Beija-Flor," I added. Ridiculous, Sidney said dismissively. Pompous old Joãozinho was doing another one of his play-to-the-foreign-tourist numbers, and he was really going to get himself into trouble this year. The samba might be popular, but the theme was mystifying, what with all that stuff about being black from Egypt to Liberty. Unbelievable sums were supposed to have been invested in the parade, and the Hummingbird of Nilópolis school was going to end up paying the bill for all the years Joãozinho had determinedly ignored the root traditions of carnival. As for Império Serrano, Sidney lamented, it seemed destined to sink. A pity, because if Mangueira did not exist, Sidney would happily throw his loyalty behind it. The interesting parades to look for, he concluded, would be Portela's and Tradição's. The breakaway school of Tradition was to open the first parade night, and Portela would close it with a samba that directly challenged the upstart with the opening lyrics, "Who's up for a fight?" Sidney thought this was taking a poorly calculated risk: under the leadership of the son of Portela's legendary Natal, the four-year-old Tradição was already a formidable school, stuffed with celebrities, imbued with a crusading zeal against the flirtations of Portela's animal banker with the South Zone, and favoring the Grand Old School's most hallowed traditions: little nudity, lots of samba, a first-rate *bateria*.

Sidney was shivering with cold. I had not noticed the driving rain that had begun again after a couple of hours' respite, but now a drop of water landed with a thump on my head; I moved sideways and realized that the rain was beginning to drip on the okra. Shifting the plate, I saw that rain was dripping into my beer. "You should see," Sidney said, pointing to the curtained-off area where five family members shared the only bed. "The mattress is completely sodden." In fact, the rain was streaming down the inside walls.

The weather had cleared when I set out the next morning for the neighborhood where four Mangueirenses had been killed in a mudslide. The sky was a clear bright blue behind the flocked clouds that were rushing away, their crop of rain temporarily exhausted. Every one of the scanty leaves on the hill shone brightly, and the brick shacks had been soaked to a rich, deep brown. Dona Esmeralda gave me instructions on how to climb to the topmost ridge of the hill and down again to Candelária, where the landslide was. As she waved me off she warned me not to be too surprised by Mangueira's indifference to the situation there. "We're like that here, you know. When one of the rich and famous people on the hill dies, everybody comes to the funeral. When it's someone who's poor and unknown, no one even signs the contributions book to help the family pay for the burial."

Candelária, the oldest, most thickly populated part of Mangueira, turned out to be as dense and labyrinthine as a casbah. Stairs lead the twisting alleys at least three-quarters of the way up the hill, bounded on every side by houses placed tightly together and built up into haphazard second, third and even fourth stories. At many points it is possible to shake hands from house to house across the sunless alleys. The only vegetation grows in tin-can planters, which are frequently suspended from the top windowsills or second-story overhangs to keep them out of the way of passersby. Near the top of the hill the houses thin out slightly, only because the area near the ridgetop is so steep and craggy it is almost impossible to build on it.

Yet there was construction here as well. Wherever there was not enough surface to hold a house, it was projected out over the hillside and propped up on stilts. Guided by a relative of the landslide victims, I edged sideways along a narrow walkway by a row of stilt houses. The one that had collapsed had been prosperous, at least as well built as Dona Esmeralda's: one thickness of plaster-covered brick for both stories, and a tile floor that was still visible under the rubble. A nuclear family had lived here: an assistant manager at a downtown paint store, his wife and two children. Next door, in the original adobe one-room house, the man's mother lived with her two youngest sons, one of them an invalid.

There was an ongoing demarcation dispute between the neighborhood associations of Candelária and the Hot Hole regarding an area immediately above. The usual land-dispute terms were reversed: here, neither side wanted the land in question because no one was willing to deal with its problems. Candelária had gotten electricity and an open-air sewer system from the government at about the same time as the rest of Mangueira, in 1984–6, when the populist governor Leonel Brizola made a point of keeping a campaign promise his predecessors had worn thin. But the haphazard quality of the sewer system and the total absence of trash collection soon had the assistant paint-store manager complaining to the Candelária association. As everywhere else on the hill, garbage was deposited at certain commonly agreed-on spots; in this case, decades of rubbish, including everything from broken sofas to burned-out refrigerators, had accumulated just beneath an overhang and directly above the assistant manager's house. But it did no good for him to complain: the area belonged to the people from the Hot Hole side of the ridge, and the Candelária association had no control over it. Nor did they have jurisdiction over the open sewer from which water seeped directly under the foundation of the assistant manager's house, since the sewer originated on the Hot Hole side. Perhaps; but according to the Hot

Hole association, the house was in Candelária, so it was not their problem.

The neighborhood associations were usually responsive to their people's needs: the elected presidents lived on the hill and were answerable to their electorate in ways the thousands of public officials just elected to Brazil's incipient democratic regime were not. The associations settled land disputes, handled bureaucratic tangles on their affiliates' behalf, mediated between the drug traffickers and the rest of the community—generally to the traffickers' benefit—on issues of noise and turf, negotiated votes for politicians in exchange for the promise of an infirmary or a day-care center, and channeled emergency relief when natural disasters struck. But the associations were not skilled at handling discussions among themselves. Their presidents were facilitators, mediators between the great blank-faced powers of the bureaucracy and their own hapless communities, and thus experts only in hierarchical relationships. If a discussion about the assistant manager's problem had ever taken place between the Hot Hole and Candelária associations, it would most likely have taken the shape of a feud.

It rained all day and all night on February 10. Around midnight, a noise like magnified rolling thunder woke the neighborhood. The assistant manager's sister rushed from her own house just down the hill. A huge rock had broken free from the ridge and brought down with it an avalanche of mud and the entire weight of the garbage dump. The woman could hear her mother moaning underneath the rubble, asking for help. She scrabbled and dug with her bare hands while the neighbors tried to remove the construction blocks, and then the moans stopped. The next day, a rescue team from the fire department unearthed the survivors—the assistant manager's two brothers and one of his children—and told the neighbors that fifteen of the surrounding houses were under imminent threat of collapse and would have to be evacuated. No one had heard more from the authorities or received relocation assistance. I was told that some of the evacuees had pitched camp at the association headquarters down the hill, others were staying with neighbors and friends, and some were still at home.

I was curious about the Mangueira school's lack of solidarity or even concern about the tragedy, and wondered how people in Candelária were taking the fact that no one in the directorate had expressed the slightest interest in their situation. "What about carnival?" I asked the dead man's sister. "Oh," said the woman, her face suddenly shining. "We hope Mangueira wins."

By the time the flood had left ten thousand homeless in Rio state, Julinho Mattos had made significant progress on the painted, upholstered, curtained, mirrored and otherwise decorated floats.

At the hanger, workers equipped with blowtorches cut a hole in the corrugated-tin roof to make way for the tallest floats, but the rain poured in and the hole was temporarily covered up again. Out on the street more workers smoothed a new cement ramp to bear the decorated giants gently from hangar to asphalt. Inside, Julinho stapled a last row of huge silver-foil flowers on Slave Anastácia's float and gave orders to cover the top of the Africa float with straw matting. The long haul from December to carnival had exhausted almost everyone else, but despite his sprained ankle, Julinho remained good-natured and calm.

He showed me the drawings for the standout costumes. Marlene Arruda as Princess Isabel, of course, all in pink, and then Delegado and Nininha in pink and white, and a succession of people dressed as African gods, looking no more African or godlike than the dozens of similar sequin-covered whites the other schools would place on top of their floats. The most daring thing Julinho had done was to dress many of the plaster-cast figures on the floats in somber colors: purple and black. In a ballroom scene, a court lady dressed in black danced the minuet with a man wearing blood-red breeches and frock coat. Her neckline was trimmed in purple fur. His breeches were edged in green, purple and silver-mirror trim. A harpsichordist played for the dancers in front of a deep-purple velvet curtain. On a platform below the court scene, a black couple also celebrated, the black man's pose mirroring the white court lady's.

With the reticence he displayed whenever he was asked to explain an artistic decision, Julinho said his color choices had been dictated by purely practical considerations. "Purple and black are the colors of the Portuguese Crown, so they're historical. Besides, we can get away with it because we'll be parading in daylight; at night the colors would disappear. In any event, they'll stand out because they're all set against gold and mirror backgrounds.

"This is how it works," he went on. "You have to think of the colors for the whole parade, because to the spectators in the bleachers the school will be one long carpet of color. Here, for example, in the ballroom scene, look at what happens: here come two wings with a hundred feather headdresses, so that from the stands all you'll see will be a sea of ruffling pink, and then the floats with the dark colors."

The dark colors were also in the skin tones, now that two assistants had finished decorating all the figures: dark brown skins everywhere, to shine in the early-morning light—dancers, vendors, sprites, slaves, favela figures and, on one float all by herself, irremediably ugly, Slave Anastácia. I had often asked about this strange figure, and now I asked yet again, "Who is she?" This time somebody almost knew. "She was a slave," said one of Julinho's assistants. "I'm not sure about all the history, but there's a museum dedicated just to her in Our Lady of the Rosary Church, right in the Old City. You can find out all about her there."

Her ugliness had been a source of fascination for me ever since I saw the first shoddy plaster figurines on display in the *candomblé* supply shops. Traditionally, she was represented only from the shackled neck up: a black woman with blue eyes that stared out over what seemed to be a surgical mask. The ties of the mask cut her afro hairdo in bulbous halves and made her look distressingly like a fly. Everyone had a different story of how Anastácia had gotten that way. "She had her tongue pulled out by her owner's jealous wife." "She was gagged so she would not preach freedom to her people." "She had her tongue pulled out because she refused to say she was a slave." And the freakish blue eyes? There was no explanation. The only reliable fact about her was that she was rapidly becoming a major cult figure among the practitioners of the eclectic *umbanda* religion, whose most significant difference from the orthodox Afro-Brazilian *candomblé* is the ability to incorporate deities from every religion into its pantheon. But Anastácia was not a deity or a mythical creature, Julinho's assistant insisted. She was a real historical person, and her story was so tragic that both Mangueira and Vila Isabel were preparing floats dedicated to her. Furthermore, the Vatican was considering her beatification.

He was right about the church, which turned out to be the site of Rio's only black museum. Our Lady of the Rosary Church has a long association with blacks. During colonial times it had a potter's field for black slaves and supported one of the best-known religious *cabildos*: associations of black worshippers who devoted themselves to a given saint and staged processions on the saint's feast day with African chants and drums. During the great national abolition debate that dominated politics at the end of the Empire, Our Lady of the Rosary's *cabildo* contributed large amounts of money to the abolition movement and for the purchase of freedom for slaves.

The embroidered flags used by the abolitionist movement were on display at the entrance to the museum, a stifling narrow room on the second-floor gallery of the church. No one looked at them, because attention was focused directly across the passageway, on a glass counter stuffed with religious trinkets, votive candles and plaster figurines that were *candomblé* favorites: the Ibeji, or Twins, St. Barbara, St. Anthony, the Virgin of the Assumption. Sales were brisk.

Beyond was the museum, a single room fifteen meters long by eight wide, littered everywhere with oblong strips of paper. It did not take long to study the contents of half a dozen glass cases: neck and leg irons in one, a collection of broken or rusty metal church ornaments—a grail, a rosary, a bible stand—in another. Most of the sixteen faded prints on the wall lacked captions, but they appeared to be illustrations from nineteenth-century women's magazines, including one of a grateful black woman kneeling with her child before the portrait of Princess Isabel. One of the more carefully documented cases contained a ceremonial sword identified as the property of Colonel Armando de Moura, who, we were told, was on active service in the Rio de Janeiro Fire Department from 1936 to 1959.

A woman made her way on her knees across the ancient plank floor toward a knot of black and white women standing before the largest display case at the back of the room. On the case's top shelf was an enlarged photocopy, with a caption that clearly identified the source of the print as one of the illustrated travel accounts popular in Europe in the nineteenth century. In old-fashioned cursive typeface, the caption read simply, in French, "Punishment of Slaves (Brazil)." A mask and shackle hid a face of indeterminate gender, but it was unquestionably Anastácia's. One of her worshippers wept. Most whispered prayers under their breath, their eyes shut tight, their hands knotted together. They added bouquets of roses to the mounds of dying flowers banked along the front of the case and went to lean on another, where they copied prayers to Anastácia on the oblong strips of paper lying about.

Outside the museum I read a pamphlet biography of Slave Anastácia, a Bantu princess:

Her haughty bearing, her perfect features were outstanding. . . . Because of her physical beauty, one can assume she belonged to an aristocratic family which, upon returning to Portugal, sold her to a rich sugar mill owner. . . .

Lusted after by men, envied by women, she was loved and respected by all her brothers in pain. . . . Stoical, serene, submissive, she always lived thus. . . .

She was brutally raped . . . pursued by men all around the sugar *fazenda* where she lived. Her nights were full of anguish, fear and shame. . . . As an inevitable consequence, she had many children. Beautiful babies, all with eyes as blue as the distant sky. . . .

One day, she felt a desire to taste some of the sugar from the mill. She was seen by the brutal overseer, who called her a thief and gagged her. It was his revenge. Anastácia had never let herself be kissed. . . . This punishment drew the attention of the *fazendeiro*'s daughter, a vain and jealous woman who . . . had an iron shackle placed on Anastácia's neck. . . . Soon afterward, she died of gangrene. . . .

The overseer and the *fazendeiro*'s daugher felt such punishing remorse that . . . they provided for her proper burial as a posthumously freed slave.

I was interested in Anastácia because her legend was explicitly concerned with the relationship between black women and white men, and while that relationship is at the center of the Brazilian universe, it is rarely addressed from the black point of view. To begin with, the fundamental issue of just what constitutes blackness is confusingly blurred. Segregated as Brazilian society is, the decision about who is black and who is white seems to be made rather casually; while it is related to class, there are no fixed boundaries. I often wondered if someone described as "black" by my Ipanema acquaintances would be seen as "white" if he were wearing a linen suit, a doubt that expanded when I heard a man whom I would have described as a light-skinned member of the black race referred to as "white" because he was married to a very dark-skinned woman. Then there was the recurring, and crucial, distinction made between dark- and light-skinned black women, between black women and *mulatas*: but *mulatas* existed only, it seemed to me, in relation to whites, as when Cartola, in a song in which he impersonated a white boss, crooned dreamily to the servant he was watching scrub clothes, "Lather it up, *mulata*, lather it up." Black women auditioning for the Ôba-Ôba, Rio's famous cabaret for tourists, said they were hoping for the chance "to be *mulatas*," because, one explained in an interview in the newspaper *O Globo*, "to be a *mulata* must be the best thing in the world." In Mangueira, the fantastically beautiful Fia, light-skinned and hazel-eyed, "worked as a *mulata*," someone explained to me. She was a *mulata* when she put on net stockings and a sequined bikini and danced for the white foreigners at the Meridién Hotel. She was probably a *mulata* when, folding up a costume and pushing away from the sewing machine at Dona Neuma's, she adorned herself with lipstick and silver dangly earrings and went to meet her white boyfriend, a senior official in the Rio military police. But in the favela she was simply a black woman with light skin, black in her culture, black in her gestures, black in her view of the world, like everyone else there.

"Who invented the *mulata*?" a popular turn-of-the-century song asked, and answered smugly, "Portuguese men!" *Mulatas* are glorified sex fetishes, sanitized representations of what whites viewed as the savage African sex urge, but they are also, of course, tribute and proof of the white male's power: his sexual power, and his economic power, which allowed him to wrest the *mulata*'s black mother away from her black partner. At the same time the *mulata* serves to perpetuate one of the myths that Brazilians hold most dear, that there is no racism in Brazil, that miscegenation has been natural and pleasant for both parties, that white people really, sincerely, do like black people. In fact, the aesthetic superiority accorded to light-skinned black women—*mulatas*—underlines the perceived ugliness of blacks before they have been "improved" with white blood. The white skin also serves to lighten a sexual force that in undiluted state is not only threatening but vaguely repulsive, and at the same time, the myth goes, irresistible.

Brazilian myths, novels, films and songs have always celebrated the relationship between the passionate, sexually uninhibited woman with dark skin (the novel *Gabriela, Clove and Cinnamon*, for example) and the intellectually superior white man. But in this game two players get tossed out: black men, who are depicted as irrelevant or corrupt (or totally absent, as in the Anastácia legend), and white women, who are forced into competition with their black counterparts for the only game in town (like the *fazendeiro*'s daughter, who is unaccountably jealous of the overseer's lust for Anastácia, when according to established canon this young plantation flower should have had no interest in the sex urges of her father's flunky).

The hierarchy of class and color was institutionalized in the carnival parade. Floating above the dancing masses are the stars—white women and men, by and large, theoretically the most prestigious figures in the parade. Whether they are representing Princess Isabel or the god Xangô they hardly move or act; they glitter, virtually immobilized by the weight and volume of bulky costumes from which only faces and hands protrude. Below them on the floats are phalanxes of near-naked women, rotating their hips and smiling at the crowd. In recent years, these contingents have been almost equally divided between black and white women, but in the repetitive yearly carnival write-ups, the black women are always referred to as *mulatas*, and it took Joãozinho Trinta, the iconoclastic *carnavalesco* for Beija-Flor, to enthrone a stunning, very dark-skinned woman with a shaved head and a perfect African face at the head of his contingent of *mulatas*. She remains the exception.

Barred from the floats by the limitations on their budget, the vast majority of parading favelados occupy the dancing position on the pavement. But the only people who execute a formal dance during a parade are the flag-bearer and her partner and the *passistas*—school soloists chosen not for their looks but for their samba ability. The majordomo and the flag-bearer dress like royalty, covered from head to foot in rhinestones and feathers, and their stately performance counts for ten points in the judging. But although the *passistas* are the only members of the parade who actually samba the entire time, their performance gets no points. Frequently, both the men and women are very black indeed. The female *passistas* are nearly naked, while their male counterparts are traditionally dressed in *malandro* outfits; the archetypal *malandro*, of course, is a pimp, and the archetypal whore is a *mulata*. *Passistas* do not dance for each other, as black men and women might do in the Caribbean rumba or merengue, staring into each other's eyes and locking into each other's rhythms. They dance for the audience, which is understood to be white, male and in the market for dark flesh; if it weren't, why would the leering, outlandish black man pop his eyes and lick his lips as he leaps to kneel behind the black woman's trembling buttocks, modeling them with his hands and offering them to the crowd?

What was curious about Anastácia was that, fitting none of the contemporary Brazilian sexual stereotypes, she embodied them all: although she was chaste, she was endlessly sexually available; although she was aloof, she was sexually irresistible; and although the legend stressed her black skin and Africanness, the unaccounted-for blue eyes made her the first of a breed—a parthenogenetic *mulata*.

For weeks after my first visit to the Black Museum I hunted in the libraries for the original lithograph of Anastácia, going through the nineteenth-century travel chronicles book by book. I finally found her in the wondrously ornate Royal Portuguese Reading Cabinet, just around the corner from Our Lady of the Rosary. The interior decoration of this imperial extravagance, wrought iron from top to bottom, is what the underside of the Eiffel Tower might look like if it were painted in bright colors and turned into a library. The ancient Portuguese librarian seemed like a period piece as well, but he was efficient, and he emerged from the rows of gold-embossed leather-covered books in the upper galleries with the two volumes of the book I'd requested, Jacques Arago's *Souvenirs d'un aveugle: Voyage autour du monde*, and there, finally, on page 76, was Anastácia.

In the first place, she was a man. In the second place, she never existed. The illustration in Arago's book was a generic depiction of a male slave (as opposed to the many specific portraits of slaves and white people identified by name) drawn to show two forms of punishment common in Brazil. One was a neck shackle used on captured runaways; the other was a tin face-mask tied over the mouths of blacks who suffered from the common compulsion of eating dirt off the ground and plaster off the walls. Arago described both in the book, and explained the strange habit of eating dirt—prevalent among Indians and blacks throughout the Western Hemisphere—as an attempt to escape the miseries of slavery through suicide by gradual poisoning. He may have been right; subsequent scientific explanations attributed the compulsion to a physiological need for minerals lacking in slaves' insufficient diet; this explanation did not take into account the fact that many slaves, especially field workers, were probably better fed than today's favelados. (During the slavery period

Uruguay and Argentina became major exporters of beef jerky to the slave societies of Brazil and the Caribbean, where plantation owners knew that the only way to get maximum effort from their human property was through adequate nutrition. Dried meat, fresh fruits and greens, manioc root, coconut and sugar cane in sufficient quantity made up the plantation slaves' diet.)

Because Arago's own illustrations were lost in the shipwreck, and he was blind by the time his book was published, the French illustrator commissioned for the text had to rely on the author's summary written descriptions for his engravings, and the dainty surgical mask he drew bore little resemblance to the real thing, a cone-shaped device with breathing holes that covered the lower half of the face. As for the neck iron, Arago's illustrator drew it as a simple iron ring with a lock, whereas the real thing was more commonly equipped with a hornlike protrusion that made it impossible for the wearer to lean or lie down easily.

How had the figure in this illustration become the much-raped, proud but submissive Bantu slave princess? As it happened, just about the time that Julinho first began to sketch Anastácia's float for the abolition script, the archdiocese of Rio de Janeiro became interested in the same question, largely as a result of a petition for Anastácia's beatification that landed on Cardinal Eugenio Sales' desk. As recently as 1986 the cult of Slave Anastácia was still quite small, and it took some time before Monsignor Guilherme Schubert, a member of Brazil's Institute of History and Geography, was able to piece together the different parts of her story and publish the results of his investigation in the *Boletum da Revista do Clero* in 1987, which I read one broiling summer afternoon in the spacious, breezy corridors of the archdiocese library, eagerly drinking in the information and the leafy shade.

In 1971, Schubert reported, the bodies of Princess Isabel and her husband, the Count of Eu, were returned to Brazil by the Portuguese government, and on their way to their final burial site in Petrópolis, they spent the night of July 29 in Rio, in Our Lady of the Rosary Church. The small museum there was headed at the time by a layman, Yolando Guerra, known to have close connections to the *umbanda* religious community.

To celebrate the arrival of the princess and her consort, the church authorities put together a small commemorative exhibition on slavery, with contemporary lithographs and a few iron instruments used on the slaves. When the exhibit was being disassembled, Guerra asked the organizers to leave him a photocopy of one particular illustration, of a slave in a neck shackle and a face mask, captioned in French. It appears he had had a vision. . . .

Thus was Anastácia born, initially brown-eyed, but with the essential elements of her story largely as they stand today. Guerra was yet another black Brazilian trying to invent his missing past, but when he died in 1981 he was certainly unaware of how much he had contributed—with his fairy-tale story of Anastácia in which anyone worth knowing is royal and the wicked stepparents/owners repent and are good in the end—to hiding the real history of Brazilian blacks. For the text from which the illustration was taken is probably as scathing an eyewitness account of Brazilian slave society as we have.

Jacques Étienne Victor Arago, an illustrator for a French scientific expedition, arrived in Rio de Janeiro in 1824 during the reign of Dom Pedro I, an amiable slob whom Arago promptly provoked by beating him mercilessly at billiards. A man who stored his grudges carefully, Arago recounts this episode in his book, and then its consequence: he was forcibly evicted from the royal presence on a trivial excuse. On his return voyage to France, Arago was shipwrecked and lost the results of nearly four years' work. This violent ending to his Brazilian experience, and his encroaching blindness, help to explain the corrosive, bitter fury that informs his view of Brazil, but Arago's rage runs deeper.

Thirty-five years after the Declaration of the Rights of Man, fresh from the aftershocks of the French Revolution, the ardently republican Arago was revolted almost beyond coherence by everything he saw in Brazil. Everything was colored for him by the horror of slavery. Generously gifted with the French genius for sarcasm and snobbery, he had little time for the beauties of the Rio landscape and even less for the delights of the upper-class salons, whose taste in art, he wrote, "make[s] you want to leave town for a walk in the woods." He wrote scathingly about the ignorance of rich Brazilians and described a "magnificent and empty public library, where only the director is in the stacks." Commenting on Rio hospitality, he noted that the first de rigueur visit to a Brazilian's home was never followed by an invitation to return. He was indifferent to the beauty of white Brazilian women, and remarked instead on the vulgarity of their fingers, "crowded with rubies, pearls and emeralds." Most of all, he was unimpressed by the myth, common even then and subsequently translated into orthodoxy by sociologists like Gilberto Freyre, that Brazilian slavery was in some fashion benevolent. Brazil, he wrote, after visiting the United States and most of the Caribbean colonies, "is without a doubt the place on earth where slaves have most to bemoan, where they face the harshest labors, where their punishment is the most cruel, and indeed, the most ferocious." And yet, Arago notes, "Santo Domingo, Martinique, Bourbon [Réunion] and Île-de-France [Mauritius] have frequently seen uprisings, scorched earth and murder. In Brazil the slaves keep silent, immobile beneath the knotted whip."

Here he describes the marketplace on the rua do Valongo where slaves were sold, and where he watched a trafficker exhibit a "piece" to a prospective customer:

> "Look at that one."
> "It's not bad."
> "Walk."
> And it walks.
> "Now run."
> And it runs like a gypsy.
> "Lift your head, move your arms, stamp your feet, laugh, cry, show your teeth!"
> "Well done! Now then, how much?"
> "Six quadruples."
> "I'll give you five. . . . And by the way, what about the little mark?"
> "He's got it; look here."

And the trafficker shows the buyer the spot where the slave has been branded.

Earlier, Arago walked by a public plaza with a whipping post. The gutter running off the post, he says, is filled with blood, and the tormentor has exhausted his arm with so much effort. Now Arago spots another victim.

. . . and another (I saw him, I heard him)—another one, tied to a ladder, had just received fifty cane-blows, of which the lightest had torn off his skin. Not one gesture of pain betrayed this man's torture. When his punishment had come to an end, the black stretched, yawned as if he had just been yanked from a peaceful nap and smiled:

"Good God, a man can't even get any decent sleep around here."

I visited Our Lady of the Rosary often after my first encounter with Anastácia. Every time I went I discovered another spot in it that Rio's blacks had made sacred. There was the dark room on the ground floor dedicated to the Archangel Michael and made hellishly hot by hundreds of votive candles, so many that gigantic vats covered with grids had been provided for them to drip into. I was told there that St. Michael is associated with the cult of the dead in *umbanda*, but it took several visits before I realized that the statue was placed directly on a largish pile of bones, prayerfully described by one of the men in the crowded room as "the bones of unburied slaves." There were the votive candles themselves, for sale in the church atrium, shaped like legs, or arms, or hearts, or the head of Anastácia. Others were shaped like buttocks, and I had to call in a witness to make sure I was seeing things right. Eventually I realized that almost every one of the objects in the Black Museum had been sacralized; an old engraving of Zumbi was covered across every millimeter of its surface with the careful signatures of worshippers. A crude plaster sculpture of an old black man received the ritual offerings of cigars and money. A massive carving of a black man's head, labeled "The Unknown Slave," always had a bouquet of roses on the ground before it, and often people would stop to whisper secrets into its ear after praying to Anastácia.

The unknown slave of the unknown history of Brazil's unknown blacks. Seedy and corrupt as it was, the Black Museum was the only place in Rio where the descendants of slaves could have the sensation of physically, directly, being in touch with their own history. Lacking a Wailing Wall, a memorial, any official testimony to their suffering, they had turned the Black Museum into a shrine. And it was full of lies.

A new thunderstorm was rumbling in over the hills when I left Our Lady of the Rosary Church on precarnival Thursday. The train strike that had nearly destroyed the budget of so many Rio workers was still on, despite threats of massive firings for the miserably paid railroad employees. For North Zone commuters, the cheap train ride downtown had been replaced by two or three bus fares in each direction, and the crush of people trying to get home after work had snapped the bus lines' capacity. Rush-hour crowds now scampered across President Vargas Avenue's ten lanes of traffic, throwing themselves in the way of overcrowded buses to force them to a stop. A few dozen people assaulted the buses that went by Mangueira and held the doors open by force, but there was no room, even for those willing to hang off the sides. Several more dangerously crowded buses went by. At last I got pushed onto one that careened to a stop at the hill just as the rain started crashing.

Mangueira was one of the two schools of which Riotur asked help in checking the refurbished Sambadrome's equipment. A trial run of the parade was scheduled in the Sambadrome for the Sunday before carnival, with no costumes or floats but with Mangueira's full-strength *bateria*—all 337 members—and, of course, the samba pullers, who would travel in the sound truck about midway down the length of the formation. Although the event was free of charge and announced in the press, no public was expected and not many school members either. No one thought that the wing from flood-stricken Petrópolis would come into town for the rehearsal. Even on the hill, where two buses were waiting to take school members downtown, there was little enthusiasm. It was raining. President Vargas Avenue is normally not appealing, and a rehearsal on a drizzly Sunday night in one of Rio's least hospitable public spaces sounded like a poor idea.

Designed by Oscar Niemeyer—the architect who created Brasília—and conceived in the same Orwellian style as the capital, the official home of samba is a long, sad corridor of colorless cement that is supposed to evoke—with its rows of bleachers on one side and piled-up shoe-box balconies on the other—the nineteenth-century plazas and buildings of Rio Branco Avenue, where the parade used to take place. The dimensions of its failure cannot be adequately grasped until one has seen a busful of tourists arrive, descend and elbow each other aside in their haste to board the bus again.

The Sambadrome nevertheless looked livelier than expected on this rehearsal evening, softened around the edges by darkness and artificial lights, and with a few hundred Mangueirenses and a larger contingent from Independent Youth of Padre Miguel laughing and singing in the "concentration section," where the parade forms before entering the "avenue," or parade strip. Padre Miguel's *bateria*, long recognized by the other schools as Rio's best, was warming up in the concentration section with a virtuoso display of playful, nuanced, light-spirited *batucada*, nothing like Mangueira's train-track tattoo. This most irreverent of samba schools was as physically different from Mangueira in costume as out of it. The drummers were young and wore fashionably baggy clothes, and there were even several women in the front rows assigned to the light metal percussion instruments. One gaunt young woman, leading the *chocalho* section, was dressed in a long, gauzy cotton skirt and espadrilles, a loose tunic and chunky jewelry, with her hair pulled back in a severe knot; she would not have looked out of place on the Faubourg-St.-Denis. Across the way, the Mangueira women looked decidedly stolid in their spandex outfits and platform heels.

The Padre Miguel *bateria* was energetically going through practice riffs while the Mangueira drummers rested on the other side of the road, wearing condescending expressions that spoke of their age and experience. Padre Miguel's *passistas* practiced, Mangueira's chatted with the wing members. Now, out of the corner of our eye, we saw what we soon realized was the Independent Youth's Opening Commission, made up not of the venerable old gentlemen or celebrities who generally greet the crowd at the head of every school, bowing ceremoniously in top hats and tails, but of fourteen extremely big, black, muscled young men. They were dressed in street clothes for the rehearsal: I had heard that for carnival they would be wearing thigh-high white boots and miniskirts, trademarks of Xuxa, the pouting blonde hostess of TV Globo's morning cartoon show. In their Xuxa getup, they would perform a little routine devised for them by the late *carnavalesco* Fernando Pinto, which they were now rehearsing: "Bye-bye, Brazil," they sang, mimicking Xuxa's baby-talk sign-off. "Kiss-kiss, kiss-kiss"; and they puckered their lips and blew dainty little kisses, Xuxa style. "Here is our delight!" At which, splitting into twin rows of seven each and turning to face both sides of the audience, they joyfully placed their hands on their flies and weighed what they advertised as the not inconsiderable volume within.

"Disgusting," Guezinha thought it.

She had arrived seconds before the rehearsal began, irritable and distracted, tailed by a breathless handful of friends. At the sound truck, Percy Pires was blaring instructions, and the harmony directors were moving up and down the ranks, checking for wing chief absences. "People, it's shameful," Percy yelled out over the microphone. "The school members are here and acting responsibly, and we can't get any cooperation from the chiefs." A couple of dozen baianas were patiently waiting in their appointed place, about half the Petrópolis wing was standing quietly in formation, the *passistas* were strutting and ready to move, and some of the wing chiefs still could not be found. I was nervous, worried about stage fright and endurance. In Nilsemar's wing, directly behind Guezinha's, many of the members were also white, and first-timers. "Don't be intimidated by the Sambadrome," Nilsemar advised them. "Use this rehearsal to take its measure, and pace yourselves."

As the music started and we rounded the bend from the concentration area into full view of the avenue stretching six blocks before us, I despaired. Already I was winded, having ignored Nilsemar's warning and thrown myself into the song from the first measure and through the long time it took for our tail end of the school to arrive at the parade ground. There was nothing here but cement and desolation, I thought, made even more breathless by panic, and the night air rushed through my throat like sandpaper.

But there was more. As we passed the entrance gate we saw what had electrified the leaping, frenetic wings ahead of us: thousands of people in the bleachers, yelling, waving, singing with us, all the favelados come down from the hills where the mud was sliding, to make believe that this free rehearsal was the real parade they would never be able to afford. They cheered; we waved. They sang; we skipped. They jumped up and down, screaming hoarsely, "Mangueira!" Their arms reached out to us, and we felt the great surge of forward energy, the samba foam rising to top the cresting wave inside of us. "Black men dance, play *capoeira*, / They are the kings, pink and green, of all Mangueira!" we shouted, and rushed into the welcoming din.

This was samba now, all of us. Black and white, dancers and klutzes thrown together into the same joyous mess—free, liberated, glamorous and hilarious at the same time, returned to the innocence of pure unrestrained exhibitionism, posturing and primping and wiggling our hips, charging around in circles with our arms going like pistons, yelling at the top of our voices and flouncing our backsides, staring boldly at someone in the audience who looks at us with dazzled pride, with wistfulness, with envy for the briefest fraction of a minute before we move on and leave his gaze behind. The memory of his face evaporates and with it all memory, for we are past remembering in this river of people, this flow of present instants that sweeps us away from the past. There are tasks to accomplish too urgent to leave any room for a tugging sense of loss or the burning pain of the lives we may have lived before. We must, this very second, throw one hand up in the air, finger upright in a testifying fashion, to command the world's attention to our presence. We must immediately flutter our other hand past our face, torso, hips and legs to show how much we have to offer. We must let into the air the song bursting up through our throats. At this very moment we feel compelled to skip back and forth in straight lines with our wing partner and sudden friend, waving hips out in unison and solidarity, caught in the momentum. But then we forget about it because we have caught the eye of a cluster of teenagers looking at us with that thrilling mixture of admiration, amusement and envy, and we must dedicate a line of our song to them, no more than that, because the instant is over and now they too have vanished. Ahead is the carnival truck and even closer is a sheepdog, blowing his whistle and waving his hands at us frantically—"Move it! Move it!" We must stick out our tongues at him and flounce on.

13 *Mid-February*

In Mangueira precarnival Thursday was dominated, as the days before it had been, by the rains and television, television and the rains. The newscasts featuring carnival and flood items were followed by televised debates among the samba school presidents, and then by live broadcasts of the first precarnival costume balls, which started at midnight.

At Dona Nadir's, I watched television with the family and Eurides. She had been offered a free costume by her old wing chief that included—although children under the age of five were theoretically banned from the parade—a baby *fantasia* for Anderson. Her husband's reluctance to see her parading and the fear of exhausting the baby were the reasons Eurides gave for her continuing hesitation, but I suspected that she was concerned less with Lilico than with the burden of dancing for eighty minutes while carrying her son, who had developed into a gigantic infant. Placid and enormous, brown as a chocolate cake, Anderson gurgled at his own private jokes and benevolently accepted the hugs, squeezes and nibbling kisses Dona Nadir, her offspring and friends so ravenously bestowed on him. Occasionally he stared in amazement at his mother, who, having just learned on the evening news that a white starlet was deserting her home school for a rival, was now working herself up into a remarkable philippic.

"She decided that she had had enough of her school, did she?" Eurides asked the television set. "What I want to know is, where would that Little Miss Nobody be without her home school? Had anyone ever heard of her before she decided to parade with her breasts in the air last year? Did she have any talent whatsoever? Just listen to this! The school gives her the opportunity to be its *bateria*'s godmother; she gets five minutes of free television exposure which an up-from-nowhere like her should die of gratitude for; the next day she's in all the papers, overnight she's a star, and now she decides her school isn't treating her right! Can you believe it?"

Some of us could, because the consensus was that the woman in question was so extraordinarily pretty she could probably get away with switching schools in the middle of the parade if it came to that. But this was not a convincing argument to Eurides, who wanted us to estimate just how many pretty women there were in a country of some 150 million people, and how many of those women would sell their inheritance for the opportunity to appear as one of the sixteen samba schools' *bateria* godmothers. And anyway, she pointed out, the whole business of the godmothers was just another television scam, nonsense the drummers didn't like and didn't need and didn't understand because it had absolutely nothing to do with *bateria* tradition and everything to do with the live broadcasts. The television people thought they could hang on to the audience's attention only by putting near-naked women on the screen at every opportunity. White women, mind you, or had any of us ever seen a black godmother? Only in Mangueira, where Guezinha's oldest daughter, as light-skinned as the rest of the family, was making her debut as *bateria* godmother; Adair was probably going to be the only one of the bunch who could samba, and we could be certain the television wouldn't be focusing on her. The cameras would be preoccupied with whoever the first woman would be to parade completely naked at carnival, because, mark her words, there would be one this year, "peeled clean from top to bottom; bottom front too."

Having won her argument with the television screen, Eurides had a brighter thought. "You know, it must be the best thing in the world to be a *bateria* godmother, dancing in front of two hundred, three hundred men, keeping them happy! If I get the idea into my head I'm going to save my pennies, do a plastic job after I finish nursing

Anderson to get my bust back up, get really slim. . . ." Lilico looked at his wife in alarm, judging that the woman who had already had her breasts surgically reduced to conform with the Brazilian fashion for smallness was perfectly capable of carrying out the plan she was now outlining. Eurides, unmindful of his stare, was going into a trance. "*Ah, não!* No one is going to get in front of me if I decide to go through with this! And when I start to samba, there's nobody on the hill who can match me! . . . Can you imagine? Me in a tiny bikini, all sequins, up in front of all those men? I wouldn't eat for a whole year, just to get in shape for something like that! Just think," Eurides went on rapturously, waving an arm around Dona Nadir's tiny sitting room, "here's the drums; there's the stands, jammed with people; and here I am, entering the Sambadrome! Blowing kisses!" She blew a few to the upper gallery. "Mmuah! I love you too! Mmmuah! And everybody's cheering, and me in that tiny bikini . . . Oh *God*! I would samba until my sandals broke, my feet burst, my legs swole up." She collapsed onto the sofa and Lilico, gathering up Anderson's things, suggested that it was time to be getting back home. Eurides grinned happily at us.

Later I watched television in Dona Neuma's house, stitching a kangaroo pocket for a notebook and pen onto the underside of my costume apron, while Ceci's sewing crew continued their long haul through the hundred costumes for the warrior wing. Replays of last weekend's scenes of flooding and despair were on the late-night newscast: the governor of Rio de Janeiro state picked his way down the bank of a river that used to be a street in Petrópolis; men hip-high in mud rescued their belongings from one-room houses in the northern flatlands of the city.

Although the catastrophes on the screen provoked constant murmurs of sympathy from the sewing crew, the Mangueira school's only official reaction to the floods had been the comment by Dona Zica during a televised interview that the school was not involved in any emergency efforts to benefit hill residents left homeless by the rains. She had stated this in her usual straightforward way, somewhat to the interviewer's surprise. "But surely the Mangueira community is doing something?" he insisted. Dona Zica saw that a different response was called for. "Of course," she said. "I'm sure the neighbors have taken those poor people hot coffee and food, because the Mangueira community is very solidarity-minded."

In contrast, Portela had announced a donation by all school members to help the Petrópolis homeless, and I asked Ceci why Mangueira was not doing something similar. "Because it's all demagoguery," she snapped. And Jaime, chief of the warriors' wing, added just as angrily, "Because none of that money will ever get to the people who need it! It'll end up in the pockets of every *malandro* in the vicinity— from the relief agencies to the government social services. Or do you believe in miracles?"

"All this do-good stuff is nonsense," Ceci concluded. "The world is like that, unfortunately."

Which was more or less what Guezinha had said a few weeks earlier, when the nightly news announced that the president of the neighborhood organization of Rio's largest favela had been assassinated, together with her lover and her younger brother, in what appeared to be an act of gang warfare. The woman, who was very young and attractive, was said to have had an affair with one of the most important members of the Red Phalanx cocaine ring before she shifted her political alliance to the favela's animal bankers, the news commentator explained, and the murder had been the Phalanx's way of declaring war on the bankers. "See that?" Guezinha said. "We knew that poor girl. She was very bright, very active; she did a lot of good things for the favela, and what did it get her? It doesn't pay to try and help others. You only get into trouble."

The newscast continued with its inventory of dead and wounded, homeless and disappeared. Someone came in covered with mud up to his knees and dumped eighty-four pink parasols on the floor, just brought in from a factory in one of the hardest-hit flood areas. "Never again!" he said, shaking himself dry. "You can't imagine what it's like out there: the van wouldn't go through the mud, so we had to leave it and walk almost two blocks to the factory. You really feel the water current could pull you down in some places. And then the worst part is going through all of that in the darkness, because the lights have been out all evening. If there's anything wrong with those parasols, it's just too bad; I'm not going back there again!"

He waited impatiently for someone in the house to verify the delivery, but Dona Neuma and her daughters had just been through another outburst of mutual recrimination and were now locked in positions of wounded dignity and strict adherence to their job descriptions. At last Guezinha called Fia in from the kitchen and asked her to count the parasols. She opened each one to make sure they worked. "They're fine," Fia told the delivery man, who headed back out into the rain. Iracema's sewing machine whirred through the glum silence that fell on the household again.

"Those poor people out in the flatlands," Chininha finally said.

Oblivious to the family tensions, the upstairs crew cut out panther-print satin armbands and ankle bands, stitched them with elastic and glued silver pom-poms on the edges. It was close to one in the morning and the crew had been working since before noon, but they were determined to wrap up Jaime's wing before carnival Saturday, barely thirty-six hours away. Jorginho, the carnival connoisseur; Ana, his partner; and Dona Diva, one of the baianas, were trying to decide how I could best spend the carnival weekend. "Is this your first one?" Ana wanted to know. She was attractive and very lively, but she had an introvert's taste for speculative thought. She was curious about the difficulties of trying to report—that is, observe—an event while being a part of it. "Because on top of everything else it involves trying to understand a world that is so different from yours, doesn't it?"

She wanted to know in what ways Mexico was different from Brazil. "For one thing, it doesn't have samba," I said, meaning that it completely lacks the capacity for sustained episodes of intense unambivalent joy. "Yes, I know," she agreed. "That's something very strange and hard to understand about us. No one can easily explain to the outside world why we are willing to sacrifice so much for carnival. But we are."

We were nearly finished with the armbands, but now there was a box of silver glitter tape to cut into one-inch lengths. Someone brought up a couple of beers.

"What I would advise you to do," Ana said, "is forget about the note-taking. Stop trying to write down what happens. If you don't give in to the spirit of carnival, if you don't let it overwhelm you, you'll never understand what it's like, so how will you be able to explain it to others? If you have the experience, you won't forget a minute of it. Every detail will stay clear in your head forever."

"What does Ana do for a living?" I asked Jorginho when she went downstairs for a moment. He looked at me, marveling at how little I understood. "She's unemployed, of course," he said. "Like everybody. Like me. How else do you think we have time for this?"

Jorginho kept himself energized through the endless hours of work by remembering past carnivals, selecting among his experiences those which might be best for me to enjoy. "I once had a good little carnival out on Paquetá Island," he mused. "You would like it. Modest. Unpretentious. Very old-fashioned. I took the ferry out there and discovered that the place has no cars. Just bicycles and unpaved streets. I spent the day there, and then people came out in homemade costumes, on their little floats, drinking and having a good time. It wasn't that anything *happened*, you understand; it's just that the place felt . . . mellow. It was a very good place to drink."

I said I had heard of Paquetá Island. In fact, I added, happy to exhibit a little of my own carnival expertise, I knew that it was an indirect cause of the birth of the samba schools, because the first turn-of-the-century promenade—on which the schools later patterned themselves—was founded on the way back from a Paquetá picnic, then very popular among union members and workers' associations.

"That promenade was called Delightful Myrtle," Dona Diva the baiana interrupted. "How did you know about it?"

"It's famous in carnival history," I answered. "How did *you* know about it?"

Dona Diva drew herself up to full, diminutive height and put an assertive hand on her hip. "Because my sister was a distinguished member."

Self-effacing, silent, Dona Diva scuttled through Dona Neuma's household sweeping and scrubbing and cooking and stitching and gluing without a murmur, and when at last work was no longer possible she spread out a blanket on the hard balcony floor and slept, but she was carnival royalty. She let her voice carry with new authority as she went through her genealogy. Daughter to *jongo* singers. Sister to a member of Delightful Myrtle. Member of the earliest dirty blocks on the hill. Friend to all the authentic baianas from Bahia who made Little Africa the berth of samba. A bamba from the days when bambas were bambas, when "samba ate" at the weekend-long parties, and when men were men and women knew how to hold their drink. "There were fights then, no question about it. The knife ate. The stick ate. And nothing stopped the samba, because we knew what we were doing." Carnival had different rituals then, she said. Like the devotees of Ishtar, the sex-changing fertility goddess of Babylon, Dona Diva and her friends would switch clothing. On the first morning of carnival, the women members of her dirty block would wear men's jackets inside out, the men would dress up as women, "and then we'd party the whole day long. At night, we had the promenade to dress up for, and then we had a real parade. That was carnival. This thing they have now is a joke."

A white couple in to pick up their costumes listened to this account with great admiration. It was true, they agreed, that the samba world had gotten tamer. Even here in Mangueira and only recently, they remembered the days in the 1970s when coming to the *quadra* was a real risk, when if you tripped over somebody and didn't say "Excuse me" prettily enough, you were likely to find a knife in you. But they would have liked to see the real old days. Not that they understood how anyone could have the energy to dance all day and then parade all night; like most of us, they were still complaining about sore muscles and exhaustion four days after the Sunday rehearsal at the Sambadrome.

Not Dona Diva, who announced with an eyebrow arched in pride that she was seventy. "You've got to know what you're doing," she said, sipping her beer parsimoniously. "Then you don't get tired: I've sometimes paraded with two different schools on the same night."

Downstairs, Iracema's crew rearranged the sewing machines and equipment so they could monitor the carnival balls on television. There were half a dozen balls, including two gay events, broadcast live all night from gigantic South Zone nightclubs, and in some sense these balls represented historical continuity, connecting the present to the late nineteenth century, when carnival became a distinctive part of Brazilian life and high-society costume balls emerged as its most important activity. Every now and again, and in order to establish the link, the lens would center on one of the wealthier people in Brazil: a society widow with money in real estate, a world-famous plastic surgeon or the immigrant owner of a vast merchandising empire; but attention was only secondarily trained on these fully dressed socialites. Mostly, the lens focused on buttocks, startling numbers of them, wiggling and jiggling in front of our faces sometimes in generous profusion, sometimes in tight close-up that filled the screen with only two.

There were female, gay and transvestite buttocks for us to contemplate. Television reporters made their way through this pillowy landscape with high-technology headgear and shouted out some names through the din so that we could know whose we were looking at. The star commentators were famous transvestites who conducted kittenish interviews with the giggling, sometimes quite drunk revelers. A girl-child smiled and nodded when "Adorable" Rogéria, Brazil's most famous transvestite, asked if he could give her behind an experimental squeeze. "A real woman's fanny is never as hard as ours, that's what I've always insisted," Rogéria said, demonstrating.

Exhausted at three a.m., Iracema and her sewing crew hardly commented on the activity on the screen, but suddenly someone—Fia or Dulce, perhaps—sat up and studied one particular set of gyrating buttocks with interest. "Isn't that what's-her-name?" she asked.

"Well, look at that, I think it is," Iracema said. "She's from this hill, you know," she told me. "Sad, no? To lose all your shame like that?"

"Especially with that cellulite," said plump Chininha, emerging briefly from a sleepless daze.

Precarnival Friday found the women in the Neuma household sunk in their recent habitual silence, paying no attention to the television that was turned up loud. Despite almost forty-eight hours of uninterrupted rain there was no water on the hill, and the beautiful Fia announced from the kitchen that the noonday dishes would have to remain in the sink for the time being. A vicious stench sneaked out of the bathroom.

Iracema was stitching when I walked in. Dulce was pushing elastic drawstring through sleevebands with a safety pin and asked for help, but the one other rusty safety pin in the house snapped in two the moment I tried to use it. Dona Neuma was on the phone and could not tell me whether she had more pins; when she was off the phone briefly I was upstairs, vainly asking Ceci's crew for a pin, and then Dona Neuma was back on the phone by the time I came downstairs. Fia's daughter Danielle was teasing Chininha's son Julio César. Julio César pushed Neuci's daughter Caro. Caro shrieked. Neuci shrieked back. Fia screamed at Danielle. No one screamed at Julio César, who roared and yelled and shrieked piercingly until Neuma got off the phone and told everybody to shut up. After trying several times to push elastic tape through a sleeveband with a twisted bobby pin, I threw the sleeve on a pile of sewing next to Dulce, who picked it up wordlessly and flung it across the room to Iracema's corner. Iracema, without turning from her sewing, shoved the entire pile on the floor. Guezinha arrived and announced that the shoes for our wing were delayed for the unforeseeable future. Iracema counted a pile of pattern pieces and found that there were six sets of sleeves missing from Chininha's costumes.

Then Guezinha discovered that she had a serious problem.

As Marilia Barboza had proposed long before, the "reality" sector of the parade was to include our maids' wing, a cooks' wing and, to close the parade, two wings of fifty members each, dressed in a gold lamé version of the street cleaners' orange suit, with a band of hand-embroidered silver sequins stitched across the chest and on the sleeves. Dona Zica's granddaughter, Nilsemar, with whom Dona Neuma's household was temporarily engaged in a feud, was in charge of one of the two street cleaners' wings. Guezinha had agreed to supervise the other fifty street-cleaner costumes for her friend William, who in turn had agreed to supervise them for Percy, who was too busy supervising the entire carnival as Elíseo Dória's chief assistant to pay much attention to his wing.

Just next door, Nilsemar, a quiet, orderly person, was already delivering perfectly tailored street cleaners' outfits with richly embroidered sequin trim when, seventy-two hours before parade time, the subcontractor in charge of embroidering the silver sequin strips for Percy's wing brought them in, and Guezinha, counting, discovered that there were enough strips for only twenty-five costumes. The rest were missing, either because the subcontractor had misunderstood the instructions or because Guezinha had made a mistake. She counted the strips again on the porch, while one bright-eyed child after another popped into the yard and asked eagerly when the costumes for the children's parade would be ready. Guezinha was counting and shooing children away, with Dona Neuma hovering and coughing anxiously in the background, when Percy appeared and asked if there was anything wrong.

I decided that it was time for a visit to Celina.

Her legs were swelling badly after several hours of straightening and combing hair next to the stove. Hairdos seemed to be the hill's precarnival obsession; five-year-old girls scheduled to parade with the children's samba school the following day wanted ringleted pony-

tails with spit curls. Women who would not be parading at all nevertheless wanted smooth bouffants for their strolls downtown or for
the drinking parties in the neighborhood. Celina couldn't afford the
materials needed for the most up-to-the-minute fashion—a head of
shoulder- or waist-length artificial braids painstakingly woven into
the wearer's hair—so she stuck to her hair tongs and to the poorest
women in the community, who came in all morning and afternoon
and paid her with seventy or a hundred cruzados according to hair
length and complexity of the style. A good many customers who
promised to pay later had made and failed to keep that promise
before, and Celina took them all, shrugging that nothing was gained
by turning someone away. "At least she gets her hairdo, and that's
half of it, no?"

She had barely had time to cook, and she was hungry and hot.
As usual when it rained, Celina was also having laundry worries,
aggravated now by the lack of running water: "We should be wearing
fresh, clean clothes for the carnival, but even if the running water
returned to the sink right now and I started washing, how would the
clothes ever dry?"

The puddled room was filled with family, customers, leaks, a
swarm of kittens, and tempers were crackling. When the sun shone,
Celina's family could believe the myth that they lived outdoors because they were so gregarious, but days of forced confinement
brought the graceless truth as close as the damp walls: they lived
their lives out in the open because there was no room for them
anywhere else. "Sit down," Celina said, and Sidney moved off a chair
and wedged a space for himself on the sofa behind Marcos and next
to Bebeth, who, having fought recently with Sidney, took herself and
her transistor radio to the damp bed behind the curtain. I told Celina
I had an appointment, and after agreeing to meet at the *quadra* the
following day, when the baiana costumes were to be handed out, I
left.

A few doors down the alley, a woman I knew only by sight waved
me over. With a finger on her lips she motioned me in the direction
of her room. "He's been like this all afternoon: I can't get him to
move," she whispered, and opened the door a crack. In the gloom I
made out a few clotheslines strung from wall to wall and filled with
laundry, a huge washing machine pushed up against the damp bare
brick wall, an empty cot. "Go on," the woman said, opening the
door wider. "Go inside."

In the exact middle of the small hot room there was a boy, aged about nine, illuminated by a thrill so overwhelming he had to hold perfectly still to keep it all in place. There was no need to ask what his incandescence was about: it shone on and was kindled by the immaculate cotton-candy–pink suit he was wearing—a suit with silver-edged lapels, buttons that buttoned, a vest pocket with a handkerchief tucked in, all of it tailored over a pink-and-green-striped T-shirt with bands of green embroidered sequins, worn over pink trousers that fit precisely and grazed the tops of soft moccasins in pastel pink leather cut exactly to the size of his feet.

"My son," the woman said. "Washington Luiz."

He could barely nod. We stood in the dank windowless room, in the shadows cast by the single light bulb against the drying laundry, while his mother talked around him, about how she was new on the hill and unused to carnival, and how at first she had not been willing to let her son participate in the children's parade because spending the money seemed ridiculous, and about how even after Washington Luiz said he had been selected for the Opening Commission, which received its costumes free, she had hesitated, wondering what the school would ask for in the end, and how now she was so glad to have given in, murmuring this in perplexed amusement while Washington Luiz smiled inwardly to himself, only occasionally bending slightly to let his gaze travel from the moccasins up to his chest, which was how, in the absence of any mirror, he could look on himself and see his body clothed in the costume of a dream world— that is, of the Real World, where events happen and are remembered, where lives move forward rather than repetitively around themselves, where things look the way they're supposed to and actions have consequences, the world of which Mangueira with its trash and rags and open sewers and leaking roofs is not a part. He could look down and see himself looking like his dreams, and this was a situation so dangerously improbable he could not budge, because a movement in any direction would inevitably drop him into the chasm of either reality or illusion.

I asked if he would mind shifting a little in the direction of the light bulb so I could take his picture, and he just managed; but when I asked if we could talk, he whispered no, not right then.

His mother walked me to the end of the alley, and I asked her why she had named her son after a turn-of-the-century Brazilian president, although what I really wanted to know was why she had chosen to name him after one of Brazil's most obscure and oddly named rulers. "Brazilian?" Washington Luiz's mother said in alarm. "No, I don't think so; he was an American, wasn't he? At least I hope so."

The commotion at the Neuma household was still audible, Dona Neuma shouting hoarsely that she might no longer be in a position of power at Mangueira but she still had a sense of honor, and that if necessary Guezinha would have to embroider every one of those sequins herself, with her daughter cutting in, in a choked voice, saying that the lady her mother was very nervous and should get some rest, and Percy, who was usually superb at getting Dona Neuma to co-operate with him, repeating uselessly, in a hoarse voice to match Dona Neuma's, that she should not be so worried, because she was not helping the situation any.

The rain had slowed to a drizzle, and I decided to look for some quiet at the hangar. The train strike had ended, with no concessions to the railroad workers and under threat of massive firings; public transport was back to normal, and I rode a bus.

Earlier in the afternoon the downtown streets had been flooded ankle-high, but now they were merely wet, and a few small holes in the sky were letting the setting sun shine through. There was a holiday thrill in the crowded streets, as if some sort of erotic Christmas were about to happen. The carnival street lighting blinked on: imitation stained-glass figures of sambistas lit from inside and strung across the major thoroughfares as well as the narrow colonial streets. Beneath the colored lights hawkers offered last-minute bargains on costumes still piled high in the stores and on improvised stalls in the streets. The record shops competed with each other in blaring out story sambas, and here and there, in front of a loudspeaker, a couple or a group of friends danced.

The hangar neighborhood was not deserted. Carnival workers bustled along President Vargas Avenue carrying costumes or pieces of equipment, and a steady flow of cars streamed down the back streets toward the glowworm light emerging from within the Sambadrome's cement canal. For once, the pink door at the Mangueira hangar was unguarded, open to frantic wing chiefs, harmony directors, samba stars in to check their costumes and their float positions, carnival reporters, friends. Julinho kept himself and his workers separate from the uproar at the front by means of a rope strung across the float factory space, where he was working on the float for the children's school—a drab little car decorated only with the figure of the deceased *bateria* director, whom the children were honoring in their parade. The other members of the crew were painting the final coats of gloss and glitter on the now nearly finished floats.

A one-legged sprite in a red cap leading an elephant; full-fleshed baianas offering their sweets with generous smiles; a white couple dancing; a black couple dancing; Anastácia and two attendants; a platform with two gigantic fists and a brace of zebu oxen with incongruous and enchanting smiles painted across their muzzles; a gigantic slave ship; a stage covered in straw matting and decorated with brightly painted gourds; the five-platformed stand for the African gods; the golden throne for Princess Isabel, supported by the four black atlantes and crowned with two heraldic angels entirely covered in mirror to catch the morning sun; a platform (which Julinho had not been able to bring himself to decorate like a favela) where Nininha and Delegado would stand. A well-dressed black man who had stepped over the rope barrier took his family around from float to float, pausing to examine the details: the teeth so carefully painted on the dancing baianas, the white baby suckling at the black woman's breast. Percy ran up, his face blood-red, his neck veins swollen, and caught the intruder by the scruff of the neck, kicking and shoving him all the way back to the pink door, shouting insults as they went, before giving the man's terrified children a final shove onto the sidewalk. Above a week's growth of stubble Percy's eyes were sunken and bloodshot. His shirt was stained with sweat and his hands were shaky. He had not left the hangar for more than a couple of hours at a time for nearly a week. Now, as he berated Seu Sixteen and the other workers for their lack of attention to the door, he lost his voice. Minutes later he was asleep on an old car seat propped up against the kitchen wall. No one paid any attention to his outburst. Julinho's pal Melão, unnaturally silent, his arm still in a sling, went on painting hand-held ornaments in a corner. Julinho lit a cigarette and pressed his brush dry against the edge of the little can of gold paint he was holding. Seu Sixteen dispensed coffee.

Outside, a swelling river of people walked in the direction of the Sambadrome. There were reporters come to claim their credentials in the chaotic press room, where no credentials were ready; Riotur workers trotting with decorations with which to crest the Sambadrome; proprietors of boxes who wanted to inspect their custom-ordered decor.

Some boxes were already painted in the owners' school colors. One had been done in black and silver. Workers were smoothing down flowered wallpaper for a box that would be furnished with wicker sofas and a large refrigerator. Over the sound truck's loud-speakers Bezerra da Silva's sly voice sang about cocaine, alternating with the story-samba recordings.

The area just between the Mangueira hangar and the parade grounds—ordinarily an empty lot, lately transformed by the rains into a moldy-smelling stretch of mud and refuse—was filled with the clack and bustle of construction. Rows of beer shacks were going up, their light bulbs reflecting in the puddles underfoot. There were folding tables and chairs around each, a grill for hot dogs and shish kebab, and given pride of place on a raised shelf behind the counter, a television on which to monitor the parades.

Several Mangueira school members had half a dozen shacks in one of the choice commercial spots. Here and there I recognized faces I had seen in the vicinity of beer stands on the hill, already installed in their new location for the brief season. Looking for Delegado, who had told me he put a shack up every year, I found only his sisters—identically gaunt, toothless, energetic and unfriendly—hauling beer and soft-drink crates behind the counter and setting the first rows of skewered meat on to grill. They said Delegado was not around because he had work to do back on the hill, and I remembered that tonight was Mangueira's final *quadra* rehearsal.

One a.m. At Dona Neuma's home, Guezinha was looking devastated, ambulating purposelessly through the house, alone. Her mother was asleep. Elania had gone out for the evening with her boyfriend, just returned from a long out-of-town trip. Iracema, Dulce and Fia were stitching and Chininha was in the kitchen, making fritters. Guezinha poured herself a glass of milk, slammed the refrigerator shut, picked up a chicken-and-dough fritter from Chininha's tray and disappeared upstairs without a word. No one in the household had plans to go to the rehearsal.

Two a.m. The last rehearsal of the carnival year; from now until the next September the *quadra* was to remain empty and silent. I looked at it all again, saying my own farewells to the drummers I never talked to; to the traffickers who never agreed to talk to me and to their girlfriends whom I was never curious about; to the dancers whose movements I had memorized and tried secretly to copy in my room at night; to the school's second flag-bearer, Carlos Dória's common-law wife, who had smiled her sweet smile and twirled through all the weekends following first his estrangement from her and then his death; to Beto End-of-the-Night and his tireless assistants at the microphone; to Elíseo Dória's muscled bodyguards, and their dark green T-shirts and merciless stares; to the favelados who lived on the edge of the *quadra* and were present at every rehearsal, hanging out the windows of their shacks in full view of us, drinking in the rehearsals and thankful for the privilege of ringside seats to the commotion; to Iracema's husband, Carlinhos, who bustled among the tables in his Prince Valiant haircut all night long, hawking T-shirts, smiling and bowing to all potential customers; to the sound technician hidden in his box beneath the singers' tower, responsible for all that dreadful, distorted sound; to the squalid children, single-mindedly churning out samba even then, long after the adults had had enough and were leaning back in their chairs in a stupor of beer and fatigue.

The dance floor was nearly empty. The few non-Mangueirenses still around were getting ready to leave: beautiful black *malandros* with white linen suits and smiles like knives holding out for last-minute pick-ups; exhausted white couples groggy and graceless from beer. Nondancers had moved their chairs up from the table area to the inner side of the dance space, where some were now dozing discreetly, barricades of beer at their feet, while others slept with the desperate intensity of late-night travelers in bus stations, heads lolling back off their axis as if their necks had been broken.

Enjoying the luxury of so much space, two women danced. A small light-skinned woman in a green satin china-doll dress held the center, making sparks fly in a fast erotic samba. Her orbiting moon was tall, hefty, very black. Green eye shadow, green nails, purple lipstick, St. Teresa's smile. Green headband, bright magenta jacket over a green shirt. In contrast to her partner she was ecstatic and calm, curtsying and spinning through an imitation of the flag-bearer's dance. A headful of braids floated behind her. Occasionally the two women opened the link to admit a man, any man, turning their smiling attention briefly on his flying legs and then shutting him out with another smile, spinning inward into their own hypnotic circle.

Carlos Dória's widow danced with her frequent partner, as chubby as she and a dead ringer for the young Louis Armstrong. He danced always with uncontrollable and irresistible energy, samba popping out of him at such speed that every once in a while he was forced to look down to see what it was doing to his feet, or his hips, or his hands. Then he would shrug happily—"Oh, what the hell"— and give in, letting the dance work its will with him. Dória's widow floated at his center, her smile open in a gesture of pure delight.

Almost four a.m. Delegado took the floor with a young girl—his niece or granddaughter, someone murmured—and led her to the center of the space. She had remarkable speed and a complicated repertory of movements, all of which she performed with fullness and grace, caught up in the pleasure of dancing to a degree that overcame any awareness of the audience. She must have been about fourteen years old, but there was none of the sharp-edged busyness of the mosquito brigade's dancing in her movements, and none of the blatant sexual appeal coached into sambistas from toddlerhood. Delicately, she explored every interstice in the rhythm, dancing first to the light metal instruments, then to the drums, reshaping the music into movement and making all its different parts visible: the song line's rise and fall, the changes in rhythm, the backbeat of the mandolin.

Delegado guided her gently, effortlessly, not working, dancing little jokes to himself as he went.

A teenage majordomo had been practicing on the sidelines of this exhibit, and now Delegado turned to him, pulling him into the center and dancing alongside. The boy followed out of the corner of his eye while Delegado waved his glittery baton—scolding, urging, remonstrating, demonstrating with a dazzling display of his eternally long legs which seemed to climb on top of each other and then down the same ladder again, all the while spinning counterclockwise and swiveling his torso 180 degrees right and left. The kid imitated more than passably, a little frightened and a little proud, aware that the rest of the dancers in the *quadra* had gradually come to a halt, closing into a breathless circle around the trio's magical performance.

The music stopped. The crowd burst into applause while Delegado hugged his pupil. For the first time ever, I saw his smile.

A little past four a.m. The table on Dona Neuma's porch was littered with beer bottles and shrimp shells. Fia was out with her police chief for the evening. Dulce had gone home, but Iracema was still stitching and Chininha was keeping her company, dozing on a chair. Images of breasts, painted bodies, sweat-shined hips flickered on the television screen. Somebody had turned the sound off. Red G-strings. Black G-strings. A man slurped beer off of a woman's body.

Upstairs, Dona Diva had already laid out a blanket on the porch for the night. Ceci, who had emerged earlier from the shower sweet-smelling and in full makeup, was out for the evening. The wing was finished, wrapped up, she had said, but Ana and Jorginho were still at work. He looked exhausted, coked up, stoned out, weird, wired, tense as I'd never seen him, but thus far unflagging in his determination to finish the work before carnival Saturday, which was now about four hours away.

He had a plan, he said. Throughout the following day, enjoy his sleep. Then, around five p.m., when he was rested, showered, dressed up, hit one of the little downtown samba clubs and stay there until closing time, whenever that was. The end of the club night would be his cue to embark on some serious drinking, wherever fate and the flow of carnival took him. This stage should last until late Sunday morning, when he would be in exactly the right state of mind to put on some women's clothing, head for the northern suburbs around Portela and Império Serrano and join up with the Piranhas' block, the best of all the cross-dressing blocks, except for the Ipanema band, which was good, he thought, but really mostly for gays. In the afternoon it'd be time to go downtown to join a couple of the traditional downtown blocks, after which he'd probably rest a little before the parade.

He smiled a tight smile, his eyes glittering and shifty, focused suddenly on Fia's hips as she walked in, studying them with a lascivious intensity that turned his sharp-featured face, with its high cheekbones and carved mouth, into a mask of the lewd Exu. "From here until Thursday, nobody's going to get in my way," he announced in an even, chill voice, and as I left he did not say "God bless you."

In the predawn drizzle I climbed home by way of the Hot Hole. From somewhere on the other side of the *quadra* there was a burst of machine-gun fire, the "peal of laughter" of the *malandros'* celebrations. A last straggle of coke sniffers huddled under a narrow awning, but the path up the hill was deserted. A song was going through my head, one that was popular back in the 1930s, before Carmen Miranda joined the roster of Hollywood's Latin American mascots alongside Pepe Carioca and Speedy Gonzalez. It was written by Assis Valente, the man who wrote most of her Brazilian hits, and she used to sing it in a sweet, slow, playfully indignant voice:

> He put on his best party clothes
> And went to see what he could see.
> He'd already drunk hard liquor
> Instead of taking toast and tea.
> He carried a switchblade and a tambourine.
> And he smiled when people said: "Easy, Lion. Relax."
>
> He tore up my velvet curtain
> And made it into a skirt.
> He put on my best camisole
> Instead of his shirt.
> He took off all his ID and put it under lock,
> And he even grabbed the broomstick to make a flagpole
>   for his parade block.
>
> He turned my hot-water bottle
> Into a baby's pacifier,
> And then he ran out of here
> As if he'd caught fire,
> Yelling, "I want to suck, Momma, I want to suck,
> Momma, I want to suck!"
> He carried a switchblade and a tambourine.
> And he smiled when people said: "Easy, Lion. Relax."
>
> I know he's going to rig himself up
> Like Marie Antoinette,
> And I know just how crazy my baby can get.
> But I'll tell you one thing:
> He's not getting out of my sight.
> Because now that the batucada's getting hot,
> He's going to want to dance until he drops tonight
> At the Club Polka Dot.

14 *Carnival Saturday*

A beautiful black youth with a blank face and a body like a snake's weaves through the early-morning drinkers with a friend. The friend, an ostrichlike bird with sparkling midnight-blue plumage, emerges from the back of the minute, flesh-colored bikini the youth is wearing and rears its richly feathered neck along the boy's supple spine, peering over his head with large vacant eyes very like the boy's own. The only other things the boy is wearing, aside from the bikini and his friend, are a pair of thigh-high snakeskin boots in matching midnight blue, a metal-studded dog collar and blue glitter powder on his eyelids and perfect cheekbones.

An early mist coats the walkway in front of the Polka Dot Club. Bright sunlight pierces and melts it where revelers converge along Rio Branco Avenue. A lone black woman walks through the thick light: Tina Turner hair and a black lace slip. A drinking party of men: white polka-dot shirts, black shorts. Someone in polka-dot boxer trunks. Someone else—also a man—in black lingerie, garter belt and high heels. There are a few families, the children smeared in greasepaint: black on white, white on black. The harsh contrasts and the glare of the brand-new sun on the sidewalk wound the eye.

A red wig. Big red breasts. High heels with pom-pom tops. Screams. Giggles. Whoops.

A huddle of transvestites is making an anarchic entrance on the avenue. The tallest one skitters up to a group of men and cradles her anatomically correct falsies in her hands, offering them with an arch lipsticked smile. Refused, she flounces off but soon returns again, this time with her coterie in tow, all tottering on their spike heels. They block off the men's progress, pouting, posing, offering plump backsides, snaking hands along stockinged legs. Delighted to spot a camera, they shift their attention and head for the lens, jockeying for the foreground spot, pushing each other aside with a forceful shift of the hip. Someone is laughing in the crowd. They wink in her direction, flutter their tongues lasciviously, rub their breasts and shudder.

The sun coaxes coils of steam up from the sidewalks, the heat intensifying by the minute, as if downtown Rio were a pot just placed over a nice slow fire to stew. A man pours a plastic cup of beer over himself. The very drunk appear to be having a better time than those of us who have turned up for the official inauguration of carnival still blinking, dazed, sleepless, straight out of the shower. To catch up, a few men order beer at the nearest counter.

Beer drinking against a backdrop of loud music. Today it is under the auspices of the Polka Dot Club, which has staged the first carnival frenzy—at eight on Saturday morning—for going on seventy years. These days the Polka Dot Club joins forces with Riotur to inaugurate carnival with a program that includes a vintage car caravan, the surrender of the city keys to King Momo and a parading madness led by the Polka Dot band. The cars are the same ones that paraded in the days when following a caravan of fancy new Model Ts was one of the major carnival thrills.

Predictably, the ceremony is delayed an hour or two.

Waiting, I scan the magazine racks at a newspaper stand just setting up for the day. Already it is aflower with special carnival issues devoted to the South Zone balls. In the establishment publications, it is possible to count row after row of perfect teeth and identical buttocks displayed by marvelously similar young women lined up in G-strings and tops designed with as much variation as can be coaxed out of such a small amount of material. Smaller layouts are devoted to society notes and a few previews of school parades, along with coverage of the costume balls: arcane rituals in which a few aging men and even fewer women glide down a runway bearing the weight of as much as a hundred pounds of sequins that have been sewn, stretched and buttressed into extravagant shapes.

Specialized magazines focus exclusively on the more titillating activities at the South Zone balls. My favorite is one whose title translates roughly as "Only Filthy Lewdness," but I can't find it on the stand. There are adequate clones: seedy two-toners with runny-inked photographs of sozzled men crowding desperately smiling women and performing various gynecological examinations on them. What makes the images odd are the people jumping and waving their arms in the background, like fans at a football stadium. I wanted to check if the same participants appear in the photographs from one year to the next, but it's hard to tell. The microphone at the parade stand gears into action and I put the magazines back.

King Momo, the obese ruler of carnival, descendant of Momus, the Greek god of pranks, materializes in the yellow haze. His nearly spherical face is pleasant and alert, reflecting neither gluttony nor sloth. He is slightly made up for the television cameras, and his costume is elegant: a gray satin tunic trimmed in white fur, flowing trousers, Louis XIV slippers.

Nimbly he hoists himself up on the stand where the carnival queen and her entourage are already poised. The queen is very pretty and she is required only to smile, which is fortunate, since she's probably been up all night promoting Riotur at a succession of balls. She smiles. King Momo smiles and does a little samba shuffle. The president of Riotur gives a brief speech, distorted past comprehension by the microphone. Most of the crowd is edging away from the stand and toward the back of the parade, where the Polka Dot band has formed ranks.

The crowd has swelled to several hundred, and almost everyone is wide awake again. There is a busy, eager hum of chatter and giggling. Last-minute arrivals come running up to join the cortege, the transvestites' ankles wobbling dangerously under the strain of their costumes, their high-heeled shoes and their haste. I run into a couple of Mangueirenses, emerging with renewed energy from a nightlong daze of beer, and I seem to recognize a blond man I have spotted before, looking respectable in Ipanema, now in the latter stages of euphoric dissipation. The crowd is about evenly divided between whites and blacks. All the new arrivals look clean, freshly pressed, ready for Sunday school.

The beauty queens are climbing onto the backs of lined-up convertibles, flipping mirrors out of some hidden pocket and checking their makeup. Sensing a camera, they flex themselves into soft angles. Not a false move. Thigh folded lightly against thigh, hips swiveled at a three-quarter angle to the torso to make the waist look slimmer, shoulders back, chin slightly up and a choice of smiles, sixteen or twenty teeth showing. The smaller, friendlier smile predominates at this early hour; the wide, reckless smile with its promise of debauchery is deemed more appropriate for the evening. The beauty queens change poses, cross their legs carefully, keeping their muscles tense so the flesh doesn't spread. Around them the transvestites howl and bump and grind.

The number of drag queens will multiply throughout the day. There will be a pert-bottomed one in high heels, naked except for a *cache-sexe* fashioned like a bunch of grapes, running through an extraordinarily accurate imitation of Betty Grable poses, if you ignore the fellatious tongue that lolls out of her mouth now and then. And a gigantic one in roller skates dressed like a miniskirted Red Cross nurse, needle at the ready, red light flashing on her helmet, emitting a shrill ambulance wail as she rolls. And one I want to hug, tiny and also naked under her fake-fur coat except for a lavishly curled pubic wig, importuning a man with a shy "May I?" and locking her legs around his waist for a frantic three-second hump, then climbing down again with a blushing, whispered "Thank you!" before he's had time to react.

The band is tooting a few trial notes. King Momo receives the keys to the city from a city official and promises to rule with no regard for law, decency, decorum or propriety. The crowd is jumping, impatient with these formalities. King Momo climbs on his Momobile and all the cars rev up. With a piercing metallic cry, the band blasts the day in half. The past is behind us: carnival has begun.

In the Hot Hole a corpulent man sits with his wife. He is wearing her clothes, a sprig of rue stuck behind one ear. They play cards.

A din of clashing metal and drums announces the Folia de Reis, literally, the craziness of kings. Carnival revelers dressed in brightly colored dominos; a flag-bearer in a cardboard crown and eyeglasses leading the procession, guitar and cymbal players following behind. This form of celebration died out in the 1930s, I'd read, but the ghosts are here in Mangueira, solemn and primitive in their progress down the viaduct.

More men in their wives' clothing, one with a smear of red lipstick across his mouth, swigging *cachaça*. Even those who aren't cross-dressed sport a sprig of rue, sacred to the warrior god Ogun.

Not quite noon yet, but there is cocaine everywhere. A half-dozen white youths standing next to a beer shack are drinking and snorting as if they were in a hurry. The hill kids race around on their motorcycles, Tuchinha recklessly going beyond his usual boundary at the edge of the Hot Hole and onto the viaduct, back and forth along the edge of the hill.

Dona Esmeralda feeds me a carnival lunch as follows: fried rice with a slight tomato cast; mashed potatoes; beans with bits of salt pork; fried manioc flour; fried plantains; spinach crêpes with white sauce; oven-roasted chicken; orange soda pop; and for dessert, orange pound cake.

Each mouthful of cholesterol, refined carbohydrates and sugar makes me swoon with pleasure and guilt. Greedily, I sink into a second plateful, paying attention to the chicken for decorum's sake but longing to drown in manioc—its gritty, nubbly taste of pure starch—and the delight of the bacon's hot juices. Dona Esmeralda, who has seen me breakfast every morning on dry black stuff I call bread and she feels sure is toxic, looks on with great satisfaction.

She learns in the course of the meal that my next stop will be the *quadra*, where the baiana costumes are to be distributed. The announcement knifes through her and leaves her wincing. "Have you seen them?" I haven't yet, but I understand they are an improved version of the sample copy. "I've heard it was very beautiful." Yes, I say. Indeed.

She leans forward hungrily. "How?"

What?

"How is it beautiful?"

It's hard to say, I think, fumbling for words and a napkin, wondering if I can manage more fried plantains. Pink and green. Frothy.

"It's my understanding that although it's very pretty it has some problems as well," I say finally. "People seemed to think the African shoulder cape wasn't long enough, and there wasn't enough material in the skirt. I'm sure last year's was better."

"No," she says, no longer trusting me. "Last year's baiana left some people unhappy."

This is the first I've heard of that, I assure her.

Dona Esmeralda instructs me. "No one liked the materials," she says. "They were . . . cheap. Not worthy. Baianas like to be dressed in the best there is, and last year the lace, particularly, was very poor quality. It was curtain lace, to put it bluntly, vulgar and cheap."

Nevertheless, I insist, the problem this year was that the costumes were farmed out to a couturier who didn't know all that much about baiana tradition.

This is the first Dona Esmeralda has heard about the controversy. She had restrained herself from asking even that much. "Oh well," she says, and sighs. "I don't care for such things now, anyway. Before, of course, I took a great interest. Last night—this morning, really—you would have found me down at the *quadra*, right until the rehearsal broke up, because, you see, this morning is the time for the nostalgia block. We call it that because there won't be another rehearsal until September. So you stay in the *quadra* all night, drinking plenty of beer, and then at dawn the *bateria* leads the school out into the street, and everybody follows behind, up and down the viaduct, dancing and playing, and then you hang around the Hole, drinking beer, getting a good party going." Her whole body is straining forward, taut with memory.

She draws a deep, painful breath. "But now that I reflect on it, I think that probably that whole part of my life was a waste of time, because carnival is exhausting, you know. For example, if I had joined the baianas this year, right now I would be so tired! And yet I'd still have to cook and wash clothes so that everybody could be nice and clean for the parade. That's not a way to live, wasting your time on foolishness that gets you nowhere and just makes you tired."

I wait for the "Praise the Lord!" end to her speech, but it never comes. Dona Esmeralda slumps in her chair, lost in thought.

Tiny green Indians dance around me. Pink fairies float down the hill. Children stream out of Dona Neuma's and Dona Zica's in their shiny

costumes. Combed, washed, glittering in brand-new costumes delivered just in time for the parade. The mosquito brigade zooms around
in dizzy circles, crazy with the excitement of the afternoon to come.
Tuchinha's housekeeper beams down on them from his lanky height.
An outrageous queen, the only flamboyant gay grudgingly accepted
in homophobic Mangueira, he is bursting with pride today. He claps
his hands together, chivying and shushing and scolding the unruly
membership of the children's wing he presides over, herding them
together for one final run-through of the baby samba school's story
samba.

On a stoop, Ademar the sambista watches disdainfully.

Cars pull up at Dona Neuma's and Dona Zica's, pull away again
laden with costumes, the backseats a foam of tulle, glitter and ruffles.

The baiana costumes have not arrived from the couturier's shop.
There is no sign of him or of the baiana wing chief, and Dona Neuma
is wisely keeping away from the *quadra*. Messages have arrived sporadically via the directorate office phone since early in the morning,
when the first baianas clambered down from the North Zone buses
and waddled happily into the *quadra*. "The costumes will arrive at
eleven." "They'll be here at noon." "Three at the latest." While
members of the *bateria* zigzag down rows of pink suits and top hats
laid out in the directorate meeting room, looking for the outfit with
their name on it, the baianas grow cross.

Wisely, Celina has not wasted any time at the *quadra*. She is
sitting next to the stove with her tongs, fixing her own hair. The
costumes, she says, will be ready when they're ready, because the
only thing that is not possible is for them not to be ready in time for
the parade. Someone will be sure to let her know when they arrive.
Of course, if Dona Neuma had been in charge things would be
different, but she isn't. At least it's stopped raining.

Washington Luiz, who has been tagging around behind me in his
pink suit all afternoon, pops his head in the door to announce that
the children's school is almost ready to leave for the Sambadrome.
He stares at Celina and her tongs. "Why is the lady making her hair
stand up on end like that?" he wants to know. "Little boy, you don't
need to be asking dumb questions," Celina says dryly. "Soon enough
you'll be grown up, and you'll marry a nappy-haired woman of your
own, and you'll have the rest of your life to figure out why she does

the way she does." Under her cool stare, Washington Luiz vanishes.

She is in an odd, harsh mood. "Poor kid," she says, going back to her hair. "He's not going to be around long on this hill. I was just like his mother: always getting into trouble, never able to make the rent. He's older than he looks, you know, about twelve, and he hasn't yet made it to first grade. I could never get my children through school either. Always getting evicted, moving from one hill to another, struggling just to keep everybody fed. A child with a mother like that doesn't have much of a future."

In the *quadra*, mutiny is in progress. Grumbling and loud protest. If Dona Neuma were here . . . If Dória were still alive . . . If Mangueira thinks I have the money and the time to spend getting myself here and waiting all day when I should be washing clothes, just wait until next year. If that insignificant couturier thinks we're not worth his time . . . Someone in the directorate has the inspired idea of getting the kitchen to work. Soon enough Celina appears. "They're giving out free lunches!" she exclaims, offering me a plate of macaroni. Shortly afterward, a van full of costumes arrives.

Now the *quadra* is in chaos. The costumes have no names on them. The numbers on the bags don't match a list. The headdresses are being handed out separately. Dona Neuma puffs into view, answering the wave of greetings and hugs distractedly, looking for an end of the raveled thread she can pull and start to order. Impossible. For hours, the costume distribution continues while the baianas, who as a rule dislike the use of foul language, mutter nasty things. Despite the meal.

The porch and the stairs and the bedrooms at Dona Neuma's are packed with school members trying on costumes. The beautiful Fia helps three-year-old Julio César with his miniature *bateria* costume: pink suit with green sequin trim, a top hat half as tall as he is, a pacifier. He poses for a picture on the porch, perfectly immobile until one of the street kids sneaks up and pops a balloon behind his ear. He wails in terror.

In the living room, Iracema is still stitching, glued to her chair with a last costume she is just starting to work on: hers. Friends and relatives have set up camp here, equipped with drink, shrimp, turnovers. Iracema laughs, sips beer, trades jokes. Dulce, who is not parading, is unsteady on her feet. Numbly, she pushes sleeves right side out and tugs the elastic drawstrings close.

Upstairs, Guezinha and Elania hand out costumes and check off lists, barely looking up as they pass out the bulging plastic bags. The maids' wing members pick up costumes complete with green shoes, the street-cleaners' wing members are receiving gold lamé outfits with silver trim. Not a shoe, not a band of silver is missing.

Behind them, Ana and Jorginho work in silence, gluing silver pom-poms on leopard-skin armbands. Over the porch railing, Jorginho sees a car arrive, calls out to the driver, hastens out.

A few minutes later he is back again, strung tight as a crossbow, his eyebrows arched into a point, lips strained white against his teeth. His breath comes short. "Just wait, just wait!" He walks up and down the chaotic hallway, muttering about buddies, and traitors, and the man in the car who bought a silver chain from him some time ago and owes him to this day. Ceci tries to calm him, but Jorginho is out of control. "He drives up here in a fancy red car and tells me, 'I'm just going over to Beato's to pick up some blow,' and then he says he still doesn't have money to pay me? The bastard is going to pay!

"I know people! I know who to talk to! The bastard thinks he's going to parade with Portela? I'm going to get two of my friends and I'm going to walk right up to him in the Sambadrome, just when he's getting ready to come out, and I'm going to have them put a gun to either side of his head, and I'm going to say, 'Get the fuck out of those clothes. Take off that costume this minute. You're not parading, asshole!' "

I never see him again.

The hill is changing colors. Awash in pink and green.

Children stream down the hill toward the waiting buses.

Dusk. In Dona Neuma's front room, Iracema is wrapping up the sewing amid a blithe racket of laughter and cooking and the blare of the television set, continuously broadcasting last year's parades. Those who show up at this hour to pick up costumes tend to stay, this being as good a party as any. A dizzily elated couple waltzes in, middle-aged, black, middle-class. Paunchy and prosperous both. Black and white polka dots on his shirt, her skirt. They have spent the day with the Polka Dot band and are euphoric. Hugs. Handslaps. Cheers and jokes. A great carnival. They unload beer they've brought. Iracema, smiling, banters with the man, who yanks her out of her chair and spins her around the floor. Who's up for a dance? Iracema is back at her sewing, his wife is tired, all the women are busy. Alone, chattering a samba rhythm to himself, he bippity-bops, his shoes snaking a fast sandy shuffle on the tile floor. Bippity-bop, bippity-bop. A nice little rhythm we've got going here. He chatters on. Stops. Turns cigarette-ash gray. Totters backward and grabs the air looking for somewhere to fall. Calmly, his wife pushes a chair out and pulls him down on it. He slumps, sweating.

"I'm tired," he says. "Let's go home."

15   *Carnival Sunday*

Out on the viaduct with my sudden companion for the evening, a boy of marvelous beauty and *malandro* style. No taxi will stop for us in the reeling night. The boy is too tall, too black, too crazy. "I have ID, man!" he yells after a taxi that speeds by. "I'm somebody here in Mangueira!" His speech is slurred.

Eventually a taxi driver stops, parleys, asks for ID, lets us in. "To the Sambadrome!"

We crawl out at Beer Shack Row, sink into the mud, slog through the soup of people, our immaculate white outfits already sullied, our bearings lost. I trip in the shapeless crowd, which has suddenly veered off in crazy directions. He catches me. At the center of the turbulence, a huge man built like a cop is pistol-whipping a small pickpocket-shaped man, pressing him against the side of a car with one meaty hand. "Don't worry," my companion says, and from the pocket of his Bermudas he pulls out a towel wrapped around a gun. "You're safe with me." I want to go away. He wants to watch. We stay to watch the pistol-whipping until the crowd's attention falters and we drift away.

Midnight on carnival Sunday. First night of the first-division schools' parades. Drunks. Dancers. Brawls. Couples pressing against each other in the shadow of the beer shacks. Men drinking in the shacks' glaring light. Noise. Too many people. More people. We pick and shove our way through the multitude. I trip again. He whirls to look for a culprit, one arm around me, the other eagerly reaching for the heavy towel. "Are you all right?" He smiles down on me, standing back a little so I can get the full impact of his beauty—the sleek muscles, the perfect round head, the long yellow eyes set almost flat on the surface of his face.

People have changed dimensions, and I can't figure out the new measurements. In the narrow passageways between shacks, women as wide as trucks steer by, preceded and followed by their voluminous skirts. Near-naked wraiths sprout headdresses like forests. Ducking, I clatter into a wall of shields, behind which a phalanx of golden warriors drink and laugh.

Ragged threads of music weave into the alleyways from every shack and, at the crossroads, ravel. Here there is a *pagode*, the tambourine rattling gaily under the singer's mournful voice. There, a radio pounds out sambas. Everywhere, television sets multiply parade images to the din of the *bateria*.

Next to us, in a ring defined by light bulbs, dancers from Bahia. In flowing African robes a circle of men dance and clap an intricate beat. The dance is low-down, funky, carried from the pelvis in a weighted crouch. My companion, desperately bored in my unadventurous company, eager to deposit me in Mangueira territory and be off, stops to admire this. It isn't samba, and he doesn't know how it's done. Around the green-and-white *afoxê* dancers a larger circle forms. Paraders limp out of the Sambadrome, sweaty and dazed, cooling quickly in the evening drizzle, and stop for a look. Large old women from Rio dressed like large old women from Bahia and men with gigantic birds on their heads pause briefly and move on. There is a deeply held conviction among blacks that Bahia is more root than Rio, and the slow carnival *afoxês*, with their African look and their lack of dazzle and extravagance, are much admired.

My companion suggests a beer but refuses to pay for it when he finds out the hawker's price. Our progress to the Mangueira side of the shacks has been beset with obstacles—samba parties, unnavigable mud banks, African *afoxês*, drunks my companion would like to pick a quarrel with. Now, as the first Mangueira barracks glows within reach, I see on the nearest television screen that the Independent

Youth of Father Miguel's parade is starting, and I want to watch.

The blond-wigged, miniskirted Opening Commission is on, but it doesn't appear to be doing its crotch dance, or perhaps it simply isn't being shown on the screen. So little is. Fernando Pinto's floats, full of detail and minor jokes, look neither witty nor impressive in their broadcast version. A float featuring Brazil's leading statesmen as the Four Horsemen of the Apocalypse looks heavy-handed, the star-crossed mounts of indeterminate genus poorly made. There are no more floats, or the camera doesn't bother to show them. We see only close-ups of the stars on them, and then, in greater close-up, many buttocks. Infrequently, the camera eye blinks in the direction of the school's ground troops, who look, amazingly, like a lot of people marching in not very well made carnival costumes. My companion is not impressed and is pleased to think the blame lies exclusively with the Independent Youth. "Is that all they've got?" he says scornfully. "Where's their samba?"

He steers me in the direction of the Mangueira shacks, runs into a friend of the family, exchanges greetings, introduces me as someone who "is not used to carnival and should sit here and rest a little bit," parks me on a wobbly bench in the back part of the shack, where a samba party is in progress, and, visibly relieved, withdraws.

I hardly notice his departure. I am thinking of the beige fingernails and half-moons on Julinho's gigantic fists, the exquisite suit with which the white dancer on the minuet float has been so painfully outfitted, the smiling cows. All of them will be lost on the screen, along with Fia's samba, Guezinha's outrageous smile, Waldir's strut. Gone. I make an inventory of the things television will render invisible—everything the Mangueira school cherishes about itself, everything the *carnavalesco* has lavished care on, almost everything the jury gives points for. No points for buttocks, I am thinking bitterly, but an animated talker's elbow on the same bench keeps jabbing into my ribs, threatening to edge me directly onto the mud. A woman's elbow, attached to a skinny body with a wig. I peer around the halo of the wig.

"Nininha!"

She puts on her glasses. A loud whoop. Chortles. Hand-slaps. Another whoop, with a crouch and a slap of the palms on the thighs. A cackle. Now let's have a hug. I haven't seen her for ages. "Girl, girl," she says, shaking her head. "So you are really parading!" If I last that long, I say. She pours me a beer, we chunk plastic glasses in a toast. "Mangueira Triple Crown!" Who would stint on the energy needed to make Mangueira champion for the third time in a row?

She pours me another beer, introduces her friends, talks about her costume. Nice, she says, very luxurious. Sequins from neckline to hem, she exclaims, her eyebrows arched in amusement and surprise. And Delegado's too. He's going to look like the king in a deck of cards, magnificent. "The only thing is," she finally admits, "I wish it weren't all pink and white. I don't feel right unless I'm wearing pink and green." But your teeth, Nininha, I say. And the wig! She smiles and poses to show off the brand-new dentures the school has paid for, the head of curls she can toss and shake. Yes, the teeth are good. Very good indeed. So good that now that she's reminded of them, she might as well do a little dance, and she gets up, calls the *pagode* singers' attention to herself, asks for the Mangueira story samba.

Nininha stands in the drizzle, dancing in the mud, shaking her hips, rolling her eyes, rubbing her pot belly lewdly, hands spread wide now at the sides of her head, rolling her eyes again in shock at her own naughtiness, oh my oh my.

I laugh so hard I nearly slip off the bench. "Have another beer," Nininha says.

Her daughter is standing in front of us, a strapping big girl, as Nininha must have been, with a wicked, friendly smile. She is leading a man by the hand, skinny but fantastically good-looking. "Think so?" she says quizzically. "There's not very much to him." Her boyfriend flashes a *malandro* smile. There's enough. Nininha wanders off looking for a public bathroom. By the smell, there appears to be one a few shacks away. She is gone a long time. I pour myself some more beer and stroll over to the front of the shack to watch the screen.

Independent Youth's parade has ended uneventfully. Its story samba was too short, is the comment, and the audience got tired of hearing it repeated for eighty minutes as much as the school's energy flagged from singing it. It was also emotionally monotonous, unlike Mangueira's samba, which has a part where we can all be sad evoking slavery days, a part where we get to be indignant denouncing racism, a part for us to jump and bounce talking about black dances. And

Fernando Pinto's death detracted from the floats' visual sharpness; he had the designs set by the time of the car crash, but the light, irreverent touch he was famous for is missing.

The Sambadrome clears. The street cleaners' brigade fans out on the avenue with brooms and a giant brush. In the beer shack area there is a temporary flood of dispirited green-and-gold dancers. A limping Tinkerbell heads for an upturned crate and slumps in a dark corner, unstraps her pointy high heels, rubs her feet. The next parade begins.

The harmless drizzle is turning into full-out rain. On the bench, wondering whether to stay or look for cover, I say that rain tonight is fine, as long as it doesn't rain tomorrow. "Oh, no," says Nininha. "If it's going to rain on this poor little school that's had such hard luck all this year, then I hope it rains on us too. It's only fair." União da Ilha, a minor school from Governor's Island, lost 2 million cruzados in a robbery at its hangar, after which a fire destroyed about a third of the costumes. But the school's singing is spirited. After a couple of minutes of pouring down in earnest, the rain trickles away. A flurry of pirates and shepherdesses who have been huddled under the beer shacks' skimpy awnings rustle out again into the mud.

In a white turban, perhaps tipsy and definitely close to tears, is someone people address as Xangô, from Salgueiro. He is not parading this year, someone murmurs, after a lifetime spent with the Acadêmicos do Salgueiro. He has resigned over a matter of principle, which he grievingly explains to his friends from Mangueira. It's the floats, he says. They're not the parade, they're not the school; we are, the school membership, the people with roots. But the big schools have forgotten that, crowded us out. All they want is to make a big impression on television, and all they spend their money on is the biggest floats available and big-name stars to ride on them. Just look at Salgueiro this year! Twelve floats? Sixteen? Sixty-four? He no longer cares, but he is not about to parade as ornament and backdrop for some inanimate monster made out of papier-mâché, to benefit a school that no longer cares about its root. He sobs and moves on, disconsolately. The cluster of sympathizers that has formed around him disbands. Attention focuses once again on the television sets.

After many years of working up to this moment, and as Eurides has predicted, the spectators of the Rio carnival are finally able to see their first fully nude woman parading down the avenue. The television broadcasters announce her as a "painter" or perhaps an "artist." And she considerably livens up interest in what until then has been the undistinguished presentation of the Governor's Island school. An artistic arrangement of red greasepaint flames covers her entire body, including (we all crane to see) her pubic hair. It's hard to tell whether she is having fun. On the one hand, I know from the evening rehearsal at the Sambadrome how hard it is not to enjoy oneself prancing down the avenue with adoring throngs screaming from the bleachers. On the other hand, her smile is extremely practiced, and her eyes look bewildered. Perhaps she knows how to dance, but tonight she is moving very carefully, stiff from the hips up, as if she were carrying a sandwich-board advertisement and pointing to the text: "See Naked Women for Free!" The men who had clustered around the television set in response to this appeal scrutinize her carefully and wordlessly. "What's that got to do with samba?" one man eventually asks, but the others remain tense and silent. Even Nininha comes up to take a look. "Poor thing," she says after a few moments, and wanders away again.

Feeling unexpectedly dizzy, I decide it's time for a walk. Much drinking and merrymaking at Delegado's shack, where in his absence his sisters and a fat man in shorts slam beer on the counter and stretch their palms out for money. Shouted conversations that sound like violent arguments are in fact exultant, with the participating men yelling over each other in their eagerness to berate Independent Youth. Not a winner. What a dud. Brother, did you see those wings, no energy at all. The first potential rival is not even in the running. "Mangueira Triple Crown!"

Mangueira Triple Crown. It could be. Little champagne bubbles of excitement fizz up at the possibility. Perhaps it's time to check out the Sambadrome.

A drunkenly friendly police officer waves me directly onto the parade area, although my credentials are for a stuffy box far removed from the avenue, where no self-respecting bamba would deign to sit. In a burst of great conspiratorial feeling the cop and I smile, nod, smile again, wave at each other. Smug with achievement and carnival savvy I weave my way to the concentration area behind the gates where the São Clemente samba school is forming.

A disaster is in the making here. The only South Zone samba school has got itself a leftist *carnavalesco*, who last year put together an unlikely parade about abandoned children and this year has decided to denounce violence. A fitting subject, since much of the school's favela element comes from Dona Marta hill, where the drug traffickers Cabeludo and Zaca fought it out earlier in the carnival season and from which the defeated Cabeludo fled before his death in January. The mad One-Arm Beto, who was accused of shooting Aromatic Maruf at the Império Serrano school, has written songs for São Clemente, and he has family on Dona Marta, a hill with its own modest samba tradition. During the August cocaine wars on the hill, one of the local TV newscasts ended its coverage with a spectacular panoramic shot from the hilltop that showed the slum, the fancy apartment buildings and the ocean and, in the foreground, one of São Clemente's composers singing his candidate story samba about violence. Because I feel that Dona Marta played a significant role in my own samba history, I am eager to see this parade.

The *carnavalesco*, Carlos d'Andrade, in a tailored cream-colored linen suit with Bermuda-length trousers and knee-high socks, is running up and down, checking the ranks. The ranks are terribly depressed. The parade theme is depressing. The song is nice, but a little mournful, what with one verse after another denouncing "our suffering flora and fauna" and "our Indians who lost their land and are now being murdered." The floats, lined up in the concentration area, are strange and ugly, with gigantic foam-rubber guns pointing out from the center and a foam crablike creature waving its claws at the audience. The costumes—in black and ocher, gray and burnt orange, solid black and solid gray—are incredibly depressing. A float standout waiting in the wings covered in a black veil adds a killing edge of grimness.

Sitting at the entrance to the avenue, sharing a beer with someone who has come out of the little police booth just behind, I watch the beginning of the fireworks display that opens each parade. It fizzles in the rain. Then the sound goes. D'Andrade looks strangled.

A covey of transvestites dressed in elaborate feathered costumes prepare for their entrance. The gray, dark blue and ocher of their elegant attire blend wonderfully into the general theme, and as a whole they seem more wired, and vastly more cheerful, than anyone else in the parade so far. But just as they ease into place in front of a dark feathery wing, a harmony director marches over and yanks them out of line, getting everybody in the wing out of step. Infiltrators.

They had talked their way into the concentration section—perhaps with help from my friend the cop—and are now ruthlessly evicted.

The feathery wing recovers its step, followed by a *bateria* dressed as stormtroopers. The audience's discomfiture is by now excruciating. Surprised by a fit of giggles, I discover that I'm laughing alone; my temporary drinking partner on the curb is gone.

The debacle unfolds. Toward the middle of the parade, the forces of evil depicted on the floats give way to the forces of light, beginning with a beautiful Adam and Eve on an Eden float done in white, gold and glowing orange. But it's too late. The stunned audience, having sat through the first half in painful silence, cannot escape from its fog of gloom in time to cheer for the second part. As one wing after another emerges from the concentration area to brave the withering stillness in the avenue, they cloak d'Andrade in murderous looks.

A new, magical thought propels me toward the beer shacks again, exploring each in turn, from the southern sector near Mangueira, to the opposite side of the Sambadrome, where I eventually locate Portela. My obsession is to find Argemiro. Argemiro is a member of Portela's Old Guard, whom I once visited with a crowd from Mangueira. He was skeleton-thin and his old, dry skin felt like paper. In his neat cement-block house he received us and called his cronies over, boasted about his teenage girlfriends, and told stories and remembered the good old days in the 1970s when the Portela Old Guard reinvented the *pagode* in somebody's backyard. Despite his terrible hangover he laughed so much his ribs hurt, and when one of our crowd went to use the bathroom and came back remonstrating that the door didn't shut and that the women friends who came to visit would not appreciate this, Argemiro gave him a sly look and said, deadpan, "Honey, the young ladies who visit me don't *need* to shut that door."

A photograph of that happy afternoon just happens to be floating in my purse, and my fixed idea is to find Argemiro in the night and surprise him with it. At least one other person among the tens of thousands of revelers milling through the Sambadrome area tonight is bound to know him, I reason, and eventually, after stopping at shacks selling sausages and shacks selling fried fish, and asking men dressed in blue-and-white women's clothing and women wearing blue-and-white-striped T-shirts, and baianas in blue and white with trays of fake sweets glued to their turbans and old men in blue suits with blue-and-white-striped shirts, I find someone who does, a Portela man who says he doesn't think Argemiro is around but that some of his buddies are partying next to one of the school floats.

Portela does not have the privilege of a hangar within walking distance of the Sambadrome, and so the floats have been brought down earlier in the day from the North Zone to the concentration area, where Portelenses are assigned to guard them. Argemiro's friends are here, expansive, dizzy, full of news and elation: Argemiro has new girlfriends, the Portela Old Guard may indeed bring out a record with the help of a Japanese samba enthusiast. They study the photograph as if it were a book; that's Dona Zica's granddaughter Nilsemar? Look at that; we'd always heard she was very pretty, but here's the proof. And just look at old Argemiro! Cuddled right up. And her fiancé, huh? Too bad. And this woman Marilia wrote a book about Portela? And another one about Mangueira? Doca looks good here, doesn't she? She's the one we were telling you about, who had the backyard where all the Old Guard started getting together to sing and revive the *pagodes* after people had practically forgotten how to live with samba.

It's time for Argemiro's friends to get ready. The float they're about to push to the Sambadrome gates is not quite so plain as the Mangueira standard, but it is oddly lifeless. It has a confused scene of desert and outlaws, unmagical, unenchanting. Certainly, on the basis of floats alone, Portela will represent no threat this year to Mangueira's Triple Crown, but will both be crushed by the Salgueiro steamroller? And what about Beija-Flor, whose floats are reportedly so monumental there has been concern about maneuvering them down some of the smaller streets from their hangar to the Samba-drome? Monitoring Mangueira's parade chances now seems the night's most urgent task, and I head back toward the Sambadrome.

I am watching Estácio de Sá's parade when I get evicted. The old mother favela of all the samba schools may be poor and unfashion-able, but its *carnavalesca*, Rosa Magalhães (the only woman in the first division), puts together unique parades. Following on the heels of São Clemente's disaster, this jolly, colorful script about—of all things—cattle has the audience cheering. There are benign white oxen guarding miniature Egyptian temples lovingly painted in trompe-l'oeil marble; the bull that Maurice of Nassau is supposed to have made jump across a precipice during the Dutch conquest of northern Brazil; baianas dressed in the patchwork costumes of a northeastern chase-the-bull folk dance; and toward the end, a float representing a gigantic pot-au-feu. The parade evokes strange adjectives for a carnival context. I think: *cozy, charming, endearing.*

It is my last clear thought. A Riotur inspector has asked for my credentials and, unexpectedly argumentative, I am disputing her right to do so. Smiling, she listens to the flow of invective I cannot seem to stanch—diatribes against her, the police, the incompetent organization she works for. Smiling still, she informs me that I will have to produce credentials for the parade area, leave, or be escorted out by the police. I leave, clambering over the spike-tipped fence that separates the parade grounds from the public exit area, puncturing my legs dramatically. The back alleyways leading out of the Sambadrome are full of menace and darkness, suddenly empty. Near tears, I wonder where Nininha is, the woman who could have taught me how to drink without making a fool of myself.

She isn't in the Mangueira section of the beer shacks, nor is anyone else I know. The night has gotten rougher, dawn is about to break, the party seems over. I've lost the key that let me into carnival's secret. Looking for a way to recover it, I run into Salgueiro's monumental floats just as the sun edges into the sky and hits the golden structures with its own dazzling light.

The floats tower like magical kingdoms in the glorious morning that is breaking, and a mute, awed crowd stands around them, still for once, just staring. A pyramid of mirrors, with niches where behemoth feathered beings preen and tremble in the morning breeze. Mile-high stacks of gold coins, each topped with mysterious, solemn women, their skin gleaming gold. An open-pit gold mine, the gold-besotted miners shining in its crevices, covered only in loincloths and glitter, every muscle glowing. Ahead of us, the parade gates open and the floats first lurch slightly and then glide in stately procession toward the waiting crowd. A collective gasp is almost audible from the bleachers.

The city is in ruins. Through the jumble of filth and beer cans, bedraggled revelers make their way unsteadily toward the train station, their costumes streaked with mud. There is no more music. The beer shacks are empty of customers, drained of noise. I am, I realize, as filthy and raw with sleeplessness as anyone in the crowd. A taxi driver pulls up, agrees to take me home for twice the usual amount, pulls over to the curb after a while and, with apologies, announces he must have a brief nap if he is to continue driving. After a few minutes he wakes up, drives on.

16 *Parade*

Many hours later Seu Tinguinha is on his way home down the viaduct with the week's groceries. The courtly old *bateria* director stops in front of the Samba Palace, puts his bags down to shake hands. Tuchinha, directly behind him, dressed for carnival in a pink-and-green crocheted T-shirt, whirs his Honda around in circles. No bodyguards.

Seu Tinguinha has been up all night, watching the parades on television, and he is not impressed. Ruffianish displays like the one put on by Independent Youth do not even deserve his comment, but what has him dispirited about the entire evening are the costumes. Not luxurious enough? That wasn't exactly the problem, he says. It was more the design, the fact that so many of them were open around here—he points to his chest. Does he mean the number of bare-breasted women on display? Something like that. He clears his throat, finally says it. "It's a disgrace, all that nudity. It doesn't have anything to do with us sambistas. And it's all because of television and tourists. Look at the way the parade is judged! There's no points for samba, no points for the soloists, but any day now there's going to be points awarded for naked women. And I don't go along with that at all."

Would he mind the nudity so much if the television also showed what sambistas are proud of? The dancing, the way the story is told

through the floats, the wings and their costumes in detail? Seu Tinguinha shakes his head. That's not it. It's the whole idea of nakedness
that offends him. It's hard for him to see anything in Salgueiro's
gleaming parade beyond shamelessness.

He is not impressed by Portela's showing either. That school is
in trouble and had better watch out for Tradição. Lifeless, unimaginative, he says. They're not even in the running. Less competition
for Mangueira, then, I say. Seu Tinguinha shrugs. He too appears to
be uncertain about Mangueira's fate, along with crusty old Vovó
Lucióla, who from the center of her African compound of shacks
has stated flatly that Mangueira simply does not have a winning
parade this year. "We'll see," says Seu Tinguinha. "The big competition is tonight." He means Beija-Flor. I remember the New Year's
prediction by a father-of-a-saint that a blue-and-white school would
win this championship. It won't be Portela, that's certain, but there's
still Beija-Flor.

Seu Tinguinha has picked up his bags, wishes me a good parade.
"And my best to your wife. How is she doing?"

The old man smiles, shrugs again. "Blinder every day."

On the viaduct, the slow infiltration of the color spectrum by
pink and green is almost complete. Everyone who can is strolling in
a costume from some previous year, or in a pink shirt and green
shorts, or at the very least, in green flip-flops or a pink felt hat. There
are street costumes—bow ties and bikinis with silver fringe purchased
from the downtown hawkers; for the children, harlequin suits, crazy
wigs and masks made of cheesecloth stretched and shellacked over
a mold, painted with rudimentary geometrical features: circles for
the eyes, triangles for the cheeks. Hidden safely inside, small terrorists
rush their victims with explosive noisemakers, prancing about in
demonic joy each time they manage to make someone jump.

A last gaggle of transvestites, now that the time for cross-dressing
has passed, flag down the stray car that ventures this way on a
carnival Monday and leap around it, lift up their nightgowns to
display their behinds. But they steer clear of Tuchinha, who is riding
the wind, his head thrown back in a surfer's triumphant smile.

What, I ask Celina, is that bunch of *malandros* doing at her door?
"What do you think they're doing? Snorting coke. But am I supposed

to turn down the thousand cruzados they offered me not to get in their way?"

We have arranged to take a picture of her in her new costume, foreseeing chaos at parade time on carnival morning. Most people think it's bad luck to wear a costume before parading in it. Dona Neuma certainly doesn't like it, but Celina thinks if we do it quickly there won't be a problem. Her entire family is out enjoying carnival and the sudden burst of splendid weather, but even so, Celina can hardly find room for herself and her dress in the confines of the shack. She carries the front of her hoop skirt while I compress the back, and we maneuver her out the door and past the *malandros*. She drops her silver turban in the alley, and I trip and let the hem of her skirt skim the mud. The costume doesn't fit here either; we'll have to go all the way to the clearing. We snap a hurried, guilty shot there and scramble back into the alley before anyone at Dona Neuma's can spot us. The *malandros* are interested.

"Take a picture of us," the biggest one says. He is built like a safety vault, dressed in a Mangueira-colored muscle shirt and a small matching straw hat that sits ludicrously on his large head. I demur. "Come on, just one." Quickly shuffling themselves into soccer-team rows, they pose, barring the entrance to Celina's. Washington Luiz speeds in, still on his costume high, eager for a photograph. The big *malandro* yanks him out of the air and pulls him into the picture pose.

I snap. There they are. Happy goons in celebration, facing the lens with manly stares and puffed-out chests, offering the camera a drink, cocaine tucked out of sight. In the back row one of them holds up a Brazilian flag. In the front, two of them throw their arms around Washington Luiz in a protective embrace. "Mangueira Triple Crown!" we all cry. They clear the way to Celina's door and let me through.

The sun is setting pinkly in a cloudless sky. Dona Neuma sits in a chair on her porch, one foot soaking in a big tin bucket, the other already pedicured, the nails filed to a point and painted bright red. The manicurist sits on a stool in front of her, tending to her fingernails. Dona Neuma is tired but pleased. "You know what I saw yesterday, when those children set out to parade? I saw myself and Seu Tinguinha and Delegado as we all were. I remembered what it was like to go out on my first parade. That excitement! Incredible that big fat old me could once have been small like that, isn't it? But I was, and yesterday I remembered. I had more fun watching them than I'm going to have tomorrow morning."

Guezinha is sipping a beer, still looking bedraggled and stressed. Her wing is delivered, Percy's wing is wrapped up, the last of Chininha's costumes was delivered at three p.m., and the chaos is still too recent. While her sisters and friends nap or concentrate on their nails, she hunches in a corner, listening distractedly to the conversations around her. Well-wishers in Mangueira colors drop by to cheer the school on, but the greetings are received absentmindedly. It's getting late, and it's time to rest before the parade. Shortly after nightfall the viaduct clears of revelers, the Hot Hole falls silent. At every shack on the way up the hill, television sets flicker.

Dona Esmeralda displays the results of her extravagant carnival cooking: tripe stew prepared with sausage and beans and whatever else will fit in the pot. The reticulated oblongs of stomach lining float heavily in a thick bean gruel. Not on a hangover.

She watches sadly as I eat boiled rice and a sliced tomato. She admits after some urging that she watched last night's parade from beginning to end, and having confessed that much, she goes on to provide a critique of it, school by school. Portela was terrible, she says sorrowfully. The harmony evolution was unbelievably poor, coming from a school with so many decades of practice. Big gaping holes in the ranks everywhere, wings falling behind, running to catch up. The aerial shots showed how ragged it all was. And the costumes! Never a sadder baiana, in pale unimaginative blue and white, no flounces, not enough volume to the skirt. Portela is Mangueira's best rival—a sister, really, after so long—and it's sad to see it collapse like that, but the parade was really very bad. So bad that she now feels it her duty to watch the rival Tradição just for comparison.

When I go upstairs for a couple of hours' sleep she is already in place in front of the television set with two grandsons and one of her many children-in-law, the only one who is not out on carnival night.

She is by my cot with fresh hot coffee by one in the morning, anxious lest I miss the parade. It doesn't start until five-thirty, I point out groggily. "Better to have time to check your costume than to be in a rush," she says firmly. Hands me the hairbrush, a towel, walks me to the shower.

She yells through the bathroom door that Tradição was fantastic. An ocean of blue and white! Beautiful costumes! Not a single gap in the ranks! In every group shot you could see the school's energy, all the members singing the story samba with all their heart. Beautiful floats, but not too many. Zumbi and Slave Anastácia and an impressive wing-opener, the float that carries the school's symbol and announces the theme. Not yet a winner, but definitely a major school.

The television is carrying the tail end of Beija-Flor. The huge, darkly glittering floats fill the screen, emit the starry glow of alien vehicles, seem to shudder with so much light and movement. Dark blues and gold, black and silver. Like Mangueira, Beija-Flor looks very much the same from one parade to the next, but unlike Julinho Mattos, Joãozinho Trinta tends to drown his dancers in their costumes. And unlike most *carnavalescos*, who take at least occasional advantage of the floats' satirical and farcical possibilities, Trinta sets his up as solemn monuments to Art. The effect is impressive but not catchy, yet there is no denying the dazzling beauty of what is happening on the screen. Julinho's showiest float, the Princess Isabel golden temple, is pitiful compared to the poorest of Trinta's.

So Mangueira will not triumph on the basis of lavish costumes or floats. But it won't win on originality either: two other schools have similar floats, almost every school is at least referring to the hundredth anniversary of the abolition decree, no school has taken so traditionalist a stand on Princess Isabel as Mangueira, and hardly any school can have the total absence of thematic connection between floats and costumes that, with the exception of the reality segment, is affecting ours. What, after all, do Chininha's soubrettes have to do with slave ships or Princess Isabel? Mangueira will have to earn its victory on the basis of samba, root and spirit alone.

At the door Dona Esmeralda, disappointed that I've decided to change into my costume at Dona Neuma's, pats my hair, motions her hand in blessing. "Samba a lot!" she says. "I'll be watching."

On a knoll off the side of the Hot Hole footpath, a couple embraces tenderly, the taller of the two cradling his lover's face in his hands, stooping down for a last kiss. A glistening crescent moon floats atop his partner's headdress. The moon shivers, sensing my approach, and the two separate with animal speed. The smaller man crashes through the bushes in flight. His lover glances calmly at me from heavily made-up eyes, vanishes into the shadows.

The path is otherwise deserted all the way downhill. In the shacks, screens glow with the light from the evening's fourth parade, an unambitious presentation by a school in the suburb of Cabuçu in homage to a quartet of Brazilian comic actors. The parade is important to Mangueira, though, because the large fat member of the quartet grew up in Mangueira as one of Dona Neuma's innumerable semiadopted charges. Her presence as a standout in Cabuçu's parade has been announced earlier, but her legs can't get her through two parades in a single night. Cabuçu's *bateria* rolls out over Mangueira's silence.

Silence also at Dona Neuma's.

The front room is as full of people as it has ever been. Two or three dozen women squeezing their feet into pink ankle boots, zipping themselves into their sequins, tightening the elastic on a puffed sleeve for a friend, fixing their curls, dusting glitter powder on their cleavage. Half a dozen words, occasionally. "Glitter, please?" "Not so tight." "Thank you."

Outside, pale shadows are converging on the viaduct from every point, streaming down the footpaths in hushed sequins and rustling satins. The five buses parked outside the Samba Palace are filling up. I kick a dog and a hen out of the backyard bathroom and struggle with my costume, sticky with sweat. Then I pester Dulce until she agrees to stitch the bow on to the back of my skirt.

Dona Neuma emerges from her room and stops short in front of the television set, considers what is happening on it, turns up the volume. A war cry fills the room. "Hail Zumbi!"

A phalanx of mahogany-colored warriors, tall as trees, their headdresses bristling with straw ornaments, is striding into the living room at the head of a fantastical African procession. "The loud cry of Palmares crossed the oceans and the continents," Vila Isabel sings, roars, howls. The warriors stomp. There is a rustling and shaking of straw and rattles. "Hail Zumbi!" Gigantic African wood carvings stare out from the center of a float. No sequins. No mirror trim. The camera pans briefly across a mesmerized audience.

Vila Isabel sings. "This is our magic! Prayers, ritual, *orixás*!" In straw-colored costumes, on an enormous straw-covered and ornamented seven-pedestaled float, the *orixás* stand majestically, adorned in cowrie shells, crowned in scarlet and gold feathers.

"Hail Zumbi!" A palisaded village is floating into view, pulled and centered into place by straining men in dashikis. The village has straw huts, white pigeons. In ocher robes the woman warrior Dandara shakes her spear and hurls the song out: "Look at the strength of our culture, our art and our courage!" On a lookout post, Zumbi stands with shield and spear.

Dona Neuma turns the television back down, to no volume at all, and walks away.

The audience knows the song: "Today Vila is a black feast: *batuque*, song and dance; *jongo* and *maracatú*!" Down on the ground, kingly Africans in all-male wings prance and shake. Women with beaded headdresses holding in place masses of tiny braids cut swaths through the air with their hips, raise their arms high, shake their breasts free in the night wind. Guezinha stops in front of the screen for a long look, chews on a cuticle, turns her back. "The priest raises the chalice; this gathering is a feast for every race." In a mixed-race wing, camouflaged guerrillas chant and wave the portraits of Martin Luther King, Jr., Samora Machel, Nelson Mandela. "Moon of Luanda, shine on us! We are thirsty for a home, we long for the death of apartheid!" The women guerrillas carry plastic babies on their shoulders and in back-slings. I think with a pang of Eurides, who is not parading, and her real baby. Anderson would have loved it.

Gradually, the house is divided between the nonparading members, who watch the remainder of the Vila Isabel parade transfixed, and the paraders, who leave as soon as they are finished changing. Dona Neuma and Guezinha have gone to change. The room is nearly empty, the few remaining women engaged in a last-minute round of glitter and lipstick. I have not even finished dressing. Outside, the buses are revving their motors; of the two left, one is already pulling away. The sky is silvery on the horizon. I stuff a notebook into my secret apron pocket, grab the jewelry, magenta-pink feather duster and head ornament, and without stopping to say good-bye to Guezinha or Dona Neuma fly out the door and onto the last bus, crowded as a rush-hour commuter line.

Wedged between a warrior's spear and a pink metal lollipop, I disentangle the tulle ruffle on my apron from a sitting passenger's pom-pom–tipped headdress. Two pink *bateria* members come running down from the Hot Hole, waving the bus to a halt with their

gigantic pink top hats and grabbing the back door handle as the bus
swings around and onto the viaduct underpass.

Império Serrano's pretty, unpretentious reproductions of Rio land-
marks are in parade formation outside the Sambadrome gates, two
hours behind schedule, as dawn breaks. Mangueira is forming on
the opposite side of the stadium. A man in a costume from Imperatriz
Leopoldinense, another unlucky school this year, stops to shake
hands and wish Mangueira a good parade. Others set up a cheer—
"Mangueira Triple Crown!"—at the sight of my pink maid's outfit
and green high heels. A small group, in costumes whose colors I can't
identify, is sarcastic. "Call that a costume? And I bet you think
Mangueira can win!" It feels terribly late; broad daylight now, and
the clock on the Central Station tower is signaling six-thirty. Vila
Isabel's parade must be about to end. There, at last, are the Mangueira
floats, the modest white wing-opener with a gilt chair for Dona Zica,
Slave Anastácia, the slave ship that towers over the others' unpretentious height. Between them, sheeny pink brigades of paraders.
Rushing into the Mangueira crowd from the empty silence of President Vargas Avenue, I nearly collapse with nausea.

A fetid stench to suffocate in. Clinging and cloying, overpowering,
inescapable; the accumulated miasma of seventy-two hours of beer
and urine flooding out of every sewer, a murky liquid that runs down
from Beer Shack Row and overflows onto the cobblestones of the
school formation area. Paraders pick their way gingerly over the
rivulets, among the beer cans, the mounds of plastic cups. The smell
is rising with the sun, growing solid as the crowd thickens. In the
midst of it, exhausted, frayed, Percy Pires goes through his usual
litany of entreaties from the slight elevation on which the school
sound truck is parked. "People, let's form the school! Império is
about to go on! It's very simple, look for the floats! It's time!" Complete indifference.

Fleeing the smell I cross back onto the avenue's central divide, a
grassy stretch where cars are parked and a few people are casually
changing into costume, pulling a dress or a tunic on over their heads,
peeling away the shorts underneath. Some have brought picnics, and
here and there the remains of a breakfast of beer and sandwiches are
spread out on the lawn. Because the enormous spread of President

Vargas Avenue is free of traffic, and because people are converging close to the bronze head, Zumbi is temporarily noticeable. "That's Zumbi, isn't it?"

The formation area is suddenly overflowing with Mangueira. Quickly, effortlessly, the wings have formed between floats, the lineup now extending six blocks along the avenue between the Sambadrome and the train station. Back in the thick of the stench, Percy continues his hoarse appeal, "People! Império is in the Sambadrome and we aren't even ready! It's very simple: I call out the float and wing and you look for it! Please hurry!" Despite the urgency of this call no one is running around witlessly except me, trying to figure out front and back and order and sequence in this tangle of familiarity so oddly transformed. The formation of a few hundred people I had come to identify as the school is no longer there. Instead there are thousands of remote, aloof, benign princes and princesses, smooth sparkling expanses of satins and sequins where I am used to seeing faded denim and stained rag. From beneath kingly headdresses purple-shadowed eyes meet mine with amusement. A woman with a careful, orna-mented face touches a lace glove to the corner of her mouth and curls her lips into a smile as practiced as a duchess's. It's Iracema, perfect as porcelain in her sequin-thronged bodice and dainty pink booties, standing high above the sewer trickle. Her husband stands protectively beside her, Carlos today, not Carlinhos, a proud, erect lord trimly encased in his white directorate suit. We wish each other a good carnival and I thread my way front to back through the wings, looking for anchor, failing to recognize anyone, lost in the crowds of white strangers who have taken over so much of the space. The pink-and-green pom-pom headdress I got entangled in earlier has multiplied into a forest. I wander through a dale of pink feathers and gauzy capes, among near-naked women who look like statues, through columns of warriors and salonfuls of stately black men in pink tailcoats, dazed and dazzled, sliding in the mud and beer cans, trying to keep my beautiful green shoes out of the filth while simul-taneously scanning the faces, hoping to recognize anyone at all.

"What a change, no?" a voice says. It's Ceci, her prettiness spar-kling under a pink lace parasol, escorted by Jaime, king of African kings in his blinding smile and a warrior's outfit. They are rushing through the forest of spangles to their places at the front. Dona Neuma trudges purposefully in the direction of the children's wing, her pedicured nails hidden by sensible shoes, her stout body in a standard white directorate suit with a pink blouse. She waves absentmindedly, concentrating on the parade.

Back again on President Vargas Avenue, searching for bearings. The school looks different from the outside: an ensemble of performers waiting their turn in the wings, touching up makeup, smoking cigarettes, chatting in quiet groups. The array of floats is visible from here, and on top of one, a glittering couple. "Nininha!" I shout to the heights, and she turns around, consults with Delegado, establishes my identity and grins down, flinging up her arms to display her costume with delight and self-mockery. Delegado, looking drawn and frail under the weight of his outfit, tries to smile but can't: he has finally acknowledged what he had refused to admit before, that there is no way, on that small platform on a moving vehicle, he will be able to dance. Nininha tries, essaying a brief shuffle that barely manages to move the stiff skirt. Delegado stands still, staring in the opposite direction.

At the next float Marlene Arruda has just finished applying false eyelashes. The clock reads just past seven, and she motions to a crew of assistants to lift Princess Isabel's massive dress onto her. In white slacks and a striped shirt, she's as composed and professional as a chanteuse, and too late I remember her advice to keep a caramel tucked in the back of my mouth during the parade. The hawkers have nothing but beer to offer.

The baianas, finally. Calmly in place hours before anyone, standing isolated from each other by the circumference of their skirts, 250 of them. "Where's Celina?" I skitter through the mud from one to another, spinning them around to look for Celina's face. Not here. Not here. But here's Dona Jurema beaming in all her pink magnificence, exulting in her hoarse voice about the good weather and the lovely costume and the luck of it all. And here is Dona Diva, the shortest one, the carnival queen, not a seamstress this morning but a benevolent witch in her cone-shaped turban and African cape. "Aren't you going to get ready?" she asks, with a speaking look toward my unadorned head, the plastic bag full of poison-green jewelry clanging around in my hand.

No makeup. No glitter. No headdress. I take the outside route and sprint toward the back of the formation, where Guezinha's wing has to be. Over five thousand people to get past and it's almost seven-thirty. Starting time. Skid to a stop at the street cleaners' wing, Nil-semar's impeccably sequined half and Guezinha-William-Percy's dull troops, skimpily adorned with a band of not very shiny silver tape across the chest. Back one wing to where the maids are all a-gaggle, chattering and whooping and chugging beer, fifty women most of whom I've never seen before, but oh, aren't we pretty: the way the pert apron and back bow sit on the frilly skirt; the bounce in the short little petticoat as we walk; the magical daintiness of the green platform heels, the glitter of the emerald jewels, the furl of silver ribbon on the head. I twist the ends of the head ornament into my hair, fumble with the jewelry, drop a bracelet into the steaming mud, consider it gone, hand the rest to a boy looking on at the edges and instruct him to fasten the necklace around my neck, realizing too late that he is willing but in a stultifying fog of alcohol, yank the jewelry back and manage to attach it myself, borrow a tube of glitter gel and lather on in a sticky mixture of glue and sweat. Who cares, we're all so lovely!

Amid the beer shacks a Vila Isabel baiana wearily tugs off her robes—in the school's blue and white—to reveal the shorts and T-shirt underneath, emerging once again a favelada. Next to her I finally spot Guezinha, staring intently at a television screen. She barely notices me as I slide in next to her, see what she is seeing: the parade has started, and in the aerial shot of the Sambadrome I realize the screen has never looked like this. Pink dots fill every inch of it, squiggle and bounce and sheer off every which way. The whole school looks as if it's gone insane. The crowd too is crazy, roaring its approval, cheering dementedly, possessed by the school's frenetic energy. We move back into the center of our wing, distractedly pushing aside a wall of people in our way, check our ranks. Any minute now the float ahead will start to move. We're ready. "Beauties!" someone yells. "Go get it!" "Mangueira Triple Crown!"

I look out and realize that the people we just pushed through are our own private parade, rows three and four deep of fans along the entire length of the formation, come here just to wave us in. The float ahead of us shudders and lurches, begins its glide forward. Although the official sound truck is too far away to hear, we catch the wave of song from the ranks ahead, lock into their movement with a rush of fear and excitement, mouths open to catch the words and pass them on. "I dreamt," we sing, "of Zumbi of Palmares'

240 · S A M B A

return, that the sadness of blacks was over." Very fast now, we trot behind as the float gathers speed, rushing over the beer cans, the cobblestones, past the shacks, past Zumbi, past the throngs of waving, cheering well-wishers, past the entry gates and the latrines to where the din of the *bateria*, the deafening, welcoming roar of the crowd are waiting. We're on.

Epilogue

Mangueira lost the championship to Vila Isabel, 112 to 111 points. The rains began again a couple of days after the jury announced its decision. In seventy-two consecutive hours of downpour, floods and landslides swept through greater Rio and left 213 dead, including 11 dwellers of Vila Isabel's root favelas on Ant and Borel hills. The only real help received by the forty-five families forced to evacuate their homes in Mangueira came from Ricardo Lion-Heart, who ferried medicines and paramedics back and forth in his bottle-green car to the emergency refugee centers set up by the neighborhood associations in Olaria and the Hot Hole.

Two weeks after carnival, the beautiful Fia was murdered in the house next door to Dona Neuma's, which her police-chief boyfriend was restoring for her to move into. She had been bound and strangled with wire. The workman who had been repairing the house, a former convict in the police chief's employ, was gone from the scene of the crime when Dona Neuma and her daughters forced the door of the house open and found Fia's corpse in a back room. The workman was never arrested. His employer was never seen around the favela again.

The guest of honor at Elíseo Dória's birthday party was Tuchinha.

Carlinhos Dória's brother led the school to a stunning eleventh-place defeat in the 1988 carnival with a theme honoring one of Rio's most well-known nightclub operators. A few weeks later the directorate voted him out of the presidency. Soon after, Tuchinha was arrested and sentenced to six months in prison. In August 1988, Elíseo Dória was shot to death.

Beato Salú's plans for a nursery and day-care center for his side of the hill were temporarily interrupted when he was arrested during a North Zone drug raid and sentenced to six months in jail.

Washington Luiz entered school and was quickly promoted to second grade, with the promise that if his good grades continued, he would be skipped another year.

Eurides' son, Anderson, caught pneumonia and was hospitalized twice. Eurides was offered a job as a day maid, but when she subtracted the new bus fares from the standard maid's salary and added the amount she would have to pay someone to care for Anderson during the day, she discovered she could not afford to work. A few months later, as a partial side effect of Brazil's raging economic crisis, the aerobics studio where Eurides' husband Lilico worked as a guard went bankrupt.

Acknowledgments

To encourage means literally to give one the courage—the heart—to do something. This book would not have been even a project if Penny Lernoux had not so doggedly made me brave. Other dearly loved friends—Susan Meiselas, Michael Jacobs, Anne Reid, Tim Golden, John Rettie, Richard Gott, Ramón Jimeno and Marcela Caldas, Mary Helen Spooner and Alan Stevens—provided strength and logistical support through this time.

Heartfelt thanks go also to Heloisa Fontes, who skillfully put together a bibliography; Anthony Henman, who corroborated my findings in the chapter dealing with Rio's nascent cocaine culture; the staff of the archbishopric library in Rio de Janeiro, whose help was essential in putting together the pieces of the Slave Anastácia puzzle; Marilia Barboza, who shared her years of knowledge of Mangueira with such warm enthusiasm; and Sergio Cabral and Nei Lopes, carnival experts who let me ransack their files and their memories. Yvonne Maggie and Clóvis Moura were generous with their knowledge and patient with me as I struggled to understand Brazilian black history and religion. Liz Darhansoff and Elisabeth Sifton made this book happen, and I cannot thank them enough for their trust.

Very special thanks go to Peter Fry, whose understanding of all things Brazilian is surely unequaled. If the steps he and my other carnival coaches taught me are here put together clumsily, I must apologize and assume the blame; the dance is mine alone.

The people of Mangueira have more than my gratitude: they have my admiration, and my heart.

ABOUT THE AUTHOR

From 1962 to 1973 Alma Guillermoprieto was a professional dancer. Since 1978, she has worked as a staff
reporter for many English-language media in Central and
South America, most recently serving as South American
Bureau Chief for *Newsweek*. She now lives in Bogotá and
writes for *The New Yorker* and other publications.